JIHAD

READYMADE FACTORY AGAINST TERRORISM

Col. S.P.Bahera (Retd.)

NEHA PUBLISHERS & DISTRIBUTORS

DELHI

Publisher
NEHA PUBLISHERS & DISTRIBUTORS
4832/24,Prahlad Lane,S-207 Ansari
Road, Daryaganj, Delhi-110002
Ph.: 43570976, 23278261
Email: nehapubdistributors@gmail.com

Edition: 2015

ISBN: 978-93-80318-59-2

Laser Typesetting
JEE-VEE Graphics, Delhi

Price: 1195/-

Printed
Vikas Computers, Delhi

Contents

Preface

The word Jihad stems from the Arabic root word J-H-D, which means "strive." Other words derived from this root include "effort," "labor," and "fatigue." Essentially Jihad is an effort to practice religion in the face of oppression and persecution.

The beginnings of Jihad are traced back to the words and actions of Muhammad and the Quran. This encourages the use of Jihad against non-Muslims.The Qu'ran, however, never uses the term Jihad for fighting and combat in the name of Allah; qital is used to mean "fighting." The struggle for Jihad in the Qu'ran was originally intended for the nearby neighbors of the Muslims, but as time passed and more enemies arose, the Quranic statements supporting Jihad were updated for the new adversaries. The first documentation of the law of Jihad was written by 'Abd al-Rahman al-Awza'i and Muhammad ibn al-Hasan al-Shaybani. The document grew out of debates that had surfaced ever since Muhammad's death.

Assessed from the Qur'anic point of view, the word "jihad" can also mean a struggle carried out on intellectual grounds against those who oppress people, treat them unjustly, subject them to torture and cruelty and violate legitimate human rights. The purpose of this struggle is to bring about justice, peace and equality. Apart from these ideological and spiritual meanings, struggle in the physical sense is also considered as "jihad". However, as explained above, this has to be a struggle carried out solely for defensive purposes. The use of the concept of "jihad" for acts of aggression against innocent people, that is for terror, would be unjust and a great distortion of the true meaning of the term.

The present book aims at catering to this curiosity of the readers.

—Editor

1

Islam and War: The Beginnings of Jihad

The beginnings of Jihad are traced back to the words and actions of Muhammad and the Quran. This encourages the use of Jihad against non-Muslims.The Qu'ran, however, never uses the term Jihad for fighting and combat in the name of Allah; qital is used to mean "fighting." The struggle for Jihad in the Qu'ran was originally intended for the nearby neighbors of the Muslims, but as time passed and more enemies arose, the Quranic statements supporting Jihad were updated for the new adversaries. The first documentation of the law of Jihad was written by 'Abd al-Rahman al-Awza'i and Muhammad ibn al-Hasan al-Shaybani. The document grew out of debates that had surfaced ever since Muhammad's death.

EARLY INSTANCES

The first forms of military Jihad occurred after the migration (hijra) of Muhammad and his small group of followers to Medinafrom Mecca and the conversion of several inhabitants of the city to Islam. The first revelation concerning the struggle against the Meccans was surah 22, verses 39-40: To those against whom war is made, permission is given (to fight), because they are wronged;- and verily, Allah is most powerful for their aid. (They are) those who have been expelled from their homes in defiance of right,- (for no cause) except that they say, "our Lord is Allah". Did not Allah check one set of people by means of another, there would surely have been pulled down monasteries, churches, synagogues, and mosques, in which the name of Allah is commemorated in abundant measure. Allah will certainly aid those who aid his (cause);- for verily Allah is full of Strength, Exalted in Might, (able to enforce His Will).

At this time, Muslims had been persecuted and oppressed by the Meccans. There were still Muslims who could not flee from Mecca and were still oppressed because of their faith. Surah 4, verse 75 is referring to this fact: And why should ye not fight in the cause of Allah and of those who, being weak, are ill-treated (and oppressed)?- Men, women, and children, whose cry is: "Our Lord! Rescue us from this town, whose people are oppressors; and raise for us from thee one who will protect; and raise for us from thee one who will help!

The Meccans also refused to let the Muslims enter Mecca and by that denied them access to the Ka'aba. Surah 8, verse 34:

But what plea have they that Allah should not punish them, when they keep out (men) from the sacred Mosque—and they are not its guardians? No men can be its guardians except the righteous; but most of them do not understand.

However hadith from Sahih al-Bukhari formalized the rules for warfare, which legitimized warfare against hypocrites. It has been reported from Sulaiman b. Buraid through his father that when the Messenger of Allah appointed anyone as leader of an army or detachment he would especially exhort him to fear Allah and to be good to the Muslims who were with him. He would say: Fight in the name of Allah and in the way of Allah. Fight against those who disbelieve in Allah. Make a holy war, do not embezzle the spoils; do not break your pledge; and do not mutilate (the dead) bodies; do not kill the children. When you meet your enemies who are polytheists, invite them to three courses of action. If they respond to any one of these, you also accept it and withhold yourself from doing them any harm. Invite them to (accept) Islam; if they respond to you, accept it from them and desist from fighting against them. Then invite them to migrate from their lands to the land of Muhairs and inform them that, if they do so, they shall have all the privileges and obligations of the Muhajirs. If they refuse to migrate, tell them that they will have the status of Bedouin Muslims and will be subjected to the Commands of Allah like other Muslims, but they will not get any share from the spoils of war or Fai' except when they actually fight with the Muslims (against the disbelievers).

If they refuse to accept Islam, demand from them the Jizya. If they agree to pay, accept it from them and hold off your hands. If they refuse to pay the tax, seek Allah's help and fight them. When you lay siege to a fort and the besieged appeal to you for protection in the name of Allah and His Prophet, do not accord to them the guarantee of Allah and His Prophet, but accord to them your own guarantee and the guarantee of your companions for it is a lesser sin that the security given by you or your companions be disregarded than that the security granted in the name of Allah and His Prophet be violated When you besiege a fort and the besieged want you to let them out in accordance with Allah's Command, do not let them come out in accordance with His Command, but do so at your (own) command, for you do not know whether or not you will be able to carry out Allah's behest with regard to them."

The main focus of Muhammad's later years was increasing the number of allies as well as the amount of territory under Muslim control. The Qu'ran is unclear as to whether Jihad is acceptable only in defense of the faith from wrong-doings or in all cases. Major battles in the history of Islam arose between the Meccans and the Muslims; one of the most important to the latter was the Battle of Badr in 624 AD. This Muslim victory over polytheists showed "demonstration of divine guidance and intervention on behalf of Muslims, even when outnumbered." Other early battles included battles in Uhud (625),Khandaq (627), Mecca (630) and Hunayn (630). These battles, especially Uhud and Khandaq, were unsuccessful in comparison to the Battle of Badr. In relating this battle, the Qu'ran states that Allah sent an "unseen army of angels" that helped the Muslims defeat the Meccans.

CRUSADES

The European crusaders re-conquered much of the territory seized by the Islamic state, dividing it into four kingdoms, the most important being the state of Jerusalem. The Crusades originally had the goal of recapturing Jerusalem and the Holy Land(former Christian territory) from Muslim rule and were originally launched in response to a call from the Eastern Orthodox Byzantine Empire for help against the expansion of the Muslim Seljuk Turks into Anatolia. There was little drive to retake the lands from the crusaders, save the few attacks made by the Egyptian Fatimids. This changed, however, with the coming of Zangi, ruler of what is today northern Iraq. He took Edessa, which triggered theSecond Crusade, which was little more than a 47-year stalemate. The stalemate was ended with the victory of Salah al-Din al-Ayyubi (known in the west as Saladin) over the forces of Jerusalem at the Horns of Hattin in 1187. It was during the course of the stalemate that a great deal of literature regarding Jihad was written. While amassing his armies in Syria, Saladin had to create a doctrine which would unite his forces and make them fight until the bitter end, which would be the only way they could re-conquer the lands taken in the First Crusade. He did this through the creation of Jihad propaganda. It stated that any one who would abandon the Jihad would be committing a sin that could not be washed away by any means. It also put his amirs at the center of power, just under his rule. While this propaganda was successful in uniting his forces for a time, the fervor burned out quickly. Much of Saladin's teachings were rejected after his death.

WAR IN THE QURAN

According to the Qur'an, war represents an "unwanted obligation" which has to be carried out with strict observance of particular humane and moral guidelines and which must not be resorted to except when it is absolutely inevitable.

In one Qur'anic verse, it is explained that those who start wars are the disbelievers and that God does not approve of wars:

> *...Each time they kindle the fire of war, God extinguishes it. They rush about the earth corrupting it. God does not love corrupters. (Qur'an, 5:64)*

In the case of a conflict, before engaging in a war, believers must wait until fighting becomes compulsory. Believers are allowed to fight only when the other party attacks and no other alternative except war remains:

> *But if they cease (fighting), God is Ever-Forgiving, Most Merciful. (Qur'an, 2:192)*

A closer examination of the Prophet Muhammad's life reveals that war was a method resorted for defensive purposes only in unavoidable situations.

The revelation of the Qur'an to the Prophet Muhammad continued for a period of 23 years. During the first 13 years of this period, Muslims lived as a minority under a pagan order in Mecca and faced much oppression. Many Muslims were harassed, abused, tortured, and even murdered, their houses and possessions plundered. Despite this, however, Muslims led their lives without resorting to violence and always called the pagans to peace.

When the oppression of the pagans escalated unbearably, the Muslims emigrated to the town of Yathrib, which was later to be renamed Madinah, where they could establish their own order in a freer and more friendly environment. Even establishing their own system did not prompt them to take up weapons against the aggressive pagans of Mecca. Only after the following revelation, the Prophet commanded his people to prepare for war:

> *Permission to fight is given to those who are fought against because they have been wronged – truly God has the power to come to their support – those who were expelled from their homes without any right, merely for saying, "Our Lord is God"... (Qur'an, 22:39-40)*

In brief, Muslims were allowed to wage war only because they were oppressed and subjected to violence. To put it in another way, God granted permission for war only for defensive purposes. In other verses, Muslims are warned against the use of unnecessary provocation or violence:

> *Fight in the Way of God against those who fight you, but do not go beyond the limits. God does not love those who go beyond the limits. (Qur'an, 2:190)*

After the revelation of these verses, several wars occurred between the Muslims and the pagan Arabs. In none of these wars, however, were the Muslims the inciting party. Furthermore, the Prophet Muhammad established a secure and peaceful social environment for Muslims and pagans alike by signing the peace agreement of Hudaybiya which conceded to the pagans most of their requests. The party who violated the terms of the agreement and started hostilities once again were the pagans. With rapid conversions into Islam, the Islamic armies mustered a great force against the pagan Arabs. However, Muhammad conquered Mecca without bloodshed and in a spirit of tolerance. If he wished, Muhammad could have taken revenge on pagan leaders in the city. Yet, he did not do harm to any one of them, forgave them and treated them with the utmost tolerance. In the words of John Esposito, a Western expert on Islam, "eschewing vengeance and the plunder of conquest, the Prophet instead accepted a settlement, granting amnesty rather than wielding the sword toward his former enemies."

Pagans, who would later convert to Islam of their own free will, could not help admiring such nobility of character in the Prophet.

Not only during Mecca's conquest, but also in the course of all the battles and conquests made in the time of the Prophet Muhammad, the rights of innocent and defenceless people were meticulously protected. The Prophet Muhammad reminded believers numerous times about this subject and by his own practice became a role model for others to follow. Indeed, he addressed believers who were about to go to war in the following terms: "Go to war in adherence to the religion of God. Never touch the elderly, women or children. Always improve their situation and be kind to them. God loves those who are sincere." The Messenger of God also clarified the attitude Muslims must adopt even when they are in the middle of a raging battle:

> *Do not kill children. Avoid touching people who devote themselves to worship in churches! Never murder women and the elderly. Do not set trees on fire or cut them down. Never destroy houses!*

The Islamic principles God proclaims in the Qur'an account for this peaceful and temperate policy of the Prophet Muhammad.

In the Qur'an, God commands believers to treat the non-Muslims kindly and justly:

> *God does not forbid you from being good to those who have not fought you over religion or driven you from your homes, or from being just towards them. God loves those who are just. God merely forbids you from taking as friends those who have fought you over religion and driven you from your homes and who supported your expulsion... (Qur'an, 60:8-9)*

The verses above clarify how Muslims should behave towards non-Muslims: A Muslim should treat all non-Muslims kindly and only avoid making friends with those who show enmity towards Islam. In a case where this enmity causes violent attacks against Muslims, that is, where they wage a war against them, then Muslims should respond to them justly by considering the humane dimensions of the situation. All forms of barbarism, unnecessary acts of violence and unjust aggression are forbidden by Islam. In another verse, God warns Muslims against this and explains that rage felt towards enemies should not cause them to fall into injustice:

> *You who believe! Show integrity for the sake of God, bearing witness with justice. Do not let hatred for a people incite you into not being just. Be just. That is closer to heedfulness. Heed God (alone). God is aware of what you do. (Qur'an, 5:8)*

THE MEANING OF THE CONCEPT OF "JIHAD"

Another concept that deserves clarification due in the context of our discussion is that of "jihad". The exact meaning of "Jihad" is "effort". Thus, in Islam, "to carry out jihad" is "to show effort, to struggle". The Prophet Muhammad explained that "the greatest jihad is the one a person carries out against his lower soul". What is meant by "lower soul" here is selfish desires and ambitions.

Assessed from the Qur'anic point of view, the word "jihad" can also mean a struggle carried out on intellectual grounds against those who oppress people, treat them unjustly, subject them to torture and cruelty and violate legitimate human rights. The purpose of this struggle is to bring about justice, peace and equality. Apart from these ideological and spiritual meanings, struggle in the physical sense is also considered as "jihad". However, as explained above, this has to be a struggle carried out solely for defensive purposes. The use of the concept of "jihad" for acts of aggression against innocent people, that is for terror, would be unjust and a great distortion of the true meaning of the term.

Killing Oneself, In Other Words Committing Suicide, is Forbidden in the Qur'an

Another important matter that arose in the wake of the latest terrorist assaults against the United States is that of suicide attacks. Some people who are ill-informed on Islam have made utterly erroneous statements to the effect that this religion of peace allows suicide attacks, whereas in Islam killing oneself and killing other people are both prohibited. In the words, "Do not kill yourselves." (Qur'an, 4:29) God has declared suicide to be a sin. In Islam it is forbidden for anyone to kill himself or herself, for no matter what reason. The Prophet reveals suicide to be a sin in a parable, when he says that those who commit suicide will be punished:

> *Indeed, whoever (intentionally) kills himself, then certainly he will be punished in the Fire of Hell, wherein he shall dwell forever.*

As this makes clear, committing suicide, and thus carrying out suicide attacks, and causing the deaths of thousands of innocent people while doing so, is a total violation of Islamic morality. God says in the Qur'an that it is a sin to put an end to one's own life. For that reason, it is quite impossible for someone who believes in God and says he abides by the Qur'an to do such a thing. The only people who can do such things are those who have a very mistaken perception of religion, have no idea of true Qur'anic morality, fail to use their reason and conscience, are under the influence of atheist ideologies, and who have been brainwashed with feelings of hatred and revenge. Everybody must oppose such actions.

Compassion, Tolerance and Humanity in the History of Islam

To sum up the facts we have seen so far, we can say that the political doctrine of Islam (in other words, Islamic rules and principles regarding political matters) is exceedingly moderate and peace-loving. This truth is accepted by many non-Muslim historians and theologians. One of these is the British historian Karen Armstrong, a former nun and an expert on Middle East history. In her book Holy War, which examines the history of the three divine religions, she makes the following comments:

> *... The word 'Islam' comes from the same Arabic root as the word 'peace' and the Koran condemns war as an abnormal state of affairs opposed to God's will... Islam does not justify a total aggressive war of extermination... Islam recognises that war is inevitable and sometimes a positive duty in order to end oppression and suffering. The Koran teaches that war must be limited and be conducted in as humane a way as possible. Mohammad had to fight not only the Meccans but also the Jewish tribes in the area and Christian tribes in Syria who planned on offensive against him in alliance with the Jews. Yet this did not make Mohammed denounce the People of the Book. His Muslims were forced to defend themselves but they were not fighting a 'holy war' against the religion of their enemies. When Mohammad sent his freedman Zaid against the Christians at the head of a Muslim army, he told them to fight in the cause of God bravely but humanely. They must not molest priests, monks and nuns nor the weak and helpless people who were unable to fight. There must be no massacre of civilians nor should they cut down a single tree nor pull down any building.*

After the death of the Prophet, the Caliphs who succeeded him were also very sensitive in exercising justice. In conquered countries, both the indigenous people and the newcomers led their lives in peace and security. Abu Bakr, the first Caliph, demanded his people adopt just and tolerant attitudes in these lands. All these attitudes were in compliance with the values of the Qur'an. Abu Bakr gave the following command to his army before the first Syrian expedition:

> *Stop, O people that I may give you ten rules to keep by heart: Do not commit treachery, nor depart from the right path. You must not mutilate, neither kill a child or aged man or woman. Do not destroy a palm tree, nor burn it with fire and do not cut any fruitful tree. You msut not slay any of the flock or herds*

or the camels, save for your subsistence. You are likely to pass by people who have devoted their lives to monastic services; leave them to that to which they have devoted their lives. You are likely, likewise, to find people who will present to you meals of many kinds. You may eat; but do no forget to mention the name of Allah.

Umar ibn al-Khattab, who succeeded Abu Bakr, was famous for the way he exercised justice and made contracts with the indigenous people of the conquered countries. Each one of these contracts proved to be an example of tolerance and justice. For instance, in his declaration granting protection to Christians in Jerusalem and Lod, he ensured that churches would not be demolished and guaranteed that Muslims would not worship in churches in groups. Umar granted the same conditions to the Christians of Bethlehem. During the conquest of Medain, the declaration of protection given to the Nestorian Patriarch Yeshuyab III (650 - 660 AD) again guaranteed that churches would not be demolished and that no building would be converted into a house or a mosque. The letter written by the patriarch to the bishop of Fars (Persia) after the conquest is most striking, in the sense that it depicts the tolerance and compassion shown by Muslim rulers to the Book of People in the words of a Christian:

They [Abbasids] have not attacked the Christian religion, but rather they have commended our faith, honored our priests... and conferred benefits on churches and monasteries.

All these are very important examples revealing the understanding of justice and tolerance of true believers. In a verse God commands the following:

God commands you to return to their owners the things you hold on trust and, when you judge between people, to judge with justice. How excellent is what God exhorts you to do! God is All-Hearing, All-Seeing. (Qur'an, 4:58)

Canon Taylor, one of the mission leaders of the Anglican Church, expresses the beauty revealed by the Islamic morality in one of his speeches as follows:

It [Islam] brought out the fundamental dogmas of religion – the unity and greatness of God, that He is merciful and righteous, that He claims obedience to His will, resignation and faith. It proclaimed the responsibility of man, a future life, a Day of Judgment, and stern retribution to fall upon the wicked; and enforced the duties of prayer, almsgiving, fasting and benevolence. It thrust aside the artificial virtues, the religious frauds and follies, the perverted moral sentiments, and the verbal subtleties of theological disputants... It gave hope to the slave, brotherhood to mankind, and recognition to the fundamental facts of human nature.

The false assertion that people in conquered countries converted to Islam under threat has also been disproved by Western researchers, and the justice and tolerant attitude of Muslims has been confirmed. L.Browne, a Western researcher, expresses this situation in the following words:

Incidentally these well-established facts dispose of the idea so widely fostered in Christian writings that the Muslims, wherever they went, forced people to accept Islam at the point of the sword.

In his book The Prospects of Islam, Browne goes on to say that the real motive behind the Muslims' conquests was the brotherhood of Islam. The vast majority of Muslim administrators who have reigned over the Muslim lands throughout history continued to treat the members of other religions with the utmost tolerance and respect. Within the borders of all Islamic states, both Jews and Christians lived in safety and enjoyed freedom.

Georgetown University's Professor of Religion and International Relations John L. Esposito describes how Jews and Christians who came under the administration of Muslim states met with enormous tolerance:

Muslim armies proved to be formidable conquerors and effective rulers, builders rather than destroyers. They replaced the indigenous rulers and armies of the conquered countries, but preserved much of their government, bureaucracy, and culture. For many in the conquered territories, it was no more than an exchange of masters, one that brought peace to peoples demoralized and disaffected by the casualties and heavy taxation that resulted from the years of Byzantine-Persian warfare. Local communities were free to continue to follow their own way of life in internal, domestic affairs. In many ways, local populations found Muslim rule more flexible and tolerant than that of Byzantium and Persia. Religious communities were free to practise their faith-to worship and be governed by their religious leaders and laws in such areas marriage, divorce, and inheritance. In exchange, they were required to pay tribute, a poll tax (jizya) that entitled them to from Muslim protection from outside aggression and exempted them from military service. They were therefore called the "protected ones" (dhimmmi). In effect, this often meant lower taxes, grater local autonomy, rule by fellow Semites with closer linguistic and cultural ties than the hellenized, Greco-Roman elites of Byzantium, and greater religious freedom for Jews and indigenous Christians. Most of the Christian churches, such as the Nestorians, Monophysites, Jacobites, and Copts, had been persecuted as heretics and schismatics by Christian orthodoxy. For these reasons, some Jewish and Christian communities aided the invading armies, regarding them as less oppressive than their imperial masters. In many ways, the conquests brought a Pax Islamica to an embattled area.

Another "Pax Islamica" brought by Islam was to women, a segment of society that was tremendously abused in the pre-Islamic times. Professor Bernard Lewis, known to be one of the greatest Western experts on the Middle East, makes the following comment:

In general, the advent of Islam brought an enormous improvement in the position of women in ancient Arabia, endowing them with property and some other rights, and giving them a measure of protection against ill treatment by their husbands or owners. The killing of female infants, sanctioned by custom in Pagan Arabia, was outlawed by Islam. But the position of women remained poor, and worsened when, in this as in so many other respects, the original message of Islam lost its impetus and was modified under the influence of pre-existing attitudes and customs.

The reign of the Seljuk Turks and that of the Ottoman Empire were also marked by the just and tolerant outlook of Islam. In his book, *The Spread of Islam in the World,* Sir Thomas Arnold, the British researcher, explains the Christians' willingness to come under Seljuk rule because of this attitude:

> *This same sense of security of religious life under Muslim rule led many of the Christians of Asia Minor, also, about the same time, to welcome the advent of the Saljuq Turks as their deliverers... In the reign of Michael VIII (1261-1282), the Turks were often invited to take possession of the smaller towns in the interior of Asia Minor by the inhabitants, that they might escape from the tyranny of the empire; and both rich and poor often emigrated into Turkish dominions.*

Malik Shah, the ruler of the Islamic Seljuk Empire during its brightest age, approached the people in the conquered lands with great tolerance and compassion and thus was remembered with respect and love by them. All objective historians refer to the justice and tolerance of Malik Shah in their works. His tolerance also kindled feelings of love towards him in the hearts of the People of the Book. For this reason, unprecedented in history, many cities came under Malik Shah's rule of their own free will. Sir Thomas Arnold also mentions Odo de Diogilo, a monk of St. Denis, who participated in the Second Crusade as the private chaplain of Louis VII, refers in his memoirs to the justice administered by Muslims regardless of the subjects' religious affiliation. Based on the graphic account of Odo de Diogilo, Sir Thomas Arnold writes:

> *The situation of the survivors would have been utterly hopeless, had not the sight of their misery melted the hearts of the Muhammadans to pity. They tended the sick and relieved the poor and starving with open-handed liberality. Some even bought up the French money which the Greeks had got out of the pilgrims by force or cunning, and lavishly distributed it among the needy. So great was the contrast between the kind treatment the pilgrims received from the unbelievers and the cruelty of their fellow-Christians, the Greeks, who imposed forced labour upon them, beat them, and robbed them of what little they had left, that many of them voluntarily embraced the faith of their deliverers. As the old chronicler [Odo de Diogilo] says: "Avoiding their co-religionists who had been so cruel to them, they*

went in safety among the infidels who had compassion upon them, and, as we heard, more than three thousand joined themselves to the Turks when they retired."

These statements by historians reveal that Muslim administrators who truly adopted the morality of the Islam always ruled with tolerance, compassion and justice. Likewise, the history of the Ottoman Empire which ruled lands on three continents for centuries abounds with examples of tolerance.

The way the Jews settled in Ottoman lands during the time of Sultan Beyazid II, after being subjected to massacre and exile in the Catholic kingdoms of Spain and Portugal, is a fine example of the tolerance that Islamic morality brings with it.

The Catholic monarchs who ruled much of Spain at the time brought grave pressure to bear on the Jews who had formerly lived in peace under Muslim rule in Andalusia. While Muslims, Christians and Jews were able to live side by side in peace in Andalusia, the Catholic monarchs tried to force the whole country to become Christian, and declared war on the Muslims while oppressing the Jews. As a result, the last Muslim ruler in the Granada region of southern Spain was overthrown in 1492. Muslims were subjected to terrible slaughter, and those Jews who refused to change their religion were sent into exile.

One group of these Jews without a homeland sought shelter in the Ottoman Empire, and the state allowed them to do so. The Ottoman fleet, under the command of Kemal Reis, brought the exiled Jews, and those Muslims who had survived the slaughter, to the land of the Ottomans.

Sultan Beyazid II has gone down in history as a most pious believer, and in the spring of 1492 he settled these wronged Jews who had been expelled from Spain in certain parts of his empire, around Edirne, and Thessalonica in present-day Greece. Most of the 25,000 Turkish Jews living in Turkey today are the ancestors of those Spanish Jews. They have adapted their religion and customs, which they brought from Spain some 500 years ago, to the conditions in Turkey, and continue to live most comfortably with their own schools, hospitals, old people's homes, cultural associations and newspapers. In the same way that they have traders and businessmen, they also have representatives in numerous professions, from technical subjects to advertising, with increasingly developing intellectual circles. While Jewish communities in many countries in Europe have for centuries been exposed to the fear of anti-Semitic racist attacks, those in Turkey have lived in peace and security. This example alone is enough to demonstrate the tolerance that Islam brings with it and its understanding of justice.

The compassion and tolerance exhibited by Sultan Beyazid II applied to all the Ottoman sultans. When Sultan Mehmet the Conqueror captured Constantinople, he allowed the Christians and the Jews to live freely there. André Miquel, who is known for the valuable works he has written about the just and tolerant practices of Muslims and the world of Islam, says:

> *Christians lived under a very well-administered government which they were unable to find in the time of the Byzantine and Latin states. They at no time saw any systematic oppression. On the contrary, the empire, and Constantinople in particular, became a shelter for those Spanish Jews who had been tortured. There was no forced imposition of Islam anywhere.*

As is clear from these facts, Muslims have at no time in history been oppressive. On the contrary, they have brought peace and security to all nations and beliefs wherever they have gone. They have abided by God's verse which says: "Worship God and do not associate anything with Him. Be good to your parents and relatives and to orphans and the very poor, and to neighbours who are related to you and neighbours who are not related to you, and to companions and travellers and your slaves. God does not love anyone vain or boastful." (Qur'an, 4:36) and have behaved well to all people. In short, friendship, brotherhood, peace and love are the bases of Qur'anic morality, and it is to these superior virtues that Muslims try to adhere.

THE REAL FACE OF THE TERRORISTS WHO ACT IN THE NAME OF RELIGION

All these examples reveal that organising acts of terror against innocent people is utterly against Islam and it is unlikely that any

Muslim could ever commit such crime. On the contrary, Muslims are responsible for stopping these people, removing "mischief on earth" and bringing peace and security to all people all over the world.

It is not possible to talk about "Christian terror", "Jewish terror" or "Islamic terror". Indeed, an examination into the background of the perpetrators of these acts reveal that the terrorism in question is not a religious but a social phenomenon.

CRUSADERS: BARBARIANS WHO TRAMPLED THEIR OWN RELIGION

The true message of a religion or a system of belief can be at times distorted by its own pseudo-adherents. The Crusaders, whose period constitutes a dark episode in Christian history, are an example of this type of distortion. The Crusaders were European Christians who undertook expeditions from the end of the 11th century onwards to recover the Holy Land (Palestine and the surrounding area) from the Muslims. They set out with a so-called religious goal, yet they laid waste each acre of land they entered spreading fear wherever they went. They subjected civilians along their way to mass executions and plundered many villages and towns.

Their conquest of Jerusalem, where Muslims, Jews and Christians lived under Islamic rule in peace, became the scene of immense bloodshed. They massacred all the Muslims and Jews in the city without mercy. In the words of one historian, "They killed all the Saracens and the Turks they found... whether male of female."16 One of the Crusaders, Raymond of Aguiles, boasted of this violence:

> *Wonderful sights were to be seen. Some of our men (and this was more merciful) cut off the heads of their enemies; others shot them with arrows, so that they fell from the towers; others tortured them longer by casting them into the flames. Piles of heads, hands and feet were to be seen in the streets of the city. It was necessary to pick one's way over the bodies of men and horses. But these were small matters compared to what happened at the Temple of Solomon, a place where religious services*

are normally chanted... in the Temple and porch of Solomon, men rode in blood up to their knees and bridle reins.

In two days, the Crusader army killed some 40,000 Muslims in the barbaric ways just described. The Crusaders' barbarism was so excessive that, during the Fourth Crusade, they plundered Constantinople (present-day Istanbul), a Christian city, and stole the golden objects from the churches.

Of course, all this barbarism was utterly against Christian doctrine. Christianity, in the words of the Bible, is a "message of love". In the Gospel according to Matthew, it is said that Jesus said to his followers, "Love your enemies and pray for those who persecute you" (Matthew, 5:44). In the Gospel according to Luke, it is said that Jesus said, "To him who strikes you on the cheek, offer the other also." (Luke, 6:29) In no part of the Gospels is there any reference to the legitimacy of violence; thus murdering innocent people is unimaginable. You can find the concept of "murdering the innocent" in the Bible; but only in the cruel Jewish King Herod's attempt to kill Jesus while he was a baby.

If Christianity is a religion based on love that accommodates no violence, how did Christian Crusaders carry out some of the most violent acts in history? The major reason for this was that the Crusaders were mainly made up of ignorant people who could better be defined as "rabble". These masses, who knew almost nothing about their religion, who had probably never read or even seen the Bible once in their lifetime, and who were for the most part completely unaware of the moral values of the Bible, were led into barbarism under the conditioning of Crusaders' slogans which presented this violence as "God's Will". Employing this fraudulent method, many were encouraged to commit dreadful acts strictly forbidden by the religion.

It is worth mentioning that in that period, Eastern Christians – the people of Byzantium, for instance – who were culturally far ahead of Western Christians, espoused more humane values. Both before and after the Crusaders' conquests, Orthodox Christians managed to live together with Muslims. According to Terry Jones, the BBC commentator, with the withdrawal of the Crusaders from Middle East, "civilized life started again and members of the three monotheistic faiths returned to peaceful coexistence." The example of the Crusaders is indicative of a general phenomenon. The more the adherents of an ideology are uncivilised, intellectually underdeveloped and ignorant, the more likely they are to resort to violence. This also holds true for ideologies that have nothing to do with religion. All communist movements around the world are prone to violence. Yet the most savage and bloodthirsty of them were the Red Khmers in Cambodia. This was because they were the most ignorant.

THE BEDOUIN CHARACTER IN THE QUR'AN

In the period of the Prophet Muhammad, there existed two basic social structures in Arabia. City-dwellers and Bedouins (desert Arabs). A sophisticated culture prevailed in Arab towns. Commercial relations linked the towns to the outer world, which contributed to the formation of "good manners" among Arabs dwelling in cities. They had refined aesthetic values, enjoyed literature and especially poetry. Desert Arabs, on the other hand, were the nomad tribes living in the desert who had a very crude culture. Utterly unaware of arts and literature, they developed an unrefined character. Islam was born and developed among the inhabitants of Mecca, the most important city of the peninsula. However, as Islam spread to the rest of the peninsula, all the tribes in Arabia embraced it. Among these tribes were also desert Arabs, who were somehow problematic: their poor intellectual and cultural background prevented some of them from grasping the profundity and noble spirit of Islam. Of this God states the following in a verse:

> *The desert Arabs are the worst in disbelief and hypocrisy, and more fitted to be ignorant of the limits which God has sent down to His Messenger. But God is Knowing, Wise. (Qur'an, 9:97)*

The desert Arabs, that is, social groups who were "worst in disbelief and hypocrisy" and prone to disobey God's commands, became a part of the Islamic world in the Prophet's time. However, in later periods, they became a source of trouble for the house of Islam. The sect called "Kharijis" that emerged among the Bedouins was an example. The most distinctive trait of this perverse sect (which was called "Kharijis", the "rebels", because they greatly deviated from Sunni practices), was their wild and fanatical nature. The "Kharijis", who had little understanding of the essence of Islam or of the virtues and the values of the Qur'an, waged war against all other Muslims basing this war on a few Qur'anic verses about which they made distorted interpretations. Furthermore, they carried out "acts of terrorism". Ali, who was one of the closest companions of the Prophet and was described as the "gate of the city of knowledge", was assassinated by a Kharijite.

In later periods, "Hashashis", another brutal organisation, emerged; this was a "terrorist organisation" made up of ignorant and fanatical militants bereft of a profound understanding of the essence of Islam and thus who could be readily influenced by simple slogans and promises.

In other words, just as the Crusaders distorted and misinterpreted Christianity as a teaching of brutality, some perverted groups emerging in the Islamic world misinterpreted Islam and resorted to brutality. What is common to these sects and the Crusaders was their "Bedouin" nature. That is, they were ignorant, unrefined and uncultivated, lacking a true understanding of their religion. The violence they resorted to resulted from this lack of understanding, rather than from the religion they claimed to espouse.

A TERRORIST IS WTIHOUT PITY WHOSE ONLY PURPOSE IS TO DESTROY

The founder of Russian Anarchy, Michael Bakunin and his disciple Nechayev define an ideal terrorist in this way:

> *The whole work of his [a revolutionist's] existence, not only in words, but also in deeds, is at war with the existing order of society, and with the whole so-called civilized world, with its laws, morals and customs, he is an uncompromising opponent... He knows only one science; the science of destruction.* (The Alarm *Newspaper Article, "Bakunin's Ground-Work for the Social Revolution," 1885 Dec. 26, 8 p.)*

As understood from these words of Bakunin and Nechayev, terrorists are people who sever their relationship with every material and spiritual institution thereby rejecting every moral value, and who view these institutions as impediments to their designs.

Bakunin also said, "Day and night dare he [a revolutionist] have only one thought, one aim: the unmerciful destruction; while he, cold-blooded and without rest, follows that aim, he himself must be ready to die at any time and ready to kill with his own hands any one who seeks to thwart his aims." In his Ground-Work for the Social Revolution, there is this description of what kind of person a terrorist must be:

> *Stringent with himself he must also be to others. All weak sentiment towards relation, friendship, love and thankfulness must be suppressed through the only cold passion of the revolutionary work.*

These words lay bare the dark face of terrorism and show that it is completely opposed to the religion of Islam which is founded on peace, tolerance and love. In this verse, God reveals that peace is the real salvation of humanity and that pursuing the opposite, that is war and conflict, is to walk in the steps of Satan:

> *O You who believe! Enter absolutely into peace (Islam). Do not follow in the footsteps of Satan. He is an outright enemy to you. (Qur'an, 2:208)*

The Mass Psychology of Terrorism

Another important characteristic of terrorists is that they act with a collective spirit. Within this spirit, individual ideas and personal choice are disregarded as everyone is directed toward one single goal. Those who act within this collective spirit may do things they would never do in their right mind and commit acts without using their own will and consciousness. In many countries of the world, terror groups composed of a few unintelligent and uneducated people get caught up in the emotional hysteria of mass meetings, slogans, and without even knowing what they are doing or why, they get involved in committing mass atrocities. In one moment, such people can turn into killers with blood on their hands, and even terrorists who are able to commit inhuman acts. A person may seem quiet and calm when he is alone, but when he becomes a part of a terrorist group, he may become capable of committing acts of arson and assault for no apparent reason. Such spells are cast over individuals that they are even willing to be killed for their cause.

The majority of those who take part in acts of terror often have weak wills and consciences, and they become like a flock of sheep under the influence of mass psychology. Good sense and judgment are substituted by excessive and extravagant emotionalism and a tendency toward violence and aggression. Such people are easily provoked, intolerant and know no limitation set by any law. The error of this mass psychology is revealed in the Qur'an where it says that human beings must act according to their own will and intelligence:

> *Do not pursue what you have no knowledge of. Hearing, sight and hearts will all be questioned. (Qur'an, 17:36)*

One of the Sources of Terrorism: Third World Fanaticism

These examples from history may help us gain better understanding of the present phenomenon, the so-called "Islamic terror", which is nowadays at the top of the international agenda. That is because those who emerge and carry out acts of terrorism in the name of Islam and those who back such acts, representing a tiny minority in the world of Islam, stem from this "character peculiar to Bedouins", not from Islam itself. Failing to understand the essence of Islam, which is essentially a religion of peace and justice, they make it a tool of barbarism, which is simply an outcome of their social and cultural structure. The origin of this barbarism, which may well be called "Third World Fanaticism", is the benighted initiatives of people who are devoid of love for their fellow human-beings.

It is a fact that, for the last few centuries, Muslims in all corners of the Islamic world, have been subjected to violence by Western forces and their allies. The colonialist European states, local oppressive regimes or colonialists backed by the West (Israel, for example) have caused great suffering to Muslims at large. However, for Muslims, this is a situation that has to be approached and responded to from a purely Qur'anic stance.

In no part of the Qur'an does God command believers to respond to violence with violence. On the contrary, God commands Muslims to "respond to evil with goodness":

> *A good deed and a bad deed are not the same. Repel the bad with something better and, if there is enmity between you and someone else, he will be like a bosom friend. (Qur'an, 41:34)*

It is no doubt a legitimate right of Muslims to react against this cruelty. However, these reactions should never turn into a blind hatred, an unjust enmity. God warns about this in the following verse:

> *...Let not the hatred of a people [who once] obstructed you from the Sacred Mosque lead you to transgress. Help one another in benevolence and piety, and help not one another in sin and transgression... (Qur'an, 5:2)*

Consequently, carrying out terrorist acts against the innocent people of other nations under the pretence of "representing the innocent nations in the world", is by no means compatible with Islam.

Another point that deserves a special mention here is that all Western nations and communities cannot be held responsible for the aforementioned violence and oppression against Muslims. Actually, the materialist, irreligious philosophies and ideologies that prevailed in the 19th century are in the main responsible for these dismal acts. European colonialism did not originate from Christianity. On the contrary, anti-religious movements opposing the values of Christianity led the way to colonialism.

At the roots of the greatest brutalities of the 19th century lies the Social Darwinist ideology. In the Western world today, there are still cruel, mischievous and opposing factors, as well as a culture dominated by peaceful and just elements that have its roots in Christianity. As a matter of fact, the main disagreement is not between the West and Islam. Contrary to the general opinion, it is between the devout people of the West and of the Muslim world on the one hand, and the people opposing religion (materialists, atheists, Darwinists etc.) on the other.

Another indication that Third World Fanaticism has nothing to do with Islam is that, until recently, this fanaticism had been identified with the communist ideology. As is well-known, similar anti-Western acts of terror were carried out in 1960s and 1970s by Soviet-backed communist organisations. As the impact of the communist ideology faded, some of the social structures which gave birth to communist organisations have turned their attention to Islam. This "brutality presented under the guise of religion", which is formulated by the incorporation of some Islamic concepts and symbols into the former communist literature is entirely against the moral values which constitute the essence of Islam.

A last remark about this issue is that Islam is not peculiar to a particular nation or geographical region. Contrary to the dominant Western perception, Islam is not an "eastern culture". Islam is the last religion revealed to mankind as a guide to the true path that recommends itself to all humanity. Muslims are responsible for communicating the true religion they believe in to all people of all nations and cultures and making them feel closer to Islam.

Consequently, there is a unique solution for people and groups who, in the name of Islam, resort to terror, form oppressive regimes and turn this world into a dreadful place instead of beautifying it: revealing the true nature of Islam and communicating it so that the masses can understand and live by it.

One of The Methods of Terrorism is to Cause Fear and Panicin Society

One of the most important characteristics of terrorism is that it selects its targets indiscriminately. The fact that it determines these targets without discrimination is one of the most important reasons for the spread of fear, because no one can feel secure. If people know that they are possible targets for noreasons, no-one will feel safe from the terrorists. There is nothing a potential target can do to protect themselves, since terrorists act according to their own rules, in a time and place of their own choosing. Thus acts of terror in society are arbitrary and unpredictable.

The Error of Radicalism

There is another idea that we must examine together with that of terror; that is, the phenomenon of radicalism. Radicalism means supporting sudden revolutionary destructive changes in any sphere and applying a strict uncompromising policy in order to achieve them. Radicals are characterised by their desire for revolutionary change and the stern, sometimes aggressive attitude they adopt.

In this, as in every sphere of life, the guide for the Muslim is the Qur'an. When we look at radicalism in the light of the Qur'an, we see that it has nothing to do with the way in which God commands the believers to behave.

When God describes a believer in the Qur'an, He depicts him as a loving, soft-spoken person, shunning conflicts and arguments, approaching even the most hostile people with warmth and friendship. An example to guide us in this matter is the command given by God to Moses and Aaron to go to Pharaoh and speak gently to him:

> *Go to Pharaoh; he has overstepped the bounds. But speak to him with gentle words so that hopefully he will pay heed or show some fear. (Qur'an, 20:43-44)*

Pharaoh was one of the most cruel and rebellious unbelievers of his time. He was a despot who denied God and worshipped idols; moreover, he subjected believers (the Israelites of the time) to terrible cruelties and murder. But God commanded His prophets to go to such a hostile man and speak to him gently. You will notice that the way shown by God was the way of friendly dialogue, not the way of conflict with sharp words, angry slogans and agitated protests.

There are a few other examples to show Muslims how to behave in the dialogue between Shu'ayb and the deniers. This dialogue is related in the Qur'an in this way:

> *And to Madyan their brother Shu'ayb. He said, "My people, worship God! You have no deity apart from Him. Do not give short measure and short weight. I see you prospering and I fear for you the punishment of an all-encompassing Day.*

My people! Give full measure and full weight with justice; do not diminish people's goods; and do not go about the earth, corrupting it. What endures with God is better for you if you are believers. I am not set over you as your keeper." They said, "Shu'ayb, do your prayers instruct you that we should abandon what our fathers worshipped or stop doing whatever we want to with our wealth? Yet you are such a lenient, normal person!"

> *He said, "My people! What do you think? If I do possess a Clear Sign from my Lord and He has given me His good provision, I do not want to oppose you in what way I am forbidding you. I only want to put things right as far as I can. My success is with God alone. I have put my trust in Him and I turn to Him." (Qur'an, 11:84-88)*

When we examine what he says, we see that Shu'ayb invited the people to believe in God and to adopt high moral principals and he did this with friendliness and humility. We can explain some of the reasons behind of the things said in these verses:

* When Shu'ayb says "I am not set over you as your keeper." to the people, he does not want to dominate them; his only intention is to inform them of the truth that God has revealed.
* "You are clearly the forbearing, the rightly-guided": These words of the deniers to Shu'ayb show his warm, gentle and courteous character and that this was particularly appreciated by the deniers.
* "My people! What do you think?" This expression used by Shu'ayb shows that he calls on the deniers to use their intelligence and conscience. In other words, he does not use insistent pressure, but questions their ideas from an opposing stance and invites them to consider and come to a conclusion based on their own free conscience.
* "I do not want to oppose you in what way I am forbidding you". Shu'ayb's prohibition here is not actually a prohibition. He explains that some acts are sinful and invites the people to abandon them. Moreover, when Shu'ayb says "I do not want to oppose you", it is not his purpose to dispute with the people; he does not want to make them uncomfortable and incite a quarrel; he wants only to invite them to faith and the practice of high moral principles.

If you examine the Qur'an you will see that a warm, gentle and tolerant disposition characterized all the prophets. God describes Abraham as "tender-hearted and forbearing." (Qur'an, 9:114) and in another verse, the Prophet Muhammad's moral principles are described in this way:

It is a mercy from God that you were gentle with them. If you had been rough or hard of heart, they would have scattered from around you. So pardon them and ask forgiveness for them, and consult with them about the matter. Then when you have reached a firm decision, put your trust in God. God loves those who put their trust in Him. (Qur'an, 3:159)

An obvious characteristic of radicalism is its anger. This disposition can be clearly seen in the speeches, writings and demonstrations of radicals. However, anger is not an attribute of Muslims. When God describes believers in the Qur'an, he describes, "those who give in times of both ease and hardship, those who control their rage and pardon other people – God loves the good-doers" (Qur'an, 3:134)

There is no situation in which a Muslim displays anger. The only thing a Muslim wants from other people is that they believe in God and live according to moral principles, but this is possible only by the grace of God. No matter what we do, no matter how much we try to explain the truth to people, human hearts are in God's hands. God reminds Muslims of this very important fact in this verse, "...Do those who believe not know that if God had wanted to He could have guided all mankind?..." (Qur'an, 13:31)

There is another verse that emphasises this same fact;

If your Lord had willed, all the people on the earth would have believed. Do you think you can force people to be believers? (Qur'an, 10:99)

Therefore, it is the duty of a Muslim only to explain the facts and to invite people to accept them. Whether or not people accept the invitation is completely up to their own conscience. God reveals this truth in the Qur'an when He says that there is no compulsion in religion.

There is no compulsion in religion. True guidance has become clearly distinct from error. Anyone who rejects false deities and has belief in God has grasped the Firmest Handhold, which will never give way. God is All-Hearing, All-Knowing. (Qur'an, 2:256)

Therefore, there is no coercion to make people believe and become Muslims, or to make Muslims perform prayers and beware of sin. There is only advice. God reveals in a few verses addressed to the Messenger of God that Muslims are not oppressors:

We know best what they say. You are not a dictator over them. So remind, with the Qur'an, whoever fears My Threat. (Qur'an, 50:45)

Say: "Mankind! The truth has come to you from your Lord. Whoever is guided is only guided for his own good. Whoever is misguided is only misguided to his detriment. I have not been set over you as a guardian." (Qur'an, 10:108)

Muslims are responsible only for explaining their religion; they apply no pressure or coercion on anyone and are enjoined to speak gently to even the most tyrannical deniers. Such persons cannot be radicals, because radicalism stands for the opposite of those qualities we have enumerated. Indeed, radicalism is an un-Islamic current of thought and a political stance that came into the Islamic world from outside. When we examine social phenomena described in terms of radicalism, it will be seen that these are basically a collection of methods and pronouncements used by communists in the past, or an expression of the "fanatical rage" that has no place in true Islam. (The Qur'an, 48:26)

All Muslims must totally reject an angry, unbending argumentative attitude which goes against the very nature of the Qur'an and in its place adopt a friendly, gentle, tolerant, calm and compassionate one.

Muslims must set an example to the world and be admired for their maturity, tolerance, moderation, modesty and peacefulness. Muslims must live Islam in the best possible way and be its representatives to the world, not only in these things, but also by their achievements in the fields of science, culture, art, aesthetics and social order and others.

Explaining Islam to others and defending Islam against ideas alien to it are included in what we have listed above. In the verse below, God clearly reveals what attitude a Muslim must assume with regard to others:

> *Call to the way of your Lord with wisdom and fair admonition, and argue with them in the kindest way. Your Lord knows best who is misguided from His way. And He knows best who are guided. (Qur'an, 16:125)*

Terrorist Methods and Psychology

The concept of terror has a wider meaning in today's language. Generally it refers to the armed conflict carried on by radical ideological groups. In general, terror means intimidation. But this intimidation encompasses a broad field including the whole lives of people who feel the intense threat of fear and violence. Terror includes intense and systematic intimidation designed to make people adopt a certain way of thinking and behaviour, as well as every kind of violent act carried out to produce this intimidation. But in every situation, the target of terrorism is directly or indirectly the citizens themselves.

Terror organisations use terror to rally support. The intimidation they use is calculated to increase their strength and so to gain the support of some or all the citizens.

The first thing that people think of when we mention the word "terror" is generally the kind known as "leftist terror", but there is also a kind of terror found in Third World countries and practiced by dictatorial regimes. Actually the reality here is nothing other than a massive implementation of leftist terror tactics. A dictator or a group in power is oppressive, using their power only for personal gain and for this reason they experience various kinds of social opposition. In this situation, the dictatorial regime always resorts to the same formula to show that it is stronger than the opposition; they inaugurate the use of terror so that citizens will be afraid and their own power are consolidated.

Terror organisations, on the other hand, in accordance with the ideologies they espouse, claim that their aim is to remove a government and its administrators which they regard as illegitimate and cruel and, in so doing, that they will reach their goal of establishing a happier and more just way of life. However, this is not a realistic claim. In the Qur'an, in the first verses of Sura Baqara, God issues this command to those who think in this way:

> *When they are told, "Do not cause corruption on the earth," they say, "We are only putting things right." No indeed! They are the corrupters, but they are not aware of it. (Qur'an, 2:11-12)*

For terrorists, killing people is a way of life. They may shoot innocent people without pity and throw bombs at children. For them shedding blood is a pleasure. They have ceased to be human beings and turned into raving savage beasts. If there is anyone among them who shows the least feeling of compassion, they brand him as a coward or a traitor and demote him. Often they use their guns against one another and carry out bloody purges against internal factions in their own organisation.

It can be seen that terrorism is nothing other than a totally diabolical source of bloodshed. Whoever supports this cycle of savagery is defending a satanic system. If a terrorist uses religious language and symbols, this must not deceive anyone. Terrorists who hide under the cloak of false religion are doubly guilty, both of the blood they have shed and for the anti-religious propaganda they have spread while committing these crimes in the name of religion.

Terror and religion are completely opposed to each other. Terrorism adopts the way of aggression, murder, conflict, cruelty and misery. But according to the Qur'an, all these things are kinds of oppression. God enjoins peace, harmony, goodwill and compromise. He forbids terror and every kind of act that does not promote peace, and, condemns those who commit such acts:

> *But as for those who break God's contract after it has been agreed and sever what God has commanded to be joined, and cause corruption in the earth, the curse will be upon them. They will have the Evil Abode. (Qur'an, 13:25)*

The basic quality that terror and those who are infected by its cruelty have in common is that the fear and love of God is something completely alien to them. Their hearts have become hardened and they are spiritually ill. In the Qur'an, God speaks about the character of such people:

But do not obey any vile swearer of oaths, any backbiter, slandermonger, impeder of good, evil aggressor, gross, coarse and furthermore, despicable.(Qur'an, 68:10-13)

To rebel for no cause and to commit acts of assault are forbidden by God. In Islam, acts of what we call terror and anarchy today are forbidden. In the Qur'an it is said:

Say: "My Lord has forbidden indecency, both open and hidden, and wrong action, and unrightful tyranny, and associating anything with God for which He has sent down no authority, and saying things about God that you do not know." (Qur'an, 7:33)

Acts of Violance - One of the Most Important Methods of Terrorist Propaganda

Terrorists regard acts of violence as propaganda for their organisations. For them, killing innocent people, robbing banks, assassinating people, kidnapping and planting bombs all act as propaganda for their struggle. To the terrorist who is bent on wreaking chaos, what publicity a single act of violence can generate in one day is much more publicity than what millions of hand-out brochures could do.

This idea is totally foreign to every kind of human feeling of compassion, mercy, concord and tolerance; it is alien to the moral teaching of the Qur'an and can gain a following only in those societies in which anti-religious ideologies hold sway. For this reason, the only possible solution that can save humanity from this benighted way of thinking is the widespread acceptance of the moral teachings found in the Qur'an and taken as a way of life.

THE OUTLOOK OF ISLAM ON THE PEOPLE OF THE BOOK

Another important topic that has been on the agenda with the acts of terrorism against the United States is the relation between the Western and Islamic worlds. As is known, by the 90s, some intellectuals were suggesting that the world was due for a struggle that would take place between the West and Islam. This is the basic theme of Samuel Huntington's well-known thesis "The Clash of Civilisations". However, this thesis—better called as "Clash of Ignorance" by Edward W. Said—rests on an imaginary scenario generated by the exaggeration of the influence of some radical and ignorant factions to be found in these two civilisations. Actually, there can be no clash between the Western civilisation and the Islamic civilisation, because the beliefs of Judaism and Christianity, the tenets upon which Western civilisation is based, are in perfect harmony with Islam.

In the Qur'an, Jews and Christians are called the "People of the Book". This is because the members of these two religions abide by the Divine Books revealed by God. The outlook of Islam on the People of the Book is extremely just and compassionate. This attitude towards the People of the Book developed during the years of the birth of Islam. At that time, Muslims were a minority, struggling to protect their faith and suffering oppression and torture from the pagans of the city of Mecca. Due to this persecution, some Muslims decided to flee Mecca and shelter in a safe country with a just ruler. The Prophet Muhammad told them to take refuge the Christian king of Ethiopia. The Muslims who went to Ethiopia found a very fair administration that embraced them with love and respect. The King refused the demands of the pagan messengers who had travelled to Ethiopia and asked him to surrender the Muslims to them, and announced that Muslims could live freely in his country

These Christian attitudes of compassion, mercy, and justice, are referred to in a verse of the Qur'an which states:

> *... You will find the people most affectionate to those who believe are those who say, "We are Christians." That is because some of them are priests and monks and because they are not arrogant. (Qur'an, 5:82)*

COMMON BELIEFS AND VALUES SHARED BY MUSLIMS AND THE PEOPLE OF THE BOOK

Christian and Muslim beliefs have many aspects in common. Judaism too shares many beliefs with Islam. In the Qur'an, God relates that Muslims share the same faith with the People of the

Book and that they say to them "We have faith in what has been sent down to us and what was sent down to you. Our God and your God are one and we submit to Him." (Qur'an, 29:46)

All true adherents of these three great religions:

- believe that God has created the entire universe out of nothing and that He dominates all that exists with His omnipotence.
- believe that God has created man and living things in a miraculous way and that man possesses a soul granted him by God.
- believe in resurrection, Heaven and Hell and angels, and that God has created our lives with a certain destiny.
- believe that besides Jesus, Moses or Muhammad, God sent many prophets such as Noah, Abraham, Isaac and Joseph throughout history, and they love all these prophets.

In one verse, that Muslims make no distinction among prophets is related as follows:

> *The Messenger believes in what has been sent down to him by his Lord, and so do the believers. Each one believes in God and His angels and His Books and His Messengers. We do not differentiate between any of His Messengers. They say, "We hear and we obey. Forgive us, our Lord! You are our journey's end." (Qur'an, 2:285)*

The beliefs of the People of the Book are in harmony with Muslims, not only in terms of faith-related issues, but also of moral values. Today, in a world where such immoralities as adultery, homosexuality, drug addiction and a model of egoism and self-seeking cruelty have grown widespread, the People of the Book and Muslims share the same virtues: Honour, chastity, humility, self-sacrifice, honesty, compassion, mercy and unconditional love.

The Common Forces against Faith

Another important fact that draws Christianity, Judaism and Islam together is the atheist philosophies that are so influential in our time. Among the best-known and most harmful philosophies of our age can be cited materialism, communism, fascism, anarchism, racism, nihilism and existentialism. Many people who believed in the false diagnoses, deceptive descriptions and explanations of these ideas on the universe, society and man, have lost their faith or doubted it. What is more, these ideologies have dragged people, societies and nations into great crises, conflicts and wars. Their share of the blame for the pain and troubles that humanity suffers from today is immense.

While they deny God and creation, all the above-mentioned ideologies are based on a common framework, a so-called scientific basis; Charles Darwin's theory of evolution. Darwinism constitutes the basis of atheist philosophies. This theory claims that living beings have evolved as a result of coincidences and by means of a struggle for life. Therefore, Darwinism sends this deceptive message to people: "You are not responsible to anyone, you owe your life to coincidences, you need to struggle, and if necessary to oppress others to succeed. This world is one of conflict and self-interest".

The social messages put across by Darwinist concepts such as "Natural selection", "struggle for life", "survival of the fittest" are a means of indoctrination. This evil morality advises people to be egoistical, self-seeking, cruel and oppressive. It destroys such virtues as mercy, compassion, self-sacrifice and humility, the moral values of the three great monotheistic religions and presents this as a necessity of "the rules of life." This Darwinist indoctrination is just the opposite of the beliefs of the People of the Book and the message of the Qur'an. Consequently, the Darwinist indoctrination constitutes the foundation of a world which inherently opposes all the three divine religions.

This being the case, it is necessary for the People of the Book and Muslims to co-operate, since they believe in God and accept the morality that He teaches. The followers of these three religions should expose to the world the fallacy of Darwinism, which has no scientific basis, but which people are trying to preserve for the sake of materialist philosophy. They should co-operatively carry out an intellectual struggle against all other deceptive ideas (communism, fascism, racism) that serve atheism. Once this is realized, the world will, in a very short time, embrace peace, tranquility and justice.

Antisemitism is a Racism Totally Contrary to Islam

In our times, antisemitism is an ideology which threatens world peace and targets the well-being and security of innocent people. This is racist hatred felt by some for the Jews. In the 20th century, antisemitism has signed its name to great disasters, one of the most horrible being the cruelty and murder inflicted on the Jews by the Nazis. In addition to this, in many countries authoritarian regimes have targeted Jews and subjected them to cruel treatment. Fascist organisations have harassed Jews and carried out bloody attacks against them.

So how should a Muslim regard Antisemitism?

The answer is obvious. Every Muslim must oppose antisemitism as he would oppose every other racist ideology. Although Muslims justly condemn the cruel and aggressive policies of the State of Israel together with their occupation of adjacent territory, to blanket condemn innocent Jews is not acceptable to Muslims: this would be a symptom of antisemitism. However, criticising official Zionist ideology has nothing to do with antisemitism, since to object to Zionism is to object to an intense form of racism. There are many Jews who also criticise the racist policies of Zionism, and to label them as being antisemetic would be absurd.

Never subjecting a community to a blanket criticism is a command stressed in the Qur'an, there is a need to distinguish between the righteous and the wicked, the cruel ones and the innocent. After referring to some Jews and Christians, who violated God's commands, God also mentions some other Jews and Christians who displayed moral perfection:

> *[However] They are not all alike. Among the People of the Book there is an upright community who recite the revelation of God during the night and fall prostrate before Him. They believe in God and the Last Day, enjoin what is right and forbid what is evil, and vie with one another in good works. They are of the righteous. And whatever good they do, its reward will not be denied them. God knows those who fear [Him]. (Qur'an, 3:113-115)*

Antisemitism is an anti-religion ideology that has its roots in neo-paganism. Therefore, it is unthinkable that a Muslim would espouse antisemitism or feel sympathy for this ideology. Anti-Semites have no respect for Abraham, Moses or David who were blessed prophets chosen by God to be examples for humanity.

Antisemitism and other kinds of racism (eg. prejudice against blacks) have no place in true religion; they are perversions arising from various ideologies and superstitions. Furthermore, when we examine antisemitism and other forms of racism, we see clearly that they promote ideas and a model of society that is totally contrary to the moral teachings of the Qur'an, for example, at the root of antisemitism lie hatred, violence, and lack of compassion. An anti-Semite may be so cruel as to support the murder of Jewish people, men, women, children and the aged, and condone their being subjected to torture.

However, the moral teaching of the Qur'an enjoins love, compassion and mercy for all people. It also commands Muslims to show justice and be forgiving even to their enemies. On the other hand, anti-Semites and other kinds of racists bulk at living together in peace with people of a different race or creed. (eg. German racists (Nazis) and Jewish racists (Zionists) were opposed to Germans and Jews living together; each side rejected this in the name of their respective race as a degeneration.) However, in the Qur'an, there is not the slightest distinction between races; the Qur'an advises that people of different faiths live together in the same society in peace and happiness.

According to the Qur'an, Muslims, Jews and Christians Must Live in Friendship

In the Qur'an, there is a significant difference between the People of the Book and those who have no belief in God. This is especially emphasised in the area of social life. For example, it is said concerning those who associate others with God: "(they) are unclean, so after this year they should not come near the Masjid al-Haram." (Qur'an, 9:28) Those who associate others with God are people who know no divine law, have no moral precepts and who can commit every kind of degrading and perverse deed without hesitation. But the People of the Book, while they rely basically on God's revelation, have moral precepts and know what is lawful and what is not. In the same way, permission has been given to a Muslim man to marry a woman from among the People of the Book. On this subject God commands:

> *Today all good things have been made lawful for you. And the food of those given the Book is also lawful for you and your food is lawful for them. So are chaste women from among the believers and chaste women of those given the Book before you, once you have given them their dowries in marriage, not in fornication or taking them as lovers. But as for anyone who disbelieves, his actions will come to nothing and in the hereafter he will be among the losers. (Qur'an, 5:5)*

These commands show that bonds of kinship may be established as a result of the marriage of a Muslim with a woman from the People of the Book and that those on each side of the union can accept an invitation to a meal. These are the fundamentals that will ensure the establishment of equitable human relationships and a happy communal life. Since the Qur'an enjoins this equitable and tolerant attitude, it is unthinkable that a Muslim could take an opposing view. The just and tolerant practices of the Prophet Muhammad towards the people of the Book set very good examples to Muslims. In the contract made with the Christians of Najran, who lived in the south of Arabia, the Prophet Muhammad demonstrates one of the best examples of tolerance and justice. The contract included the following article:

> *The lives of the people of Najran and its surrounding area, their religion, their land, property, cattle and those of them who are present or absent, their messengers and their places of worship are under the protection of Allah and guardianship of His Prophet.20*

By means of such contracts, the Messenger of God secured a social order for Muslims and the People of the Book alike, which was marked by peace and security. This order was a total manifestation of the following verse:

> *Those who believe, those who are Jews, and the Christians and Sabaeans, all who believe in God and the Last Day and act*

rightly, will have their reward with their Lord. They will feel no fear and will know no sorrow. (Qur'an, 2:62)

The Constitution of Madinah is the most important contract that secured justice and tolerance among Christians, Jews and pagan communities.

The Constitution of Madinah was prepared under the leadership of the Prophet Muhammad 1,400 years ago, that is in 622 AD, to meet the needs of people of different beliefs, and was put into practice as a written legal contract. Different communities of different religions and races that had harboured deep-seated enmity towards one another for 120 years became parties to this legal contract. By means of this contract, the Prophet Muhammad showed that conflicts between those societies, who had been enemies and quite unable to reach any form of compromise, could come to an end, and they could actually live side by side.

According to the Constitution of Madinah, everyone was free to adhere to any belief or religion or to make any political or philosophical choice. People sharing the same views could come together and form a community. Everyone was free to exercise his own justice system. However, anyone who committed a crime would be protected by no-one. The parties to the contract would engage in co-operation with one another, provide support for each other, and would remain under the protection of the Prophet Muhammad. Conflicts between the parties would be brought to the Messenger of God.

This contract was in force from 622 to 632 AD. Through this document, the tribal structures which had formerly been based on blood and kinship were abolished, and people of different cultural, ethnical and geographical backgrounds came together and formed a social unity. The Constitution of Madinah secured absolute religious freedom.

MONASTERIES, CHURCHES AND SYNAGOGUES MUST BE RESPECTED

Another important fact we learn from the Qur'an is that Muslims must respect Jewish and Christian places of worship. In the Qur'an, the places of worship of the People of the Book, ie.

monasteries, churches and synagogues, are mentioned as places of worship protected by God.

> *...if God had not driven some people back by means of others, monasteries, churches, synagogues and mosques, where God's name is mentioned much, would have been pulled down and destroyed. God will certainly help those who help Him – God is All-Strong, Almighty. (Qur'an, 22:40)*

This verse shows every Muslim the importance of respecting and protecting the holy places of the People of the Book. Indeed, the Prophet Mohammad also made contracts with pagans as well as the people of the Book. Pagans were always treated with justice, and when they asked to be taken under protection, their requests were readily accepted by Muhammad. This meant that these communities sought the protection of the Messenger of God in the face of an attack or a wrongful accusation. Throughout his life, many non-Muslims and pagans requested protection from the Prophet Muhammad, and he took them under his protection and ensured their security. In Sura Tawba, God advises that requests of pagans seeking protection be accepted by believers. Of this, God says the following:

> *If any of the idolaters ask you for protection, give them protection until they have heard the words of God. Then convey them to a place where they are safe... (Qur'an, 9:6)*

Jews and Christians, due to their shared commonalities with Muslims are much closer to Muslims than those who have no faith in God. Each of these religions has its book, that is, they are subject to a book sent down by God. They know what is right and what is wrong, what is lawful and what is unlawful according to their scriptures, and all revere the Prophets and Messengers that accompanied them. They all believe in a hereafter, and afterlife where they will have to give an account to God for all their actions. So, there is a shared foundation from where we all can unite upon.

Rallying to a Common Formula

Concerning the People of the Book, God gives Muslims a command in the Qur'an; to rally to a common formula:

> *Say, "O People of the Book! Let us rally to a common formula*

to be binding on both us and you: That we worship none but God; that we associate no partners with Him; that we erect not, from among ourselves, Lords and patrons other than God." (Qur'an, 3:64)

This is indeed our call to Christians and Jews: As people who believe in God and follow His revelations, let us rally to a common formula – "faith". Let us love God, Who is our Creator and Lord, and follow His commands. And let us pray to God to lead us to an even straighter path.

When Muslims, Christians and Jews rally to a common formula this way; when they understand that they are friends not enemies, when they see that the real enemy is the rejection of God, then the world will become a very different place. The wars in many parts of the world, enmities, fears and terrorist attacks will come to an end, and a new civilisation based on love, respect and peace will be established upon this "common formula".

There are important facts to consider for Muslims. What God teaches us in the Qur'an about different peoples and creeds is clear:

* The morality of the Qur'an excludes every kind of racism.
* It is commanded in the Qur'an that, so long as they show no hostility to Islam or Muslims, a tolerant and friendly attitude must be maintained toward other religions.

It is evident that the Jews have committed many errors which the Qur'an points out, criticizes and about which it gives a warning. The crimes committed by Israel in the present day against humanity are painfully well-known, but all this must not be taken by Muslims as a cause to feel hostility against all Jews. Again a basic vantage point prescribed by the Qur'an is not to make judgements about people just because they belong to a particular race, nation or religion. In every community, there are good people as well as wicked people. The Qur'an draws attention to this differentiation. For instance, right after mentioning the rebellious nature - against God and His religion - of some People of the Book, there is reference to an exception and, said thus:

[However] They are not all alike. Among the People of the Book there is an upright community who recite the revelation of God

during the night and fall prostrate before Him. They believe in God and the Last Day, enjoin what is right and forbid what is evil, and vie with one another in good works. They are of the righteous and whatever good they do, its reward will not be denied them. God knows those who fear [Him]. (Qur'an 3:113-115)

In another verse, God commands:

We sent a Messenger among every people saying: "Worship God and keep clear of all false gods." Among them were some whom God guided but others received the misguidance they deserved. Travel about the earth and see the final fate of the deniers. (Qur'an, 16:36)

God revealed to all messengers that He is the Unique and that there is no-one but Him whom people must worship, serve and obey. The divine message, conveyed to the people by God through His messengers, has been communicated to people since the creation of man. Some societies have accepted the message and followed the right path while others have denied and swerved from it. This also holds true for the present day. Some people will side with the righteous, whereas some others will plunge into mischief. This is the law of God. Those who believe should also adopt such an outlook and never forget that there may be sincere, pious people who have fear of God among the members of all religions as well as those who are far removed from the religious tenets.

Our hope is that a world will be established in which people will be able to live together in peace, no matter what race or religion they belong to, in which every racist perversion will be rejected, everyone's rights will be safeguarded and everyone will be respected. The struggle that will have to take place on intellectual grounds against all anti-religious ideologies will hopefully establish the peace that has been longed for. Of this God relates the following in the Qur'an:

Those who disbelieve are the friends and protectors of one another. If you do not act in this way (be friends and protectors of one another) there will be turmoil in the land and great corruption. (Qur'an, 8:73)

> *Would that there had been more people with a vestige of good among the generations of those who came before you, who forbade corruption in the earth, other than the few among them whom We saved. Those who did wrong gladly pursued the life of luxury that they were given and were evildoers. (Qur'an, 11:116)*

ISLAMIC SPAIN AND PORTUGAL

Muslims conquered Spain in the year 711. The medieval Iberian Peninsula was the scene of almost constant warfare between the Muslim al-Andalus (and later Taifas) and Christian kingdoms. Periodic raiding expeditions were sent from Al-Andalus to ravage the Christian Iberian kingdoms, bringing back treasure and slaves. In raid against Lisbon, in 1189, for example, the Almohad caliph Yaqub al-Mansur took 3,000 female and child captives, while his governor of Córdoba, in a subsequent attack upon Silves in 1191, took 3,000 Christian slaves.

The Almohad Dynasty, was a Berber, Muslim dynasty that was founded in the 12th century, and conquered all Northern Africa as far as Libya, together with Al-Andalus (Moorish Iberian Peninsula). The Almohads, who declared an everlasting Jihad against the Christians, far surpassed the Almoravides in fundamentalist outlook, and they treated the *dhimmis* harshly. Faced with the choice of either death or conversion, many Jews and Christians emigrated. Some, such as the family of Maimonides, fled east to more tolerant Muslim lands, while others went northward to settle in the growing Christian kingdoms.

INDIAN SUBCONTINENT

Sir Jadunath Sarkar contends that several Muslim invaders were waging a systematic Jihad against Hindus in India to the effect that "Every device short of massacre in cold blood was resorted to in order to convert heathen subjects." In particular the records kept by al-Utbi, Mahmud al-Ghazni's secretary, in the Tarikh-i-Yamini document several episodes of bloody military campaigns. In the late tenth century, a story spread that before Muhammad destroyed the idols at the Kaaba, that of Manât was secretly sent to a Hindu temple in India; and the place was renamed as *So-Manât* or *Somnath.* Acting on this, the Shiva idol at the Somnath temple was destroyed in a raid by Mahmud Ghazni in CE 1024; which is considered the first act of Jihad in India. In 1527, Babur ordered a Jihad against Rajputs at the battle of Khanwa. Publicly addressing his men, he declared the forthcoming battle a Jihad. His soldiers were facing a non-Muslim army for the first time ever. This, he said, was their chance to become either a *Ghazi* (soldier of Islam) or a*Shaheed* (Martyr of Islam). The Mughal emperor Aurangzeb waged a Jihad against those identified as heterodox within India's Islamic community, such as Shi'a Muslims.

West Africa

The Fula or Fulani jihads, were a series of independent but loosely connected events across West Africa between the late 17th century and European colonization, in which Muslim Fulas took control of various parts of the region. Between 1750 and 1900, between one- to two-thirds of the entire population of the Fulani jihad states consisted of slaves.

Caucasus

In 1784, Imam Sheikh Mansur, a Chechen warrior and Muslim mystic, led a coalition of Muslim Caucasian tribes from throughout the Caucasus in a ghazavat, or holy war, against the Russian invaders. Sheikh Mansur was captured in 1791 and died in the Schlüsselburg Fortress. Avarian Islamic scholar Ghazi Muhammad preached that Jihad would not occur until the Caucasians followed Sharia completely rather than following a mixture of Islamic laws and *adat* (customary traditions). By 1829, Mullah began proselytizing and claiming that obeying Sharia, giving zakat, prayer, and hajj would not be accepted by Allah if the Russians were still present in the area. He even went on to claim that marriages would become void and children bastards if any Russians were still in the Caucasus. In 1829 he was proclaimed imam in Ghimry, where he formally made the call for a holy war. In 1834, Ghazi Muhammad died at the battle of Ghimri, and Imam Shamil took his place as the premier leader of the Caucasian resistance. Imam Shamil succeeded in accomplishing what Sheik Mansur had started: to unite North Caucasian highlanders in their struggle against the

Russian Empire. He was a leader of anti-Russian resistance in the Caucasian War and was the third Imam of Dagestan and Chechnya (1834–1859).

MAHDISTS IN SUDAN

During the 1870s, European initiatives against the slave trade caused an economic crisis in northern Sudan, precipitating the rise of Mahdist forces. Muhammad Ahmed Al Mahdi was a religious leader, who proclaimed himself the Mahdi—the prophesied redeemer of Islam who will appear at end times—in 1881, and declared a Jihad against Ottomanrulers. He declared all "Turks" infidels and called for their execution. The Mahdi raised an army and led a successful religious war to topple the Ottoman-Egyptian occupation of Sudan. Victory created an Islamic state, one that quickly reinstituted slavery. In the West he is most famous for defeating and later killing British general Charles George Gordon, in the fall of Khartoum.

Wahabbists

The Saudi Salafi sheiks were convinced that it was their religious mission to wage Jihad against all other forms of Islam. In 1801 and 1802, the Saudi Wahhabists under Abdul Aziz ibn Muhammad ibn Saud attacked and captured the holy Shia cities of Karbala and Najaf in Iraq, massacred the Shiites and destroyed the tombs of the Shiite Imam Husayn andAli bin Abu Talib. In 1802 they overtook Taif. In 1803 and 1804 the Wahhabis overtook Mecca and Medina.

Ottoman Empire

Upon succeeding his father, Suleiman the Magnificent began a series of military conquests in Europe. On August 29, 1526, he defeated Louis II of Hungary (1516–26) at thebattle of Mohács. In its wake, Hungarian resistance collapsed and the Ottoman Empire became the preeminent power in South-Eastern Europe. In July 1683 Sultan Mehmet IVproclaimed a Jihad and the Turkish grand vizier, Kara Mustafa Pasha, laid siege to Vienna with an army of 138,000 men.

On November 14, 1914, in Constantinople, capital of the Ottoman Empire, the religious leader Sheikh-ul-Islam declares Jihad on behalf of the Ottoman government, urging Muslims all over the world—including in the Allied countries—to take up arms against Britain, Russia, France, Serbia and Montenegro in World War I. On the other hand,Sheikh Hussein ibn Ali, the Emir of Mecca, refused to accommodate Ottoman requests that he endorse this jihad, a requirement that was necessary were a jihad to become popular, due to British pressure and on the grounds that:

'the Holy War was doctrinally incompatible with an aggressive war, and absurd with a Christian ally: Germany'

Afghanistan

Ahmad Shah, founder of the Durrani Empire, declared a jihad against the Marathas, and warriors from various Pashtun tribes, as well as other tribes answered his call. The Third battle of Panipat (January 1761), fought between largely Muslim and largely Hindu armies who numbered as many as 100,000 troops each, was waged along a twelve-kilometre front, and resulted in a decisive victory for Ahmad Shah.

In response to the Hazara uprising of 1892, the Afghan Emir Abdur Rahman Khan declared a "Jihad" against the Shiites. The large army defeated the rebellion at its center, inOruzgan, by 1892 and the local population was severely massacred. According to S. A. Mousavi, *"thousands of Hazara men, women, and children were sold as slaves in the markets of Kabul and Qandahar, while numerous towers of human heads were made from the defeated rebels as a warning to others who might challenge the rule of the Amir"*. Until the 20th century, some Hazaras were still kept as slaves by the Pashtuns; although Amanullah Khan banned slavery in Afghanistan during his reign, the tradition carried on unofficially for many more years.

The First Anglo-Afghan War (1838–42) was one of Britain's most ill-advised and disastrous wars. William Brydon was the sole survivor of the invading British army of 16,500 soldiers and civilians. As in the earlier wars against the British and Soviets, Afghan resistance to the American invaders took the traditional form of a Muslim holy war against the infidels. During September 2002, the remnants of the Taliban forces began a recruitment drive in Pashtun areas in bothAfghanistan and Pakistan to launch a renewed "jihad" or holy war against the pro-Western Afghan government and the U.S-led coalition.

Pamphlets distributed in secret during the night also began to appear in many villages in the former Taliban heartland in southeastern Afghanistan that called for jihad. Small mobile training camps were established along the border with Pakistan by al-Qaeda and Taliban fugitives to train new recruits in guerrilla warfare and terrorist tactics, according to Afghan sources and a United Nations report.

Most of the new recruits were drawn from the madrassas or religious schools of the tribal areas of Pakistan, from which the Taliban had originally arisen. As of 2008, theinsurgency, in the form of a Taliban guerrilla war, continues.

Although there is no evidence that the CIA directly supported the Taliban or Al Qaeda, some basis for military support of the Taliban was provided when, in the early 1980s, the CIA and the ISI (Pakistan's Interservices Intelligence Agency) provided arms to Afghan mujahideens resisting the Soviet invasion of Afghanistan, and the ISI assisted the process of gathering radical Muslims from around the world to fight against the Soviets. Osama Bin Laden was one of the key players in organizing training camps for the foreign Muslim volunteers. The U.S. poured funds and arms into Afghanistan, and "by 1987, 65,000 tons of U.S.-made weapons and ammunition a year were entering the war."

Algeria

In 1830, Algeria was invaded by France; French colonial domination over Algeria supplanted what had been domination in name only by the Ottoman Empire. Within two years,Abd al-Qâdir was made an *amir* and with the loyalty of a number of tribes began a jihad against the French. He was effective at using guerrilla warfare and for a decade, up until 1842, scored many victories. He was noted for his chivalry. On December 21, 1847, Abd al-Qâdir was forced to surrender.

Abd al-Qâdir is recognized and venerated as the first hero of Algerian independence. Not without cause, his green and white standard was adopted by the Algerian liberation movement during the War of Independence and became the national flag of independent Algeria.

The Algerian Civil War (1991–2002) was an armed conflict between the Algerian government and various Islamist rebel groups which began in 1991. By 1997, the organized jihad in Algeria had disintegrated into criminal thuggery and Algeria was wracked by massacres of intense brutality and unprecedented size.

China

Uyghur Muslim forces under Yaqub Beg declared a Jihad against Chinese Muslims under T'o Ming during the Dungan revolt. Yaqub Beg enlisted non Muslim Han Chinese militia under Hsu Hsuehkung in order to fight against the Chinese Muslims. T'o Ming's forces were defeated by Yaqub, who planned to conquer Dzungharia. Yaqub intended to seize all Dungan territory. The Boxer Rebellion was considered a Jihad by the Muslim Kansu Braves in the Chinese Imperial Army under Dong Fuxiang, fighting against the Eight-Nation Alliance.

Jihad was declared obligatory and a religious duty for all Chinese Muslims against Japan after 1937 during the Second Sino-Japanese War.

PAST HOLY WARS

The following are some highlighted dates in timeline of violence by Muslims(it includes: Muhammad's followers in Islam's early days acting for his honor/sake, Muslims using Islamic themes, Quranic text or/and ideas, mobilized forced conversions, "religious cleansing" campaigns to *cleanse* the area of non-Muslims, attacks by Islamic religious authorities often explained with declaration of clear 'Islamic' goals, war with a clear subjugation of Dhimmitude / infidels status, [regarding the massacres in early Islam in Spain.] violence triggered by Islamic clerics preaching in mosques, battles described as Jihad or holy war and emerging of radical-Islamic movements- which take its roots from Muhammad/Quran -

inspiring source for violence) from its early days till post WW2, 622-1946.

Early Islam (622-634)

Early Islam - 622-634

1. The killing of Abu Afak. The poet who mocked Muhammad was killed with "one blow of his sword when the latter slept outside his house."
2. The killing of Asma Marwan.
3. Attack upon the 'Banu Qaynuqa' Jews
4. The killing of Kab Ashraf
5. The killing of Ibn Sunayna. The Jewish merchant who was killed at the hands of a Muslim zealot.
6. Attack against the Banu Nadir Jews.
7. Massacre of the Banu Qurayza Jews. Medina in 627, Muhammad's followers killed between 600 and 900 of the men, and divided the surviving Jewish women and children amongst themselves, after the Jewish tribe had committed treason to the treaty of Madinah and were punished according to the torah.
8. The killing of the shepherd.
9. The torture and killing of Kenana ibn al-Rabi
10. The slaying of an old woman from Banu Fazara
11. The killing of Abdullah Khatal and his daughter.
12. The attack upon Tabuk. for becoming an apostate.

Though they offered to surrender, Muhammad felt the need to make an example of them. "The adult males were condemned to death, and the women and children to slavery. Between 600 and 900 males were beheaded." Three large Jewish tribes dwelled in Medina in Muhammad's time: the Banu Nadir, Banu Kainuka, and Banu Qurayza. When war broke out between Muhammad's new supporters and the Meccans, the Jewish clans of Medina remained neutral and were at first unharmed. Nevertheless after the 627 failed Meccan siege of Medina, Muhammad accused the Jews of siding with the Meccans and ordered an attack on them. The reference to this episode in Islamic text is in Sura 33 of the Qu'ran, known as "The Clans." (The Quran tells of three Jewish tribes conquered by Mohammed near Medina, "Two were permitted to choose conversion or exile, but the third was allowed only conversion or death.").

Shia Martyrdom (680)

The Shia [Shiite] Martyrdom. - *October, 680* It began on the morning of 3 October 680 CE. Some link it to the "Roots of terror: suicide, martyrdom, self-redemption and Islam." Even outside the Shi'ite martyrdom, violent death seems to have followed the event. The Basiji in Iran, founded in 1979 by the order of Ayatollah Khomeini, invoked the 680 Shia martyrdom to its "contemporary" Iran-Iraq war in the 1980s, it promoted and established "soldiers of God," carried out and instituted self-sacrifice which was accepted by at least 500,000 Iranian Shia Muslims ready for self infliction, it created child sacrifice, thousands of children, were sent out to clear the mines at the border with Iraq. Between 700,000-800,000 Basij volunteers were sent to the front during the eight-year Iran-Iraq War, when self-sacrifice was the quintessential value of the Islamic revolution, used as cannon fodder when the Islamic regime, often with a plastic "key to paradise" hanging around their necks and the promise that they would automatically go to paradise if they died in battle."

From a research on Child Soldiers: in 1984, Iranian President Ali-Akbar Rafsanjani declared that "all Iranians from 12 to 72 should volunteer for the Holy War."

Thousands of children were pulled from schools, indoctrinated in the glory of martyrdom, and sent to the front lines only lightly armed with one or two grenades or a gun with one magazine of ammunition. Wearing keys around their necks (to signify their pending entrance into heaven), they were sent forward in the first waves of attacks to help clear paths through minefields with their bodies and overwhelm Iraqi defenses. Iran's spiritual leader at the time, Ayatollah Khomeini, delighted in the children's sacrifice and extolled that they were helping Iran to achieve "a situation which we cannot describe in any way except to say that it is a divine country."

Execution of Christians in Córdoba (850-859)

Christians beheaded in Córdoba, Spain *between 850 and 859*, accused of "blasphemy against Islam." Known among Christians as the Martyrs of Córdoba, they included women like Flora and Mary, who were beheaded in Córdoba in 851.

Anti-Jewish violence in Muslim Spain (1010-1013)

Between 1010-1013 Anti-Jewish violence in Muslim Spain.

In the 1011 massacre in Córdoba Andalusia, Muslim Spain, an estimate of about two thousand Jews perished.

Pogrom in Fez (1033)

Pogrom in Fez, Morocco, *1033*. Between five and six thousand Jews lost their lives in the hands of Muslims. The women were dragged off into slavery. According to "Islam at war" more than 6,000 Jews died.

Massacre of Jews in Granada (1066)

Granada massacre of Jews by Muslims, Andalusia Spain - *December 1066*. The 1066 Granada massacre took place on 30 December 1066 (9 Tevet 4827), when a Muslim mob stormed the royal palace in Granada, crucified Jewish vizier Joseph ibn Naghrela and massacred most of the Jewish population of the city. "More than 1,500 Jewish families, numbering 4,000 persons, fell in one day."

According to historian Bernard Lewis, the massacre - in Muslim narrative - is "usually ascribed to a reaction among the Muslim population against a powerful and ostentatious Jewish vizier." Muslims' sentiments of resentments of refusal of Jews to be subjugated by Muslims as Dhimmis can be seen in the following: Particularly instructive in this respect is an ancient Anti-Semitic poem of Abu Ishaq, written in Granada in 1066. This poem, which is said to be instrumental in provoking the anti-Jewish outbreak of that year, contains these specific lines: "Do not consider it a breach of faith to kill them, the breach of faith would be to let them carry on. *They have violated our covenant with them, so how can you be held guilty against the violator?* - How can they have any pact when we are obscure and they are prominent? - Now we are humble, beside them, as if we were wrong and they were right!"

Historian Walter Laqueur characterizes this episode as a pogrom: "Jews could not as a rule attain public office (as usual there were exceptions), and there were occasional pogroms, such as in Granada in 1066." Some 4000 Jews were massacred in the 1066 Granada pogrom, inspired in part by an anti-Jewish ode containing a line (based on aQuranic idea of referring to infidels as apes and pigs), "Many a pious Muslim is in awe of the vilest infidel ape," referring to the Jewish communal leader, the vizier Joseph b. Samuel Naghrela. (In Spain, during periods of friction between the various religious communities, the Muslims called the Jews "apes" and the Christians "pigs and dogs." Research revealed that "viewing Jews as the 'descendants of apes and pigs' is grounded in the most important Islamic religious sources.")

Almohads of Spain

The *Almohads* of Spain and North Africa between the middle of the 12th century and the 14th century. The Almohads arose in the Atlas mountains and declared a Jihad on the moderate Almoravides in order to restore the original Islamic values, conquering most of Morocco, then invading (again) Spain in 1150 to combat Christians. The fanatical warriors alienated Muslims and Jews alike, causing the Arab-Jewish cooperation and the previous usual tolerance in Andalucia came to an end.

When the liberal Almoravids came to power in 1062, conditions for Jews improved, but when the Almohades took over in the middle of the 12th century Jews were forced to embrace Islam or emigrate. It was during that time that Jews were forced to wear a particular costume a precursor of the Jewish badge. After the ouster of the Almohades in the 14th century the situation of Jews stabilized.

It was during the reign of Abu Ya'Qub Yusuf (1165–84) when the upsurge in Almohad fanaticism in Fez came about, it brought a new wave of forced conversions. It was eitherconvert or die. "Thousands of Jews in Morocco had been forced to convert at the height of the Almohade persecutions."

The Assassins (1124)

The Assassins - *1124* The fedayeen were the ardent followers of Hasan-i Sabbah (d. 1124), a leader of Ismail Shia in Iran, Iraq, and in Syria. Known to the west as theAssassins. The Assassins are regarded as "the first group to make systematic use of murder as a political weapon."

Established in Iran and Syria in the eleventh and twelfth centuries, they used assassination and terrorism with the aim of overthrowing Sunni Islam's order and establishing their own. The most open and clear religious *fedayeen* in the modern period were the Fedaiyan-i Islam.

Through assassinations of secular officials they aimed at changing the regime in Iran towards Islamization and introduce Sharia law.

In the 1890s the Shiite leadership in Iran became very involved in violence, terrorism via Fedayeen-i Islam. The "self-sacrifice" or devoutees of Islam under Shi'ite theologian, they have targeted British and Russian officials for assassination.

Ayatollah Khomeini, leader of the Shiites in Iran was from the same area as the earlier "assassins". The *Hur Brotherhood* was another group of *Assassins* that emerged from a combination of religion and politics in the 1890s, modern fedayeen, like the Assassins, find strength in the promise of a reward in "paradise."

The Ayatollah was very involved with the Fedayeen Islam who had a "network of *holy killers* engaged in repeated attempts at political assassinations." In 1944 he published:*Kashf al-Asrar* ("the Revealing of Secrets"), served as a guidance for the violent Fedayeen. Indeed, the militant group covered for the Ayatollah Khomeini until he became in power.

Forced conversions of Jews in Yemen

On both dates *1165 and 1678*, forced conversions of Jews were carried out in Yemen, Jews were given the choice, convert or die. When al-Hadi offered the Jews the choice between the sword and conversion to Islam: "Many Jews chose death and the survival of the community."

Ibn Taymiyyah

The Godfather of Islamic Fundamentalism - *1263 - 1328*

Ibn Taymiyyah, or Taq ad-Din Ahmad ibn Taymiyyah, is regarded as the Godfather of Islamic Fundamentalism. He lived from 1263 to 1328. His name by birth was Ahmad ibn Abdul-Halim ibn Abdas-Salaam. Ibn Taymiyya, dubbed 'the spiritual father of the Islamic revolution' preached that "Jihad should be waged against those who do not follow the teaching of Islam." He issued a Jihadi fatwa against the Mongols that they are not Muslim enough though they observed the Ramadan, that they are "takfir" (ex-communicated), adding that the Quran and Sunna state that those who forsake the law of Islam should be fought (without specifying what part of Sharia they violated).

According to B. Lewis, the Mongol so-called converts were not considered "true Muslims," by the Islamists "since they continued to practice and impose the laws of Jenghis Khan. "Those who follow such laws are infidels, said the Islamist jurist and that they "should be combated until they comply with the laws of Allah." He explaines that "Such a combat was therefore a jihad, with all that entailed."

Muhammad ibn Abd al-Wahhab (1703–1792) is said to be "influenced by the fundamentalist thinker, Ibn Taymiyya."

Bahmani sultans (1347-1480)

The Bahmani sultans and the genocide on Indians - *1347-1480*. The Bahmani Sultans declared Jihad against the infidels.

Every new invader of India made (often literally) his hills of Hindu skulls. The Bahmani sultans (1347–1480) in central India made it a rule to kill 100,000 Hindus (*kafir* - non-believers) every year. In 1399, Teimur killed 100,000 captives in a single day. Historian asserts that "These wars were fought in the true spirit of Jihad — the total annihilation or conversion of the non-Muslims."

Timur (Tamerlane)

The Mongol conqueror Timur the Lame, sometimes called Tamerlane, known for his ruthlessness, and his 'Islamic bigotry', carried out "blitzkrieg campaigns at the end of the fourteenth century." He earned a reputation of torturing the population which resisted his conquering wars (like using thousands alive as "bricks" in walls, outrageous torture of inhabitants like crushing in presses, scorching in flames and revive the victims when near death, in order to repeat it). Timur declared a Jihad on New Delhi in 1398.

As a "holy war" which he declared, he massacred many Hindus, not in context with battles.

Fes Massacre (1465)

Fes Massacre - *1465* Morocco.

In 1465, Arab mobs in Fes slaughtered thousands of Jews, leaving only 11 alive, for 'Islamic honor', after a Jewish deputy vizier treated a Muslim woman in "an offensive manner". (Jews were not even *supposed* to surpass a Dhimmitude status, behold, if "the dhimma had been violated", much less holding office,) The killings touched off a wave of similar massacres throughout Morocco. some six thousand Jews were murdered in 1033." and massacres look place again in 1276 and 1465.

Safavid kings (1501)

The advent of the Safavid kings Iran *1501*. In Persia 1501, Shah Esmail founded the Safavid Dynasty. He was a Shia and waged a jihad against Sunni Islam over the next decade. He eventually conquered all of Persia.

The Shiite Safavids made Shiite Islam the official religion of Iran. They created a "a rigid religious hierarchy with unlimited power and influence in every sphere of life." Minorities:Christians, Zoroastrians and Jews suffered harsh measures including strict segregation, the era brought persecutions, massacres and forced conversions to Islam. "Jews were forced to wear both a yellow badge and a headgear."

Massacre after the battle of Chitod (1568)

Islamists' Massacre of 30,000 Indians - after battle for Chitod on *24 February 1568*. It was part of Mogul Empire's atrocities on Indians, by the order of Islamic Akbar. Akbar -like all Mughal rulers- had the holy Muslim title of "Ghazi" (slayer of Kaffir - infidel). Described as a 'holy war.'

Barbary pirates

Barbary pirates - July 1625 and the 1700s. The height of North African Arab Muslim pirates' violence against Christians, mainly British, Barbary pirates called Britain's 200-year jihad. There are tales of unspeakable barbarism including the Sultan, Moulay Ismail, who tortured and butchered the captives at whim. It involved also forced conversion of the British Christians into Islam. The "Sally Rovers" were called 'al-ghuzat'— the term once used for the soldiers who fought with Muhammad—and were hailed as religious warriors engaged in a holy war against the infidel Christians who were pressurised to convert to Islam under threat of hideous punishment, writes historian Giles Milton.

In negotiating a peace treaty and protect the United States from the threat of Barbary piracy, the future United States presidents Thomas Jefferson, John Adams questioned theTripolitan ambassador to Britain Sidi Haji Abdul Rahman Adja as to "why his government was so hostile to the new American republic even though America had done nothing to provoke any such animosity." Ambassador Adja answered them, as they reported to the Continental Congress,

"that it was founded on the Laws of their Prophet, that it was written in their Koran, that all nations who should not have acknowledged their authority were sinners, that it was their right and duty to make war upon them wherever they could be found, and to make slaves of all they could take as Prisoners, and that every Musselman who should be slain in Battle was sure to go to Paradise."

Expulsion of Jews from Yemen (1679-1680)

The San'a expulsion of Jews of Yemen in the wake of Shiites' radical-Islam - *1679-1680*. Religious cleansing. In that year, the country returned to the Shi'ite rule of the Zaydi imams, and the legitimacy of Jewish presence in Yemen came under an attack which culminated in 1680 with the expulsion of the Jews from San'a and central Yemen.

Massacre of Jews in Safed (1660)

The 1660 massacre of Jews in Safed, Israel-Palestine. At that oppressive era, to buy off the Muslim attackers, Jews had to borrow money from rich Muslims at compound interest, under threats of further attacks if they failed to repay." When the Jewish community of its holy city of Safed was "massacred in 1660," and the town "destroyed by Arabs," only one Jew managed to escape.

Rise of Wahhabism (1744)

Rise of Wahabbism - *1744*. From a description of this radical Islamic movement: Wahhabism is an extremist, puritanical, and violent movement that emerged, with the pretension of "reforming" Islam, in the central area of Arabia in the 18th century. It was founded by Ibn Abd al-Wahhab, who formed an alliance with the house of Saud, in which religious authority is maintained by the descendants of al-Wahhab and political power is held by the descendants of al-Saud: This is the Wahhabi-Saudi axis, which continues to rule today.

From the more notable first wars of Wahabbi Islam, "in 1802 Wahhabi armies slaughtered thousands of Shiites in their holy city of Kerbala, situated in Ottoman Iraq." The second wave came with modern Saudi Arabia re-established the royal family ties with the Wahabbists pushing to create the fanatical Wahhabi army: the Ikhwan.

The Ikhwan waged a jihad against other Muslims in Arabia, including Sharif Hussein of Mecca, who established the Hashemite dynasty that ruled first in Arabia and then in Syria, Iraq and Transjordan. As many as 400,000 Arabs were killed or wounded in these campaigns.

el Djezzar (1783-1801)

"The Butcher" — el Djezzar - *1783-1801*. Historian J. Peters: The year 1783 brought the rise of an Albanian-born Mamluk "Arab," nicknamed "The Butcher" — el Djezzar — whose sadistic, wanton exploits became legend... The Christians in their holy town of Nazareth were also forced through maltreatment into fleeing. Even as late as 1801 Djezzar sent troops to destroy the standing crops in the environs of Nazareth. "Ramleh, however, bore the brunt of the Muslim wrath."

The term "butcher" (in Arabic el Djezzar) was given to him by Arabs, as a result of the "ferocity with which he proceeded to subdue the Bedouins of the Delta."

The Jews of Safed were attacked under the "sadistic Albanian-born Muslim" reign, as he's called. In an exchange with the "Butcher," the following text was sent by N. Bonaparte "that Islam was to be protected."

Religious cleansing: In their days of ascendancy the Muslims in the Nablus of 1783 prohibited Christians from settling. "In 1801 those Christiansnot driven out of Ramallah andNazareth were murdered."

Tetouan Pogrom (1790)

Tetouan Pogrom, Morocco *1790*. "Diaspora Research Institute" described the event: As the new ruler (Mawlay Yazid) entered the city of Tetouan, he commanded that all the Jews should be gathered and imprisoned in a house, meanwhile permitting the Moors to rob all their homes and cellars, which they obeyed with their own particular ferocity. Thus, they stripped all the Jews and their wives of all the clothes which they had on their body with the greatest violence, so that these unfortunates not only had to watch all their belongings being stolen, but also had to bear the greatest injury to their honor... But on top of this, their bestiality showed itself to such an extent that they stripped the Jewesses of their clothes, forthwith satisfied their desires with them, and then threw them naked into the streets.

This [Sultan Mawla] Yazid "had rabbis hung by their feet until they died, another burned alive for refusing to convert to Islam... had Jews crucified by nailing them to the doors of their houses... Jews were converted by force."

Jihad in Africa (1810-1818)

Jihad in Africa (Mali) - *1810-18*. Jihad was a religious war fought from 1810 to 1818 in what is now the Mopti Region of Mali. In either 1810 or 1818 (the exact date is uncertain), an Islamic fighter led a jihad against the Muslim chiefs in Masina, later the jihad expanded to include the Bambara. Seku Ahmadu established an austere Muslim empire ruled from the newly built city. He led the "second major jihad of the 19th century" beginning in 1818. "His jihad brought about an Islam theocracy as a successor to the non-Islamic empire of Segou that had been established by the Bambara."

The ruler launched from 1853 a series of expeditions against pagans, in Bambara in particular. The 1818 "Fulani" Empire of Massina fell to a more militant movement.

Java War (1825-1830)

The Java War - *1825-1830*. Fought in Java, Indonesia, this had started as an aristocratic rebellion. Under the leadership of Prince Diponegoro, it developed into a religious and cultural struggle against the Dutch.

Suleika affair (1834)

The Suleika affair - *1834*. A Jewish woman from Tangier, Morocco refused to convert and marry a high-ranking official, and was executed in Fez.

A writer has put it: Suleika, a 17-year-old girl with her entire life in front of her, offered everything under the sun if she would convert to Islam but who was beheaded on another sunny day in Morocco because she couldn't change what she was...

The martyrdom of the beautiful Suleika, who, despite torture, refused to convert to Islam left a strong impression. A song was written in her memory, it was "sung by Jewish girls in Morocco to a sad, touching melody."

Safed and Hebron violence (1834-1835)

1834-5 Safed and Hebron violence

1) The Safed plunder. 2) The massacre in Hebron, pillaging, looting, killing/rapes, in Jerusalem. The pogrom - massacre, "plunder," by Arab-Muslims on Jews in Safed. It went on for 33 days. It was incited by a highly religious cleric, a self-proclaimed

Islamic "prophet" Muhammad Damoor, who envisioned the massacre to which he agitated the "believers" to.

The attacks in Hebron, Jerusalem, that year: In 1834, Egyptian soldiers massacred Jews in Hebron on the way of putting down a Muslim rebellion, local Muslims go on rampage, pillaging, rape, killing, looting in Jerusalem at that same era.

According to professor M. Ma'oz, considered of great authority on that period, "a noticeable number of Christians and Jews, particularly children, were forced to adopt Islam....even the converts were persecuted as Jews."

Forced conversions of Jews in Iran (1838-1839)

Forced conversions of Jews in Meshed Iran and massacre - *1838/9*. There was a Massacre of Meshed Jews and forced conversions (to Islam) of the survivors. A mob was incited to attack Jews, and slaughtered almost 40 of them. The rest were forced to convert.

As a result, the entire community of Meshed was forcibly converted to Islam. However, these Persian Jews continued to practice Judaism privately in their homes. They, their descendants were called Jugutis. Under Muhammad Shah. Oppression and persecution followed the forced conversions.

Damascus Blood Libel (1840)

Damascus Blood Libel - *1840*. The Damascus affair It brought with it riots and violence against Jews. It was the beginning of a spiral of blood libels in many cities in Syria followed by outbreaks in Morocco, Algeria, Tunisia, Libya, and (other) Arab countries of the Middle East.

In his book *Blood libel: the Damascus affair of 1840* author R. Florence describes the chain of blood libels that followed all over the Islamic world, including in western Iranian city of Hamadan where Jews were killed, burned alive, "many escaped the violence only by converting to Islam."

Massacres of the Assyrians (1840-1860)

In 1842, Muslims engaged in the following massacre: Badr

Khan Bey, A Hakkari Kurdish Amir, combined with other Kurdish forces led by Nurallah, attacked the Assyrians, intending to burn, kill, destroy, and, if possible, "exterminate the Assyrians race from the mountains." At the massacre, the "women were brought before the Amir and murdered in cold blood." one incident has been depicted to illustrates the revolting barbarity: the aged mother of Mar Shimun, the Patriarch of the Church of the East, was seized by them, and after having practiced on her the most abominable atrocities, they cut her body into two parts and threw it into the river Zab, exclaiming, "go and carry to your accursed son the intelligence that the same fate awaits him."

An estimate of nearly ten thousand Assyrian men were massacred, and as many women and children were taken captive, most of the women were sold as slaves, many were presented as presents to influential Muslims.

In 1847, Muslim forces massacred 30,000 members of the Assyrian Christian community. It was an example of (Ottoman) State complicity by the Khilafah in massacres of Christians. The massacre was succeeded by another in 1896.

The Kurdish chief, Bedr Khan who [also] massacred Assyrian villagers in 1847, was "able to assemble a tribal confederacy for a 'holy war against the infidels'." A letter to the New York Times in 1860 from the American consul at Beirut, after the brutal massacre, entails the phrase "Moslem fanaticism is now fully aroused."

Jihad in Africa (1861)

Jihad in Africa - *1861,* in the region that is today an area in Mali, Toucouleur conqueror El Hadj Umar Tall took Ségou from its Bambara rulers and launched a *fresh* [second] jihad down river against the Massina.

The Islamic jihad of El Had L'mar, which defeated the Bambara Kingdom in 1861 was an attempt to establish (again) a theocratic Islamic state.

Rafin Jaki battle (1873)

The Rafin Jaki battle - *1873.* Jihadists waged war on Africa in the region of present day Nigeria. The combined ethnic communities from present day Jos area, which is: the Afizere, Anaguta, Birom, defeated the Jihadists at the battle of Rafin Jaki.

April Uprising (1876-1912)

The April Uprising - *1876-1912*. In 1876 the Bulgarians staged a rebellion (April Uprising) against the Ottoman Empire, Ottoman forces responded with a brutal massacre in what quickly became known as "the Bulgarian horrors." By 1912, as new Balkan alliances were formed in opposition to Ottoman rule, the Turks again responded with massacre. The Islamic Turks massacre 25,000 Bulgarian Christians, some claim, 100,000. Sixty to seventy villages were burned. Bulgaria, Serbia-Montenegro and some other European lands which had been under Ottoman rule declared their independence from Turkish rule, and tried to align themselves with Austria-Hungary. The Turks were outraged, and sent extra troops to the Balkans. Between 1909 and 1912, Turks massacred (at least) 25,000 Bulgarian, Kosovar andSerbian citizens, in addition to the number of casualties inflicted during the actual fighting of the war.

Historian states that "During that span of about five hundred years, the Christians of the Balkans, the majority of whom wereSlavs, lived under Ottoman Muslim rule, and were accorded the traditional Ottoman treatment of those of *infidel* status. The Balkan Christians, were subjected to heavy taxation, arbitrary violence, political disenfranchisement, and cultural oppression; some of whom converted to Islam."

Opposing view: The Ottoman reprisals to the so-called Bulgarian horrors, received great publicity in Europe where only the Bulgarian side of the story was known. Estimates of the actual number of Bulgarians killed in the suppression of this revolt vary: the Ottoman figure is 3,100; the British, 12,000: the American, 15,000: and the Bulgarian, from 30,000 to 100,000.

Jihad in Sudan and Egypt (1880)

A Jihad in Sudan and in Egypt - *1880*. What is called the (major) "First Jihad", in 1880, Muslim fighter raised the banner of holy war, and thousands of warriors flocked. "The Mahdi's army crushed forces dispatched from British (controlled) Egypt." History of Mahdist Sudan

Hamidian massacres (1894-1896)

Hamidian massacres of Armenians by the Ottoman empire - *1894-1896*. The Hamidian Massacres in 1894-1896 were the first near-genocidal series of atrocities committed against the Armenian population of the Ottoman Empire. Estimates of those killed range widely, anywhere between 100,000 and 30,000, with thousands more maimed or rendered homeless.

Scholars cite an exemplary event in 1896 as part of Turks' overall jihad on Christians in that era: "The leader of the mob cried: 'Believe in Muhammad and deny your religion.' No one answered... The leader gave the order to massacre..." Concluding that "This 1894-1896 Jihad against Christians in Eastern Turkey claimed 250,000 lives. Many Armenian women were forced into harems, and many women and children were sold as slaves. Rape, considered one of the rights of "booty" in Muslim Jihad."

Settat and Taza pogrom 1903/1907

Settat and Taza pogrom, Morocco - *1903/1907*. Prior to the 1830 French occupation of Morocco, thousands of inoffensive Jews were brutually attacked in different parts of Morocco by hostile tribesmen and uncontrolled soldiery. As Jews sought refuge by the French Christians it caused even more massacres: in Settat and Taza 1903 and in 1907.

The following text was written around that time: "We live among savages who have already tried to satisfy their ferocious hatred by making a carnage of all the Jews..."

It is listed among dates in a timeline of "The End of Judaism in Islam's land."

Greek Genocide (1914-1923)

Greek Genocide - *1922*. During the years 1914-1923, in the 1st World War and in the arena of a crumbling empire, the Greek minority of the Ottoman Empire, the Republic of Turkey's predecessor, were removed from Western Anatolia. This was done by force. An estimated 350,000 Greeks were killed between 1913-1922. Many also fled the violence back to Greece. The Turks contend that both sides were killed in warfare, atrocities were committed by both sides, and so reject the label of 'genocide' to describe these events.

Arab riots 1920-1921

Arab riots, Massacres, Pogroms on Jews in Israel / Palestine- *1920-1921*. On February 1920, the pogroms by Arabs on Jews in Jerusalem were orchestrated by two young Arab Muslim supremacists (prominent in Arab Palestine), Haj Amin al-Husseini[who later on became the Mufti] at that time served in the British army's intelligence and Aref al-Aref. A Hebron Muslim Sheik shouted: "Whoever has a stick, a gun' a knife or stone, shall go and exterminate the Jews, And in ecstasy screamed: "Adbachu Al Yahud" ['Kill the Jews!']. Amin el-Husseini was using his considerable wealth and growing power to incite the masses. Due to Haj Amin's overt role in instigating the pogrom, the British arrested him.

Arab pogroms were launched against Jews in 1920, 1921, 1929 and 1936-1939. According to the Israeli Ministry of Foreign Affairs, from 1920 to 1966, Arab terrorists murdered 1513 Jewish residents of British Mandatory Palestine.

Islamists turned mosques into hubs instigating violence, "shrine into a center of unholy activity," explaines historian, where "political intrigue and violence were hatched, as were the bloody anti-Jewish riots of 1920, 1929 and 1936. Inside the Temple Mount enclosure, fanatical preachers incited the masses who then went on the rampage with shouts of*Allahu akbar* (Allah is great) mingled with *Idbah al Yahud* (Slaughter the Jews)."

Moplah Rebellion

The Moplah rebellion - *1921*, (also known as the Mopla riots) was a British-Muslim and Hindu-Muslim "conflict" in (Malabar) Kerala that occurred in 1921. It involved forced conversion to Islam.

There were clashes that provoked arsonists who took to the street, burning and destroying government property. At first, the focus was on the British, but then it turned into a jihad against Hindus. A wave of large number of killings, massive forced conversions to Islam swept the region. Some described it as: "Muslim violence is sheer religious bigotry, an unreasoning jihad."

In Aug. 1921 the most serious of many unpardonable deeds of violence broke out. The Malabar country in Madras is occupied by 2,000,000 Hindus and about 1,000,000 Moplahs, an ignorant Mahommedan peasantry of mixed Arab and Indian decsent with an evil reputation for outbreaks of fanaticism. Among the latter the Khilafat excitement spread like wildfire... and attempted wholesale the forcible conversion of the Hindus to Islam.

"Primarily, however, it is understood the trouble arose from religious fanaticism and from the intense hatred of the Moplahs, or Mohammedans of Arab descent, for Europeans and Hindus," writes the *New York Times*. The second declaration of jihad was made by the Khilafat Committee and several Muslim groups in 1920s when the Ottoman Caliphate was abolished, consequent upon the defeat of Turkey. It resulted from the agitation carried out by two Muslim organizations, the Khuddam-i-Kaaba (servants of the Mecca Shrine) and the Central Khilafat Committee. The Moplahs of Malabar were suddenly carried off their feet by this proclamation of jihad by the Khilafat Committee. They resorted to large-scale violence which was supposed to be a rebellion against the British Government. As a rebellion against the British Government the jihad could be understandable but what shocked most people was the horrid treatment meted out by the Moplahs to the Hindus of Malabar, in this Jihad.

Pundits account that the "Moplah massacre was one of the most gruesome acts of murder by the Muslims rivaled only by the Razakars in Hyderabad in 47, and the ethnic cleansing in Pakistan and Bangladesh after partition."

Forced Conversion of Jewish Orphans in Yemen

Revival of the old custom of forced conversion of Jewish orphans in Yemen - *1922-1929*.

The 'stealing of orphans' was under the Imam Yahya, under his drastic measures the re-introduction in 1922 of the old custom of the forced conversion of Jewish orphans - was implemented in Yemen. The edict was re-promulgated in December 1928.

Muslim Brotherhood

The Muslim Brotherhood - founded - *1928*. In 1928, Hassan al-Banna founded the Muslim Brotherhood, a rigidly conservative and highly secretive Egyptian-based organization dedicated to resurrecting a Muslim empire (Caliphate). According to al-Banna, "It is the nature of Islam to dominate, not to be dominated, to impose its law on all nations and to extend its power to the entire planet." The Muslim Brotherhood, also called Muslim Brethren (jamiat al-Ikhwan al-muslimun, literally Society of Muslim Brothers), it opposes secular tendencies of Islamic nations and wants return to the precepts of the Quran, and rejection of Western influences. Al Bana was Born out of the extreme Muslim right wing's desire to counter the ideology of modernization, the Brotherhood's platform included a strict interpretation of the Koran (Quran) that glorified suicidal violence. Along with Al Banna, the grand Mufti of Jerusalem Haj-al Amin Al-Husseini was also an enormously influential Muslim leader of the time. Together, the two created a powerful and popular Islamist party by classically appealing to fundamentalist Islamic principals while blaming the world's problems on the Jews. Al-Banna also gave the group the motto it still uses today: "Allah is our purpose, the Prophet our leader, the Quran our constitution, jihad our way and dying for God our supreme objective."

An important aspect of the Muslim Brotherhood ideology is the sanctioning of Jihad such as the 2004 fatwa issued by Sheikh Yousef Al-Qaradhawi making it a religious obligation of Muslims to abduct and kill U.S. citizens in Iraq.

It advocated a war of Arabism and Islamic Jihad against the British and the Jews. The Muslim brotherhood waged a "Holy war" against Syria after the Hama massacre.

The BBC explains how the roots of Jihad and the origins of Bin Laden's concept of jihad can be traced back to two early 20th century figures, who started powerful Islamic revivalist movements in response to colonialism and its aftermath. al-Banna blamed the western idea of separation between religion and politics for Muslims' decline. In the 1950sSayed Qutb, Muslim Brotherhood's prominent member, took the arguments of al-Banna even further. For Qutb, "all non-Muslims were infidels - even the so-called *people of the book*, the Christians and Jews," he also predicted an eventual clash of civilisations between Islam and the west. "Qutb inspired a whole generation of Islamists, including Ayatollah Khomeini." The Muslim world widely accepted his ideology post Arabs' defeat in the 1967 war.

The Muslim Brotherhood has been involved in violent attacks. From its Islamic theme in its symbolism: on its flag there's a brown square frames a green circle with a white perimeter. Two swords cross inside the circle beneath a red Koran. The cover of the Koran says: "Truly, it is the Generous Koran." The Arabic beneath the sword handles translates as "Be prepared." A reference to a Koranic verse that talks of preparing to fight the enemies of God. It is among 17 groups categorized as "terrorist organizations" by the Russian government, as well as in Egypt, where they started to perform terrorist attacks, now banned by that government.

Scholar states that in "The Muslim Brotherhood's Conquest of Europe", its real goal is to extend Islamic law Sharia throughout Europe and the United States.

Contemporary Islamism holds that Islam is now under attack, and therefore -experts explain-Jihad is now a war of defense, and as such has become not only a collective duty but an individual duty without restrictions or limitations. That is, to the Islamists, Jihad is a total, all-encompassing duty to be carried out by all Muslims – men and women, young and old. All infidels, without exception, are to be fought and annihilated, and no weapons or types of warfare are barred. Furthermore, according to them, current Muslim rulers allied with the West are considered apostates and infidels. One major ideological influence in Islamist thought was Sayyid Qutb. Qutb, an Egyptian, was the leader of the Muslim Brotherhood movement. He was convicted of treason for plotting to assassinate Egyptian president Gamal Abd Al-Nasser and was executed in 1966. He wrote extensively on a wide range of Islamic issues. According to Qutb, "There are two parties in all the world: the Party of Allah and the Party of Satan – the Party of Allah which stands under the banner of Allah and bears his insignia, and the Party of Satan, which includes every community, group, race, and individual that does not stand under the banner of Allah."

In the "Holy land foundation" case of the Palestinian Arab al-Arian's involvement in funding terror organization, the Muslim Brotherhood's papers detailed plan to seize U.S. The Group's takeover plot emerged when revealed a handful of classified evidence detailing Islamist extremists' ambitious plans for a U.S. takeover. Terrorism researchers said "the memos and audiotapes, many translated from Arabic and containing detailed strategies by the international Islamist group the Muslim Brotherhood, are proof that extremists have long sought to replace the Constitution with Shariah, or Islamic law", paving its way via a plot to form "a complex network of seemingly benign Muslim organizations whose real job, according to the (US) government, was to spread militant propaganda and raise money." The Muslim Brotherhood created some American Muslim groups and sought influence in others, many of which are listed as unindicted co-conspirators in the Holy Land case, such as CAIR.

On a website devoted to Ramadhan, the Muslim Brotherhood posted a series of articles by Dr. Ahmad 'Abd Al-Khaleq about Al-Walaa Wa'l-Baraa, an Islamic doctrine which, in its fundamentalist interpretation, stipulates absolute allegiance to the community of Muslims and total rejection of non-Muslims and of Muslims who have strayed from the path of Islam. In his articles, the writer argues that according to this principle, a Muslim can come closer to Allah by hating all non-Muslims-Christians, Jews, atheists, or polytheists - and by waging jihad against them in every possible manner.

Indeed, the Muslim Brotherhood has a long-standing war on the West. From 1948 until the 1970s it engaged in assassinations and terrorism in Egypt, and has indoctrinated many who went on to commit acts of terror. Muslim Brotherhood's supreme guide issued the statement that Al Qaeda's "Bin Laden is a Jihad Fighter."

The accused mastermind of the 9/11 terror massacre, Khalid Sheikh Mohammed was raised in Kuwait and joined the Muslim Brotherhood at age 16.

Hebron Massacre

The Hebron Massacre - *August 1929*

1929 Hebron massacre ' pogrom the 'ethnic cleansing' attack upon [mostly non- Zionist, religious] pious Jews by Arab Muslims in Israel / Palestine. Agitated by the Mufti, Haj Amin al-Husseini's intentional inflammatory speeches who called the believers to rise up in *defense* of Islam's holy places. The brutality -which included beheading of babies by sword, castrating old Rabbis, body mutilation, castrating rabbis with their students before they were slain, breasts and fingers sliced off, eyes plucked from their sockets - was accompanied with cries of 'Itbach al Yahud' (kill the Jews). and "Allah akbar."

The massacres in Hebron and elsewhere of 1929, began in the wake of the Mufti's provocative speeches. The mosques were used in numerous outbreak of violence in Palestine, such as the massacre of the Jews of Hebron in August 1929 which started with leaflets handed to the Muslims while leaving the mosques. It was on August 23 (1929) when the riots erupted, as masses of Arabs, "leaving their mosques after Friday prayers, attacked Jewish neighborhoods in Jerusalem and the vicinity." The violence spread to other parts of the country, reaching a peak in Hebron on August 24, when 66 Jews were murdered, and in Safed, on August 29, where the death tall was 45. The riots lasted a full week, leaving 133 Jews dead and 339 wounded."

It started off with 2,000 Arabs bursting out of the Mosque of Omar on the Haram al-Sharif. The grand mufti Haj Amin al-Husseini admitted later on that "the speaker in the mosque that day had incited Arab worshippers to violence."

Hebron's Jewish population was not part of the Zionist movement and some link it to the unfortunate fact of its highest tall of victims. *The Forward* describes the scene:

The carnage in Hebron was particularly ugly, the mobs having sliced a variety of body parts off of their victims. Just over a half-dozen of the victims were American kids from New York and Chicago who had come to study at the famed yeshiva.

The Forward recalls:

New York's Jews were horrified by the pogroms, and the story stayed on the front pages of the Forward for nearly a month. The paper's Palestine correspondents delved deep into the issue of Arab-Jewish antipathies, discussing issues such as how Arabs were incited to violence during Friday afternoon worship in their mosques, as well as explaining to readers the concept of jihad and the 72 virgins a Muslim allegedly receives if he dies as a martyr.

Simele Massacre

The Simele massacre (Simel), Iraq - *August 1933.*

The massacre and ethnic cleansing by the Iraqi government, by Arab and Kurdish Muslim masses on Christian Assyrians, indigenous people. An estimated 3,000 Assyrians were systematically targeted by the Iraqi government to cleanse the Assyrian race."

From the British document of the time:

"Simel Massacre.. The culmination of the indiscriminate action against Assyrian men, regardless of party or guilt... Between the 8th and 10 August, widespread looting, raiding and burning of Assyrian villages in the Simel, Dohuk and Al Qosh areas had been in progress... Both Kurds and Arabs of the Shammar and Jabur tribes were implicated."

For years the scars in the region remained unhealed. The surviving Assyrians were described as, "spiritless, cowed, and apprehensive" while the Kurds and Arabs were hideously inflamed.

Jaffa Massacre

The Jaffa Massacre - *19 April 1936.*

Inspired by the religious Islamic leader the Mufti, Arab rioters attacked Jaffa and killed 16 Jews.

In September 1937, Armed Arab terrorism, under the direction of the Arab Higher Committee, was used for both; to attack the Jews and to suppress Arab opponents. This campaign of violence continued through 1938 and then tapered off, ending in early 1939. Researchers conclude about the terrible toll: "Eighty Jews were murdered by terrorist acts during the labor strike, and a total of 415 Jewish deaths were recorded during the whole 1936-1939 Arab Revolt period."

The attacks occurred as Islamic preachers incited the masses inside Mosques and the mobs attacked with the 'Islamic' shouts of "Allah Akbar!"

Rashid Ali Coup

The 1941 Iraqi coup d'état

Rashid Ali al-Gaylani declared a *jihad* against Great Britain in his pro-Nazi Golden Square coup of 1941.

On February 28, 1941, Rashid Ali as well as the following Muslim personalities: Salah ed-Din es-Sabbagh, Fahmi Said and Mahmud Salman of the Golden Square, Rashid Ali el-Kilani, Yunis es-Sebawi, Shawkat and Hajj Amin, all swore on the Koran to be faithful to the [pro-Nazi] program.

Farhud Pogrom

The Farhud pogrom on Jews in Iraq *June 1941*

It was followed agitation by the Mufti Haj Amin al-Husseini, perpetrated by a pro-Nazi Arab mob, led by Al-Muthanna club's al-Futuwwa Arab-Islamic Fascist paramilitary group. Iraqi soldiers were among the first attackers. Jews were killed randomly, hundreds were injured, "women and children were raped in front of their relatives, babies crushed, children mutilated."

The Farhud, the Mufti (who declared a jihad) inspired *Krystallnacht* in Iraq, 1941, took place Sunday and Monday, 1 June and 2 1941. The two days of murder, looting, rape and mutilation, shattered this ancient community's self-confidence, and swiftly led to the exodus of over 90 percent of Iraqi Jewry.

Nazi Germany

Arab Muslim leader the Grand Mufti Haj Amin al-Husseini meets with Adolf Hitler *21 November 1941.*

The chief Muslim, Islamic legal religious authority and Muslim leader from Palestine met the Nazi Führer.

Prior to the meeting, in June 1940 the Mufti offered his services to the Nazi *Reich* government. In 1941, he went to Berlin via Tehran, where he explained to the German ambassador, Erwin Ettel, his plan to bring all Arabs under the banner of Pan-Arabism over to the side of the Axis (25 June 1942). Here he came out unconditionally for the "final solution" of the Jewish question, calling on the Germans to wipe out all Jews, "not even sparing the children."

His meeting with Hitler evolved around Jews being "his foremost enemy". The Nazi dictator rebuffed the Mufti's requests for his empowerment. Though Adolf Hitler hated Arabs, considered them to be racially inferior just as Jews, Hitler refused to touch, shake the Mufti's hand, nevertheless, the Nazi Führer and the supreme religious authority of Islamic world were able to bridge in a common hatred of the Jews. Prof. W. Phares explaines in a paragraph:*Jihadists and World War II* that "While Nazi infidels were ultimately anathema to jihadists, the alliance answered all their practical needs at the moment."

From a description in the article "The Mufti of Berlin" (24 September 2009) in the Wall Street Journal how his legacy had an impact of future radical Islamists:...the Palestinian wartime leader "was one of the worst and fanatical fascists and anti-Semites,".... He intervened with the Nazis to prevent the escape to Palestine of thousands of European Jews, who were sent instead to the death camps. He also conspired with the Nazis to bring the Holocaust to Palestine. The mufti "invented a new form of Jew-hatred by recasting it in an Islamic mold," according to German scholar Matthias Küntzel. The mufti's fusion of European anti-Semitism—particularly thegenocidal variety—with Koranic views of Jewish wickedness has become the hallmark of Islamists world-wide, from al Qaeda to Hamas and Hezbollah. During his time in Berlin, the mufti ran the Nazis' Arab-language propaganda radio program, which incited Muslims in the Mideast to "kill the Jews wherever you find them. This pleases God, history and religion." Among the many listeners was also the man later known as Ayatollah Khomeini, who used to tune into Radio Berlin every evening, according to Amir Taheri's biography of the Iranian leader. Khomeini's disciple Mahmoud Ahmadinejad still spews the same venom pioneered by the mufti as do Islamic hate preachers around the world. Muslim Judeophobia is not — as is commonly claimed — a reaction to the Mideast conflict but one of its main "root causes." It has been fueling Arab rejection of a Jewish state long before Israel's creation.

The exiled al-Husseini fled in 1941 to Berlin, serving the Nazi regime for four years in broadcasting jihadist as well as anti-British propaganda to the entire Middle East and by recruiting Bosnian Muslims for the Wehrmacht, the SS.

Grand Mufti Haj Amin al-Husseini of 'Palestine' recruites *Moslem Holy Warriors* who fought as the Waffen SS, and the "Free Arabia." - *1943*

In speaking to potential recruits, al-Husseini stressed the connections they had to the "Muslim nation" fighting the British throughout the world. That it is about "defending Muslims."

There were three divisions of Muslim soldiers: The Waffen SS 13th Handschar ("Knife"), the 23rd Kama ("Dagger") and the 21st Skenderbeg. The Skenderbeg was an Albanian unit of around 4,000 men, and the Kama was composed of Muslims from Bosnia, containing 3,793 men at its peak. The Handschar was the largest unit, around 20,000 Bosnian Muslim volunteers. The Encyclopedia of the Holocaust states "These Muslim volunteer units, called Handschar, were put in Waffen SS units, fought Yugoslav partisans in Bosnia and carried out police and security duties in Hungary. They participated in the massacre of civilians in Bosnia and volunteered to join in the hunt for Jews in Croatia." Part of the division also escorted Hungarian Jews from the forced labor in mine in Bor on their way back to Hungary. "The division was also employed against Serbs, who as Orthodox Christians were seen by the Bosnian Muslims as enemies." All in the all, there were at least 70,000 Bosnian Muslims captured by the British. Some of these Muslim ex-soldiers participated in aiding Arabs in the anti Israel war of 1948.

2

Jihad : An Integral Part of Islam

Many people have written many books, treatises and articles for the purpose of defining the role jihad is supposed to play in the lives of the Muslims. Most writers have tried, in their own ways, to come up with the "true" meaning of the dreadful word "jihad," others took circuitous routes to emphasize on what they believed was the purpose for which God has purportedly made the launching of jihad by Muslims an integral part of their lives.

Until recently, my mind had remained in a state of dichotomy; it being the result of the inadequate attention, I admit, I had paid to the contents of the Quran while reading it a number of times. On one hand, I tended to think that jihad was a word that was used in the Quran to denote "striving" with one's inner thoughts and desires; on the other, I believed God required the Muslims to engage themselves in bloody wars in order not only to sustain their existence through plunders, but also to occupy others' lands and possessions through the use of brute force.

My dual-mindedness ended when I had the opportunity to read the book "Forbidden Love." A Jordanian woman is the writer. In it, she pointed out the meaning, as it is understood by the Arabic speaking people, of the words "qatilu" and "jihadu" that appear repeatedly in the Arabic text of the Quran.

My newly-acquired familiarity with the correct meaning of the words "qatilu" and "jihadu" made me to go over the Quran once again. Reading it this time with great care it deserves from all readers, I gleaned from it the true import and significance of both the words God had conveyed to Muhammad and his followers through His revelations.

Qatilu: Meaning to wage wars, this word appears 64 times in the Quran. Through the use of this word in the celestial book, God commanded all Muslims to wage wars on the unbelievers (kaferun in Arabic), mainly, for the purpose of plunder. In such wars, Muslims have God's permission to kill their victims in order to enable them to take over their possessions together with their female family members.

The first action enabled them to fill up their empty stomachs; the taking over of the female captives satisfied their huge sexual appetite. "Qatilu" also means a warfare that Muslims are supposed to launch on, and against the non-Muslims who live in Muslim countries, firstly, to subdue, and then to force them to pay Jizya, a protection tax, to their Islamic governments. Failure of the surviving unbelievers to pay protection tax is a ground for the Muslims either to uproot and deport them from their habitats, or to kill them 'in the cause of God.'

"Dhimmis," as the tax-paying non-believers are supposed to be called, they must live among their compatriots in total submission to them. Wearing badges of different colors to identify their religious affiliations, dhimmis should neither build tall buildings, nor should they ride horses to show their 'inferior' status to that of their 'superior' Muslim neighbors.

In order to substantiate my stated claims, citation of the following verse from the Quran should suffice:

9:29: "Fight those who believe not in God nor the Last Day, nor hold that forbidden which hath been forbidden by God and His Apostle, nor acknowledge the Religion of Truth, (even if they are) of the People of the Book, until they pay the Jizya with willing submission and fell themselves subdued."

Commenting on the above verse, Mohammed Arkoun, whose works Robert D. Lee has translated into English, says in "Rethinking Islam":

"{This verse} like the rest of Sura 9, warrant a long historical and theological commentary. They have fed an interminable polemic from which there is no escape because it is conducted at the dogmatic level. I cite them here not to touch off new controversies but to attract attention to the urgent need for a modern rereading {?} of these sacred texts that takes account of historical context and doctrinal struggles aggravated by the appearance of the Qur'an at the beginning of the seventh century."

Professor Philip K. Hitti has been candidly straight forward while drawing our attention to the historical facts that had formed the basis of the Muslims' aggressions against the non-Muslims from the time Islam was in its infancy to the time it had acquired enough military muscle that had enabled it to conquer almost one third of the world's pagan, Jewish and Christian's lands. Writing in the History of the Arabs, he says: "... Outside the Arabian peninsula and especially in the instance of the ahl-al-kitab (Christians and Jews) there was a third and, from the standpoint of the conquerors, more desirable choice besides the Koran and the sword-tribute. "Make war ... upon such of those to whom the Book has been given until they pay tribute offered on the back of their hands, in a state of humiliation."

This third choice was later by necessity of circumstances offered to Zoroastrians and heathen Berbers and Turks; in the case of all these theory gave way to expediency. ... The passion to go to heaven in the next life may have been operative with some, but the desire for the comforts and luxuries of the civilized regions of the Fertile Crescent was just as strong in the case of many.

... Al-Baladhuri, the most judicious of the historians of the conquest, declares that in recruiting for the Syrian campaign abu-Bakr "wrote to the people of Makkah, al-Taif, al-yaman and all the Arabs in Najd and al-Hijaz summoning them to a 'holy war' and arousing their desire for it and for the booty to be got from the Greeks. Rustam, the Persian general who defended his country against the Arab invasion, made the following remark to the Muslim envoy: "I have learned that ye were forced to what ye are doing by nothing but the narrow means of livelihood and by poverty. A verse in the Hamasah of abu-Tamam has put the case tersely:

No, not for Paradise didst thou the nomad life forsake;

Rather, I believe, it was thy yearning after bread and dates."

The first qatilu Muslims launched under Muhammad's leadership against the Meccan pagans, took place at the grounds of Badr in 624 A.D. It was designed to ambush an unarmed Meccan caravan, and to loot the goods and valuables it was transporting from Syria to Mecca. The caravan, however, escaped unscathed due to an evasive action taken by its leader. Had Muslims been able to lay their hands on the riches of the caravan, we would now be reading a story that would have been shorter, and different from the one we read about Islam's travails, and the opposition it supposedly endured during its rise among the pagans, Jews and Christians of the Arabian Peninsula.

The cause or causes for which God has permitted Muslims to launch "qatilu" (wars) on the non-Muslims having been made clear, let's now examine the word "jihadu" to understand its significance, true meaning and import in the context of the Quran.

Jihad: Read "jihadu" in Arabic, it is the equivalent of the word "jihad" we non-Arabic speaking people commonly use in our writings and conversation. It appears 33 times in the Quran.

In many cases, the word "jihadu" appears in the Quranic verses to gather with the phrase "fi sabil Allah." It means "in the cause of God."

Like qatilu, jihad also denotes hostile acts, in the shape of wars, which Muslims, under God's command, undertook in the past and are required to undertake even now and in future against the non-Muslims, specifically with the purpose of converting them to Islam. In jihads, Muslims should not expect to gain any booty, but should it come their way in the aftermath of their 'striving in the cause of God,' they should not only accept it gladly, they must also cherish it wholeheartedly, for all rewards and gifts come from God, and refusing them is a cardinal sin. Converting the non-believers to Islam is what the Quran subtly refers to as being the "cause of God."

Other pre and post jihad rules are like those of qatilu. Those of the unbelievers who escape death in wars must convert to Islam.

Unwilling infidels must pay protection tax; their failure to do so entitles the Muslims either to kill them or to deport them to another country that is willing to give them shelter. At the time of leaving their homesteads, deportees must leave behind what they may be forbidden by their Muslim masters from carrying with them. The list of the prohibited 'goods' may include their young mothers, sisters, wives and daughters.

In the backdrop of the above discussion, let us now explore some of the Quranic verses in which, the word 'jihadu" appears, as well as the purpose and intent for which it has been incorporated in them. While reading the verses being quoted here, we must keep in our mind the situation and the circumstances that had prevailed at the time these were 'revealed' by God to Muhammad, as well as his listeners' inability to 'dissect' each and all words to find out their etymological roots and grammatical correctness in the manner we are able to do today. They were simple folks and they took each word of the revelations in the sense they knew and believed they conveyed to them.

4:75: "And why should ye not fight in the cause of God and of those who, being weak, are ill-treated (and oppressed))? Men, women, and children, whose cry is: "Our Lord! Rescue us from this town, whose people are oppressors; and raise for us from Thee one who will protect; and raise for us from Thee one who will help!"

Two causes are mentioned in the above verse for Muslims to fight for; one to protect the oppressed, which is undoubtedly a good cause, and the second "in the cause of God," a cause that remained undefined. The following verse sheds light on what I understand to be God's cause:

4:76: "Those who believe fight in the cause of God, and those who reject Faith fight in the cause of Evil: so fight ye against the friends of Satan: feeble indeed is the cunning of Satan."

In the sight of God, the unbelievers are the friends of Satan. Fighting them, and to bring them to the fold of Islam is what the verse says is the responsibility of all the Muslims. This effort on the part of the Muslims is 'a cause of God.' Fighting for the purpose of converting non-Muslims to Islam can, in no way, be taken to mean a Muslim's struggle against his 'inner thoughts and desires.'

4:100: "He who forsakes his home in the cause of God finds in the earth many refuge, wide and spacious: should he die as a refuge from home for God and His Apostle, his reward becomes due and sure with God: And God is oft-Forgiving, Most Merciful."

As the above verse postulates, leaving one's home, taking refuge elsewhere and dying for God and His Apostle is the cause of God. It, in no way, relates to one's struggle with his "inner thoughts and desires."

9:41: "Go ye forth (whether equipped) lightly or heavily, and strive and struggle, with your goods and your persons, in the cause of God. That is best for you, if ye (but) knew."

Clearly, striving with equipment is not a struggle that can be construed to be a struggle with one's inner thoughts and desires. Striving (jihadu in Arabic) means a war against those who are unbelievers, hence they deserve to be eliminated from the face of God's earth through violent actions and killings.

29:6: "And if any strive (with might and main), they do so for their own souls: For God is free of all needs from all creation."

Striving with 'might and main' is not a struggle against one's inner thoughts and desires. It clearly means a physical war all Muslims have been ordained by God to launch against those non-believers who refuse to accept Islam and its doctrines.

66:9: "O Prophet! Strive hard against the Unbelievers and the Hypocrites, and be firm against them. Their abode is Hell,- an evil refuge (indeed)."

The above verse lays bare the true meaning of the word "jihadu." Through it, God asked Muhammad to strive hard against the unbelievers and the hypocrites. Killing by him of the unbelievers and the hypocrites is implied here; for God can consign them to the fire of hell only after their dearth. No humans can be made to take their residence in hell until they die or are killed.

In the parlance of the Quran, the torment of a sinner begins immediately after his burial. Soon after he is laid to rest, angels visit him to find out whether or not he was a God-fearing and pious Muslim in his worldly life. If he is found to have lived a sinful life, the angels curse him and leave him in the grave to suffer from all the punishments the grave is ordained by God to continually inflict on his person.

On the Day of Judgment, he would be raised and after being judged by God again, he would take up his residence in hell. It is the last scenario that the above verse refers to. And this scenario begins unfolding after one has died or been killed. Striving hard against the unbelievers and hypocrites was, therefore, a command from God to Muhammad for putting them to death; otherwise the contents of the verse under discussion would have had no justification for its inclusion in the Quran.

For those readers who like to read or hear straight forward talks or arguments, the following clear cut definition of Muslim struggle or jihad given by Abd al-Salam Faraj should be sufficient and satisfying:

"... It is our duty to concentrate on our Islamic causes, and that is the establishment first of all of God's laws in our own country and causing the word of God to prevail. There is no doubt that the first battlefield of the jihad is the extirpation of these infidel leaderships and their replacement by a perfect Islamic order, and from this will come the release of our energies." (Al-jihad: l-Farida al-Ghaiba (Amman, 1982). English translation: The Neglected Duty: The Creed of Sadat's assassins and Islamic Resurgence in the Middle East (New York, 1986), pp. 159 ff.

The first jihad that Muslims had undertaken came to be known as the 'conquest of Mecca.' Their campaign against the Meccan pagans was aimed at taking over their city, and to convert all of them to Islam. From this effort, Muhammad and his followers gained no material benefit.

INSIDE JIHAD

On 12 January 2002, Musharraf made another about-turn when he declared that no Pakistan-based organization would be allowed to indulge in terrorism in the name of religion. In a televised speech lasting well over an hour, he unequivocally condemned all acts of terrorism, including those carried out in the name of freeing Kashmir's Muslim majority from Indian rule.

He banned five Islamic extremists groups including Lashkar-e-Taiba (LeT) and Jaish-e-Mohammed (JeM), the two most powerful jihadist organizations. 'No party in future will be allowed to be identified with words like Jaish, Lashkar or Sipah,' he warned. This declaration was acclaimed as an ipso facto renunciation of jihad as a state policy. From a western perspective, Musharraf's landmark speech positioned him as the kind of leader in the Muslim world the West had been desperately seeking.

The speech marked a departure from the policy of supporting pan- Islamism and the process of Islamization. Musharraf strongly asserted that the state should exercise a monopoly over external policy and it should be determined, not by Islamic solidarity, but by the country's national interests. He vowed to suppress Islamic extremist groups challenging the authority of the state and rein in radical madrasas.

For Musharraf, the 12 January declaration was more important than his decision to support the US war on Afghanistan. 'This sets a direction for the country, that was a response to a terrorist attack,' the General told me a week after his decision that brought him into direct conflict with the militant groups once sponsored by his intelligence agencies. But he found it hard to root out a deeply entrenched jihadist culture nurtured by the state for more than two decades.

The first Pakistani jihadist group emerged in 1980 when thousands of volunteers, mainly students from religious seminaries, joined the anti-Soviet resistance in Afghanistan. By 2002, Pakistan had become home to 24 militant groups. Highly disciplined paramilitary organizations operated in every neighbourhood, pursuing their own internal and external agenda. The largest among them were LeT, JeM, Harakat-ul-Mujahideen (HuM) and Harkat-al-Jihad-al-Islami (HJI). All these paramilitary groups, originally from the same source, had similar motivations and goals, and recruited from the same kind of people (often unemployed youth from Punjab and the North West Frontier Province). The only difference was in patronage: HuM and HJI were both strongly linked with the Taliban, whilst LeT had strong links with Wahabi groups in Saudi Arabia.

These militant organizations were not clandestine nor had they sprouted surreptitiously. Their growth, if not actually sponsored, had certainly been looked upon with favour by the state. Their activities were not secret, and found expression in graffiti, wall posters and pamphlets all over the country, inviting Muslims to join forces with them. They also carried addresses and telephone numbers to contact for training. 'Jihad is the shortest route to paradise,' declared one of the many exhortations. 'A martyr ensures salvation for the entire family.' Every jihadist organization had funds to help families of 'martyrs'.

Although money was not the primary motivation of jihadists, it was essential to sustain the culture of jihad. The state's patronage helped the jihadists to raise funds at public places. The militant groups had developed a powerful propaganda machinery. Their publications had gained a large readership and their messages were also available on video and audiotapes.

During the 1980s and 1990s, the objective of jihadist movements in Pakistan was not, like that of Arab Salafists such as bin Laden, the establishment of a global Islamic caliphate. Their objectives were more in line with the regional strategy of the Pakistani military establishment: the liberation of Kashmir from India and the installation of a Pashtun Islamist government in Afghanistan. Almost all the Islamic militant groups served as instruments of Pakistan's regional policy. The army needed them as much as they needed the army. After 9/11, Pakistan's support for the American-led war on terror pitted it against its former clients.

The Wahabi-inspired LeT, the most radical face of jihad in Pakistan, was also more amenable to the ISI than any other militant outfits. After the 2002 ban, it reduced its public visibility. Instead of challenging Musharraf's military led government, it agreed to work within new parameters and restrict its activities to a 'controlled jihad' in Kashmir while keeping a low profile inside Pakistan. However, this tactical truce was a strained one. Islamist groups, even government-friendly ones like LeT, were becoming radicalized by the ideological currents of the region. Increasingly, their ambitions exceeded the goals of the ISI. Even in 2000, the founder of LeT, Hafiz Mohammed Saeed told me that he saw the struggle in Kashmir as 'the gateway to the liberation of Indian Muslims'. He went on: 'We believe in a clash of civilizations and our jihad will continue until Islam becomes the dominant religion.' A former university professor, Hafiz Saeed is not a charismatic man; he comes across as shy and self-effacing, not the ingredients that militant leaders are generally made of. Short and chubby, his long beard dyed with henna, when I met him in January 2001 he was always surrounded by his young followers. For him, killing infidels and destroying the forces of 'evil and disbelief is the obligation of every pious Muslim'. The horrors of the partition of India in 1947, which uprooted his family from their home in Simla, left a huge imprint on Hafiz Saeed's personality. Millions of people were massacred in the communal violence that followed the creation of the new Muslim state. Thirty-six members of his family were killed while migrating to Pakistan. There his family settled in the central Punjab district of Sargodha.

Farm land allotted by the government, and hard work, brought prosperity to the family. Hafiz Saeed's parents were very religious. His mother taught the Qur'an to her seven sons. Five of them were still alive. Hafiz Saeed received his primary education in the village. After graduating from the University of Punjab he joined the King Abdul Aziz Islamic University in Riyadh where he also taught for many years. During his stay in Saudi Arabia he developed close links with Wahabi clerics. After returning to Pakistan, Hafiz Saeed took up a teaching job at the Department of Islamic Studies at the Lahore University of Engineering and Technology. His two brothers lived in America. One was head of an Islamic centre and the other pursued an academic career. Hafiz Saeed himself had never travelled to the USA or any other western country.

In the early 1980s, Hafiz Saeed joined the mujahidin war in Afghanistan which also brought him into close contact with Abdullah Azzam and Osama bin Laden. Their 'dedication to jihad' inspired him immensely. 'Osama was a man of extraordinary qualities,' he recalled. Azzam, a Palestinian who had worked as a professor of Islamic jurisprudence at the University of Jordan in Amman had a huge influence on Hafiz Saeed. The Palestinian scholar arrived in Pakistan soon after the invasion of Afghanistan by Soviet forces and took up a teaching position at the Islamic University of Islamabad. But his stint was short. He shifted to Peshawar and emerged as the main jihadist ideologue. With Saudi finance he recruited volunteers for the Afghan jihad from all over the Arab world. He was assassinated in a bomb attack in Peshawar in 1989.

Azzam helped Hafiz Saeed establish Markaz Dawal al-Irshad (MDI), an organization for Islamic preaching and guidance which was ideologically affiliated with Wahabi Ahle Hadith. In the tradition of the reformist Sunni movements, the MDI sought to purify society and Islam of 'outside influences'. Its sprawling headquarters in Muridke on the outskirts of Lahore housed a university, a farm, a clothing factory and a carpentry workshop.

The objective was to create a model Islamic environment removed from any state interference. In 1994, the movement set up a network of schools across the country with the objectives of promoting the Wahabi version of Islam and preparing the students for jihad. The MDI observed a strict educational philosophy that was directed towards developing a jihadist culture and to produce a reformed individual, who would be well versed not only in Islamic moral principles, but also in science and technology.

The teaching was aimed at producing an alternative model of governance and development. These schools, located in the poorer urban and rural neighbourhoods, attracted children of families who could not afford a better education. The organization encouraged its supporters to have large families, so that more volunteers were available for jihad. Hafiz Saeed founded LeT in 1990, soon after the withdrawal of Soviet forces from Afghanistan, as a military wing of the MDI to wage jihad against the Indian authorities in Kashmir. The LeT announced its arrival on the Kashmir jihad scene on 5 February 1993 with a ferocious attack on an Indian military force in Poonch district that killed at least two soldiers.

Two of the guerrillas were also killed. Since then the outfit has been responsible for hundreds of guerrilla raids in the disputed territory. Within a short span, LeT emerged as the fiercest militant organization – it possessed not only thousands of well trained and highly motivated fighters, but also a huge propaganda network. Its several publications in different languages had a circulation of hundreds of thousands. Its main publication, Al-Dawat, had more than 80,000 copies printed and sold at major bookshops across the country.. LeT had worked in close coordination with the ISI, which also provided support to launch the militants across the border. LeT was an extremely secretive organization. Except for the top leadership, the identity of its members was not disclosed. Since its inception in 1990, it has produced thousands of highly trained fighters, who have given a new dimension to the guerrilla war in Kashmir. The earliest fighters were trained in various camps in Afghanistan. But after 1992 the camps were shifted to remote regions of Azad Kashmir (Free Kashmir) and the mountainous tribal regions of the North West Frontier Province close to the border with Afghanistan.

The procedure was simple. Any jihadist aspirant could enroll himself for training at one of hundreds of LeT centres operating openly across the country. The volunteers, most of them in their teens, were then taken to various camps for military training, conducted in two stages. At the initial level they were given basic weapons training for three weeks. The second stage of rigorous guerrilla training was restricted to those who were fully committed to jihad and were practising Muslims. At the camp, volunteers began their day with the call to morning prayers. They were then kept busy in gruelling physical and military exercise until dusk. Part of the training, included religious instruction, Qur'anic lessons and adherence to prayers. The trainees learned to transform their lives in line with the teaching of Islam. To be in the ranks of the 'soldiers of Allah', growing a beard was mandatory, shalwar (loose trousers) had to be hiked above the ankle, and watching television and listening to music were banned. Individualism was curbed, beginning with the sharing of food and drinks from the same utensils.

After the initial training, the would-be mujahid was sent back, usually to his home town, and kept under observation by senior

LeT officials for a couple of months. His conduct was closely watched as he performed routine organizational duties. He was supposed to collect funds, organize propaganda meetings and practise the preaching of Islam in his home and neighbourhood. Only a select number of volunteers were chosen for the extended programme. They returned home completely transformed after the course. They kept their hair long and stopped cutting their beards. They were identified by new names, mostly the surnames of companions of the Prophet Mohammed or of the earliest Islamic heroes. Between 10,000 and 30,000 young men were trained at LeT camps.

The extended training, however, did not ensure that a volunteer would be sent for combat operations. Thousands of trained guerrillas anxiously awaited their turn to cross into Kashmir, but not everyone was given the chance. 'I pray to Allah that my turn [to go to Kashmir] comes soon, 'said Abu Mohammed, a young college student who had already completed the second level training. Hafiz Saeed often said that he would not put a weapon in the hands of any young recruit who was not secure in his faith. To be a combatant one had to be a pious person.

LeT, unlike some of the other jihadist groups, drew its recruits from universities and colleges as well as from among unemployed youth. The traditional Islamic madrasas provided only ten per cent of the volunteers. Influenced by radical Islamic literature, many university and college students joined the group. 'Those coming from educational institutions are much more motivated and conscious of what they are doing,' said Naveed Qamar, an LeT activist and graduate of the University of Engineering and Technology, Lahore. The top leadership of the group, including Hafiz Saeed, had been on the faculty of that university. A large number of LeT activists also came from the working class or were school drop-outs. In the countryside, LeT recruits were largely from families which were influenced by Wahabi Islam.

The majority of LeT recruits came from Punjab, particularly from Lahore, Gujranwala and Multan where Ahle Hadith had its strongholds. In some central Punjab district villages LeT had considerable influence because of support for the Kashmir jihad.

Gondlawala, a small dusty village, is now called Pind Shaheedan (the village of martyrs) because at least one person from every family had fought or died in the Kashmir jihad, mainly as an LeT fighter. The group's increasing influence was indicated by the fact that the villagers would accept its arbitration in local and even in domestic disputes. In recent years, LeT had started attracting an increasing number of volunteers from Pakistan's southern provinces of Sindh and Balochistan where Wahabi influence had increased. Muslims from other countries, including Britain, had also joined LeT. Shamshur Rehman, an Afghan, was the chief commander of LeT when he was killed in Badgam district in Kashmir in May 1995 in an encounter with Indian security forces. Several foreign militants were believed to have received training at LeT camps in Pakistan. Among them were Guantanamo Bay inmates David Hicks and French terrorist suspect Willie Brigitte, who were accused of planning attacks in Australia.

LeT gave a new and more violent dimension to the Kashmiri struggle by launching Fidayin raids against Indian forces and military installations. The term 'Fidayin attack' was used by the LeT leadership for target operations well inside the Indian military bases. 'A Fidayin is one who must complete his mission even in the worst circumstances,' explained Abdullah Muntazir, an LeT spokesman. He insisted that the concept of Fidayin was different from that of a suicide bomber, who blew himself up to kill others. 'We consider suicide attacks un-Islamic. Many Fidayin come back alive after completion of their missions,' said Muntazir. The Fidayin attacks had brought an unprecedented ferocity to the Kashmir jihad.

A Fidayin is chosen from among the best and most courageous fighters and not every guerrilla meets the tough criteria. An otherworldly level of devotion to the cause is required, as I discovered when I met a Fidayin recently returned from his mission. His thin frame, gentle eyes and polite manners gave not the slightest indication of his being a guerrilla fighter. The young bearded militant, who used the nom de guerre of Abu Ukrema, had just returned from Kashmir when I met him at the LeT headquarters in Lahore in January 2001. Abu Ukrema walked with a limp because of a bullet wound, received during an encounter with the Indian troops. 'I will return to the fighting as soon as the bullet is removed and the wounds are healed,' he told me. 'It is my desire to become a martyr.' His face lit up as he narrated how he and his fellow guerrillas had destroyed an Indian army post after a fierce gun battle which lasted several hours and left many soldiers dead.

Martyrdom is not mourned as it is considered to be the sole guarantee of entry to paradise. LeT local officials visit the house of the martyr to offer congratulations to the family. Sweets are distributed to celebrate the death. The occasion is also used to solicit new recruits. Emotional speeches are delivered and then the martyr's testament, which often exhorts their kin to strictly observe the Islamic tenets and be prepared to give their lives in the way of Allah, is read in public. The men are implored neither to listen to music nor to watch films. They are asked to destroy their television sets because they 'spread the Hindu culture of singing and dancing'. LeT's sectarian tilt and ultra-orthodox ideology distinguish it from other Pakistani radical Islamists. Some other militant groups even accuse it of undermining the Kashmiri jihad by promoting sectarian division.

LeT's main stress was on jihad against Hindus, who it regarded as the worst polytheists, and against Jews who it claimed were 'singled out by the Qur'an as the enemies of Islam'. LeT leaders maintained that Hindus and Jews were their main targets because they were 'the enemies of Islam and Pakistan'. A party document, 'Why are we waging jihad', argued that jihad was the only way to avenge history and re-establish the lost glory of Islam. It vowed to take back Spain, where Muslims had ruled for 800 years, and to re-establish Muslim rule in India. It said that LeT was fighting to liberate not just Kashmir, but the whole of India. It was one of the reasons why LeT's attacks against Hindus had been so savage. In many cases the victims were beheaded. In December 2000 LeT extended its jihad from Kashmir to mainland India.

It was just before dark on 3 December 2000 when two of LeT's gunmen sneaked inside Delhi's Red Fort, which housed an Indian military unit and a high-security interrogation cell used both by the Central Bureau of Interrogation and the army. The fort, built by Mughal Emperor Shahjahan in the seventeenth century, sits on the edge of the Indian capital's old town and has a huge symbolic value for India. Traditionally, the Prime Minister hoisted the national flag here on Independence Day, and part of this historic landmark was opened to tourists in the daytime. A fierce firefight broke out after armed intruders stormed the security barracks, killing three guards. LeT claimed responsibility the next day, declaring that the guerrillas who were involved in the deadly attack were safe at an undisclosed location.

The audacious raid on the Red Fort was the first operation against an Indian military installation inside India by an Islamic militant group involved in the Kashmiri struggle. 'The action indicates that we have extended the jihad to India,' Hafiz Saeed declared when I met him a month after the incident. The attack on the Red Fort signalled a new and more aggressive phase in jihadist activities. It was incidents such as this which brought LeT to the US State Department's attention and, in 2002, it was placed on the USA's list of terrorist organizations. Musharraf, having declared his support for the war on terror, had little choice but to ban it. But the ban had little affect on LeT's power. Before it was even announced, the LeT leadership had shifted their base to Indian-controlled Kashmir. This relieved some of the political pressure from Musharraf as it made it more difficult to claim that the Pakistani government was behind the Fidayin attacks. While an entirely new Kashmiri leadership was appointed to run the military wing, in Pakistan the outfit started working under the banner of its political wing, Jamaat-ud Da'awa, with Hafiz Saeed as its head. The new organization ostensibly restricted its role to preaching, education and social welfare. But in reality it never ceased working in support of the Kashmiri jihad.

LeT leaders admit that the proscription slowed down their operation in Kashmir, but it certainly didn't stop it; a large number of its militants were still based in its camps in Muzaffarabad in Pakistani-controlled Kashmir. After initial restraint, LeT was back recruiting volunteers and its donation boxes had reemerged at public places and mosques. In a speech on March 2004, Hafiz

Saeed had declared that more than 7,000 new volunteers had received military training at LeT camps in the previous six months. The first congregation of Jamaat-ud Da'awa held in November 2002, after the government's action against LeT, attracted more than 100,000 people.

It was apparent that Jamaat-ud Da'awa was just a cover to avoid international scrutiny. Neither its militant infrastructure nor its propaganda machinery had stopped functioning. The group continued to publish several magazines and run a website. Interestingly, no LeT activist was arrested in the government's crackdown on Islamic extremists. After being detained for a few months, Hafiz Saeed was freed by a High Court order in December 2002 and then moved freely around the country, mobilizing Muslims for jihad. 'For us jihad is sacred like praying and fasting that cannot be forsaken under any condition,' he declared at the end of his detention. 'Ours is not such a cowardly party as to bow down before the US pressure for halting support to jihad. The Pakistan government placed Jamaat-ud Da'awa on the 'terror watch list' in 2003, but the action did not affect its activities, which included running a huge network of hospitals and schools. While continuing the struggle in Kashmir, LeT had its own reason not to take on the government. 'Our main objective is to wage jihad against non-Muslims,'explained Yahya Mujahid, a spokesman for the group. Indeed, unlike other militant groups such as JeM and HuM, LeT has never used its military skills within Pakistan nor did it involve itself with any sectarian or ethnic organizations. The case of LeT was indicative of Islamabad's continuing flexibility towards those organizations which had restricted their activities to Kashmir and did not indulge in terrorism at home. Pakistani authorities defended their stance saying that LeT did not present any threat to the country's internal security, so there was no need to crackdown on it. According to them the organization strictly controlled its cadres and none of its members had ever indulged in any act of terrorism inside the country.

Contrary to this claim, there is strong evidence of LeT activists providing shelter to al-Qaeda fighters fleeing from Afghanistan. Abu Zubaydah, a close associate of bin Laden, was captured in 2002 in a house in the Pakistani central city of Faisalabad rented by a LeT member. But its leaders deny any association with the terrorist network. They maintained there was a fundamental difference between them and bin Laden's views on 'jihad'. 'We do not agree with his call to overthrow the rulers of Muslim countries. Islam does not allow waging jihad against Muslims,' said Yahya Mujahid.

As well as the desire to avoid unnecessary confrontations, Islamabad's attitude towards LeT also reflected the desire to keep militancy alive until India agreed to a resolution of the Kashmir dispute. Despite an improvement in relations between India and Pakistan as a result of the peace process launched in January 2004, there has not been any substantive move on the thorny issue of Kashmir. Islamabad believed that a complete cessation of militancy in Kashmir would remove pressure on India to make any concessions.

Though its main concentration has been in Kashmir, LeT has expanded its network to several other countries. Its members were active in India, Burma, Chechnya, and Bosnia and according to some reports have also been fighting against the American forces in Iraq. In April 2004, coalition forces reportedly arrested a Pakistani Islamic fighter who was identified as Danish Ahmed. A former LeT commander in Kashmir, he was captured by British forces in Basra and later handed over to the American intelligence authorities. Ahmed is believed to be among hundreds of Pakistani volunteers involved in the Iraq war. Most of them came from religious schools run by MDI. Virulently anti- American, the party has declared that it was mandatory for Muslims to join the mujahidin fighting against the American forces in Iraq. 'Islam is in grave danger and the Iraqi mujahidin are fighting for the return of its glory. They are fighting the forces of evil in an extremely difficult situation,' Hafiz Saeed declared in his sermon at a Lahore mosque in June 2004.

Though LeT refrained from indulging in terrorist activities inside Pakistan, its leaders became increasingly critical of Musharraf's pro- American policies and move to reform the madrasas. 'Most of our leaders are lapdogs of Americans,' declared Majjalutul Dawa, a publication of Jamaat-ud Da'awa.

Despite being seen as a 'tame', controllable force, LeT is more powerful than ever, and looks set for confrontation with the government on issues which go beyond Kashmir. Simply by carrying out its recruiting, fundraising and military activities, it contributes to the radicalization of Pakistani society. Nonetheless, for as long as the Kashmiri issue remains unresolved, the government seems prepared to embrace it.

Unlike Kashmir, Afghanistan is an area where the government's objectives and those of their erstwhile jihadist allies became very different after 9/11.

However, precisely because of the extent of cooperation between the Taliban, the ISI and Pakistani jihadist groups in the 1980s, Musharraf has found it very difficult to get the state security services to effectively implement his policy about-turn. Taliban-sympathising jihadist groups, such as HuM and JeM, are now increasingly powerful on the ground in the treacherous border regions between Afghanistan and Pakistan.

The extent of Taliban/ISI/jihadist cooperation was revealed during the Indian hostage crisis of 1999, the resolution of which I witnessed first hand. I sat at Kandahar airport with a group of reporters, photographers and TV crews just 500 metres from an Indian Airlines Airbus, the only functional aircraft there. Black-turbaned Taliban soldiers guarded the plane with more than 155 passengers on board as negotiations between the hijackers and UN officials dragged on. Conditions inside the plane were stifling. The body of a passenger killed by the hijackers lay in a pool of blood.

Armed with grenades, pistols and knives, five men had seized flight IC 814 about 40 minutes after it took off from Kathmandu, Nepal on a scheduled flight to New Delhi on 24 December 1999. The plane had made stops in India, Pakistan and the United Arab Emirates before landing in Afghanistan. The hijackers, who called themselves Kashmiri freedom fighters, had demanded the release of three top Islamic militant leaders from Indian prisons. Some of the hooded hijackers would climb down occasionally to receive supplies or talk to officials. The Taliban officials were visibly warm towards them.

Interestingly, the Taliban leaders, who in the past had scorned foreign journalists and deemed photography as un-Islamic, were overly amiable, providing them with facilities. There were no restrictions on TV cameras and photography. The conservative Islamic administration appeared extremely keen to have international publicity for the event. Scores of media persons from the world over had descended on the spiritual headquarters of the regime as the hijacking drama unfolded. The eve of the new century brought an end to the hostages' eight- day ordeal when the Indian Foreign Minister, Jaswant Singh, arrived with the three men whose freedom was demanded by the hijackers. Among them was a short, stocky man with an unkempt black beard. A former leader of HuM, Masood Azhar was captured by the Indian authorities in 1994 and held in prison on terrorism charges. Along with him was a tall heavily built young man. A Pakistani-born British national, Ahmed Omar Saeed Sheikh had been detained in Delhi's high security Tihar prison for many years on charges of kidnapping three foreign tourists.

The hijackers stepped down triumphantly from flight IC 814, their faces still covered, as Indian officials handed over the freed militants to the Taliban authorities. Mullah Wakil Ahmed Muttawakil, the suave Foreign Minister of the Taliban regime, won international praise for his 'deft handling' of the hijacking episode. But the real-life drama was taking place at the far end of the tarmac. The freed militants were warmly greeted by Mullah Akhtar Usmani, the chief of Taliban forces in Kandahar, and dozens of other senior officials of the fundamentalist regime. They were joined by two of the hijackers, one wearing a western suit and the other in safari dress. 'Are you satisfied now?' a smiling Mullah Usmani asked the two men. 'Indeed,' replied one of them excitedly. They were whisked away in a window-blackened vehicle to an unknown destination. The three other hijackers also vanished from the scene.

'Everything had gone amazingly smoothly due to the Taliban's excellent political acumen and superb handling of the situation,' Azhar later recalled. It was the first time that a Pakistani-based militant group had successfully used hijacking as an instrument of terror. The well- planned action was carried out by HuM: a group similar to LeT, but which drew its recruits from less well-educated, unemployed youth, often from the North-West Frontier Province. HuM was formed by former members of Harkat-ul-Ansar (HuA) after it was put on the State Department terrorist organizations list in 1994.

The group could not have succeeded without backing from the Taliban government and its Pakistani patrons. In fact, Afghan sources, including Muttawakil, who had surrendred himself to US forces after the fall of the Taliban regime, revealed that the hijackers were taking instructions from Pakistani intelligence officials present at the airport. The hijacking was followed by an extension of militant operations well inside India. Ironically, all its jihadist 'assets' who had figured in the incident returned to haunt Pakistan with the turn of events a few years later.

It was late in the evening on 7 January 2000 when Azhar resurfaced at Al-Rasheedia mosque in Karachi's central district. Surrounded by some two dozen men dressed in camouflage-style uniforms and brandishing automatic rifles, he triumphantly declared that his freedom was a defeat for India. 'I have come here because it is my duty to tell you that Muslims should not rest in peace until we have destroyed America and India,' thundered the militant leader, his head wrapped in a chequered scarf. Some 10,000 people who had gathered there after evening prayers greeted him with chants of 'Allah o Akbar' (God is the greatest) and 'Death to India'. 'I will not rest in peace until I wrest Kashmir from India.' There was no effort from the government to detain Azhar or even to stop him from making an inflammatory speech. It was quite apparent that he enjoyed state protection. Born in 1968 in the southern Punjab district of Bahawalpur, Azhar was the third of 12 children of a schoolteacher. He grew up in an intensely religious atmosphere and most of his family members had been associated with radical Islam. Azhar received his Islamic religious education at one of Pakistan's largest and most influential Islamic seminaries, Jamia Ulumia Islamia, also known as Jamia Binoria, in Karachi, before joining the institution as a teacher. Run by a trust established by Islamic scholar Yousuf Binori in the 1950s, the school had been transformed into a centre for jihad in the 1980s during the anti-Soviet war in Afghanistan.

The seminary was the bastion in Pakistan of the fundamentalist Deobandi movement, which developed in the nineteenth century. A branch of Sunni Hanafi Islam, the creed is named after a great religious seminary established in 1867 in the Indian village of Deoband near Delhi. The founders of the seminary drew their spiritual guidance from Shah Wali Ullah, an eighteenth-century Islamic scholar who endeavoured to bind together different Islamic schools of thought. The movement, which was purely a South Asian phenomenon, sought to revive puritan Islam, but became radicalized with the call for jihad against the Soviet occupation of Muslim Afghanistan. The first squad of Pakistani jihadists came from this institution in 1980,36 and in the next two decades thousands of its students participated in 'holy wars' in Afghanistan and Kashmir. Many of the Taliban leaders were graduates of this institution. They would often consult Mufti Nizamuddin Shamzai, a widely respected cleric and dean of the school, on matters relating to Islamic sharia.

Azhar's journey into jihad started during his stay in Jamia Binoria. In the mid 1980s he went to Afghanistan to fight along with the mujahidin in the eastern Khost province. There was no going back for him from there. It was in Afghanistan that he decided to dedicate his life to the cause of jihad. He joined HuM, one of the most powerful jihadist groups involved in the Afghan war. Because of his weak physical condition he was assigned propaganda and organizational work. With his fiery speeches he soon made his mark on the movement. Audio cassettes of his speeches were used to motivate Muslims to join the jihadist cause. He was also a powerful writer and in the 1980s edited a magazine called Sadai Mujahid ('Voice of Mujahid'). He soon rose up the group's leadership ladder.

One of his tasks was to mobilize support in other countries and, during the 1990s, he made trips to several European and African countries. Some reports suggest he followed Osama bin Laden to Sudan in 1992 and fought in Somalia along with Arab fighters, most of them former Afghan war veterans, for the local warlord, Aided. He was also said to have been involved in the training of militants in Yemen before he was sent to organize the party's jihadist network in Indian- controlled Kashmir. Captured by Indian forces in February 1994 for travelling on a forged Portuguese passport, he was tried on terrorism charges. He was acquitted in that case, but remained in jail for more than six years. He made an attempt to escape by digging a tunnel, but was caught and put in a high security prison in Srinagar. During his six-year detention in Indian jails, Azhar, still in his mid thirties, wrote numerous articles on jihad, often referring in his writings to Africa. It was in July 1994 that Ahmed Omar Saeed Sheikh, then a student at the London School of Economics, was sent to Delhi by the HuM leadership with a mandate to kidnap a group of western tourists and demand as ransom the release of Azhar and some other militant leaders. Sheikh succeeded in kidnapping one American and three British nationals from a hotel in New Delhi, but the hostages were rescued by the police from a house in Sharanpur town in Uttar Pradesh. Sheikh was captured after a shoot-out in which one policeman was killed. It took another five years and the hijacking of an Indian Airlines jet to earn his and his mentor's freedom. The two probably met face to face for the first time in the plane which took them to Kandahar.

The son of a wealthy Pakistani businessman who had migrated to Britain for a better economic future, Sheikh fitted the profile of a classic politically aware Islamic militant. His passage to militancy started in 1992 when he watched a series of documentary films about the oppression of Muslims following the break up of the former Yugoslavia. In the wars in the Balkans in the 1990s, thousands of Muslims were brutally murdered in scenes of violence not seen in Europe since the Second World War.

A story gained prominence regarding Sheikh's path to extremism: moved by the plight of Muslims, it said that Sheikh travelled to Bosnia with an organization known as 'Convoy of Mercy'. The purpose of the visit was to provide humanitarian help to the victims of ethnic cleansing. But the people he had met and the things he saw during the trip radicalized him. After his return, he dropped out of the LSE and headed to a training camp in

Afghanistan where he established links with HuM. Equally important in terms of what happened next, he was recruited by the ISI in London before leaving for India.

On returning home, Azhar broke away from HuM and decided to form his own group. On 30 January 2000, flanked by his teacher and mentor, Mufti Nizamuddin Shamzai, and some other senior clerics of the Jamia Binoria, Azhar announced the formation of a new militant outfit, Jaish-e-Mohammed (JeM). The decision shocked Pakistani jihadist circles. Backing for the new party by Shamzai and other Deobandi clerics, who were considered to be very close to Pakistan's military establishment, raised many questions. Jamia Binoria had played a key role in promoting a state-sponsored jihadist culture and their support for the new militant outfit led to speculation that it was done at the behest of the ISI.

The new guerrilla group was more ambitious than any seen before, and heralded its emergence on the jihadist scene by launching a number of spectacular attacks against the Indian forces in Kashmir in mid 2000. Most of its cadres came from rural areas, small towns and from the madrasas. JeM also recruited among emigrant Kashmiris and Punjabis in Britain. One of them, Mohammed Bilal, a young man from Birmingham, drove a car full of explosives into an Indian army base in Srinagar on 25 December 2000. Pakistani and Kashmiri expatriates in Britain and other countries were the source of funding for the group.

In addition to guerrilla activities in Kashmir, JeM continued to have close ties to the Taliban regime in Afghanistan. Several of Azhar's close family members were in government jobs in Kabul. Hundreds of JeM activists received training in camps in Afghanistan, bringing them into contact with al-Qaeda. The group's newspaper, Zerb-i-Momin, became a mouthpiece of the Taliban regime and was widely read among the officials.

The weekly newspaper, published from Karachi in both Urdu and English, sold about a quarter of a million copies across Pakistan. It represented a new breed of jihadist journalism which saw huge growth during the 1990s. With the rise to power of the Taliban in Afghanistan, these publications received a massive boost and became very vocal and proactive in favour of what could be described as 'Talibanization of mind and soul' in Pakistan. More than two dozen publications representing various militant outfits had a combined circulation of around one million. They propagated a militant Islamic and anti- western world-view. Zerb-i-Momin did not publish pictures of human faces in line with the Taliban's fundamentalist interpretation of Islam. Instead, it printed images of Islam's holy places or of weapons. It regularly published news about al-Qaeda and Taliban activities. Zerbi- Momin continued its publication even after the proscription of JeM. The group also published an Urdu-language daily newspaper from four cities; Islam had a nationwide circulation of more than 100,000. JeM had expanded its activities in Afghanistan through the Al- Rasheedia Trust founded by Maulana Abdul Rasheed, a leading Pakistani cleric associated with Jamia Binoria. The Trust, which had funded JeM's jihadist activities, established a network of mosques and madrasas in Afghanistan.

The American administration in 2002 placed the Trust on the list of organizations supporting and financing terrorism. Pakistan had also frozen its funds and put a ban on it, but this action was later suspended on the orders of the High Court. After 9/11, JeM signalled their anger at Pakistan's break with the Taliban by raiding the Kashmir state assembly building in Srinagar in October 2001, killing 35 people and later launched a suicide attack on an Indian military base in Srinagar.

The attack brought the Pakistani military regime under tremendous international pressure to act against the militant organizations. The incident, which occurred a few weeks after 9/11, forced Musharraf to denounce the raid as a 'terrorist action'. A few weeks later, JeM struck again, this time extending its operations inside India. It was just before noon on 13 December 2001 when a group of gunmen wearing military-style fatigues broke through tight security and burst into the area in front of the Indian Parliament building. One of the men was wearing explosives strapped to his body and blew himself up soon after breaking in. There were about a hundred members of Parliament inside the House as an intense gun battle between the attackers and security guards raged on for thirty minutes.

The Indian Prime Minister, Atal Bihari Vajpayee, was being driven towards Parliament at the time of the assault. He immediately turned back. The gun battle left five attackers and seven guards dead and 15 others injured. A JeM spokesman immediately claimed responsibility, but its leaders later backtracked, apparently under government pressure from Pakistan. Pakistan placed Azhar under protective custody but refused to hand him over to India, saying there was no evidence of his involvement in the Parliament attack. On 12 January, Musharraf banned JeM after the US Department of State placed them on its list of terrorist groups. But the action did not affect their activities. Even before the ban, JeM had started operating under a new banner, Jamaat-e-Furqa. Azhar was released by a court order a few months after his detention. But the group retaliated against the ban by launching a series of terrorist attacks across Pakistan targeting western nationals, Christians and Shia Muslims. Many of its activists subsequently became foot soldiers for al-Qaeda operations in Pakistan. The Pakistan government had chosen to ignore Azhar's involvement in all this: he was detained only for a few months under the Maintenance of Public Order. Since then he has maintained a low profile.

JeM activists returning from Afghanistan after the fall of the Taliban regime were responsible for a suicide attack on a Christian church in Islamabad's high-security diplomatic enclave which killed several people, including two Americans, in March 2002. The group was also responsible for attacks on Shia mosques in different parts of Pakistan. These kinds of sectarian attacks inside Pakistan marked it out as differing in strategy from other hardline Sunni groups such as Sipah-e- Sahaba Pakistan (SSP) and Lashkar-e-Jhangvi (LeJ), though in reality their memberships often overlapped. JeM was also involved in a December 2003 plot to assassinate Musharraf. The plan was apparently conceived by Ahmed Omar Saeed Sheikh and Amjad Hussain Farooqi, the two main characters who figured in the December 1999 hijacking of an Indian Airlines plane.

Sheikh apparently never went back to Britain after his release in Kandahar and instead joined his mentor, Azhar. Sheikh had established links with al-Qaeda soon after his release, and Pakistani intelligence agencies believe he had travelled to Afghanistan several times since then. The 28-year-old Londoner was believed to have met with bin Laden during his last trip to Afghanistan at the time of the US invasion. Just after the Taliban were ousted, he returned to Pakistan, having shaved his beard to escape capture. He was furious with his former patrons for helping the American forces in the invasion of a Muslim country. Only a few weeks later, he was arrested for his role in the kidnapping and murder of Wall Street Journal reporter Daniel Pearl.

Farooqi was a close associate of Sheikh's and the main coordinator of the group that met in Islamabad in 2001 to plot Musharraf's murder. The militants made several plans, but the two most serious ones, which were carried out within a span of two weeks in December 2003, had nearly succeeded. The plot revealed the nature of the terrorist coalition that had emerged in Pakistan after 9/11. Farooqi represented just one more link in this new alliance, confirming the worst fears about alQaeda's successful merger with Islamic extremists in Pakistan, one that made them difficult to identify and segregate.

In his mid thirties, Farooqi had fought against Soviet forces in Afghanistan and during Taliban rule he ran a guerrilla training camp in Afghanistan for Pakistani militants. A former activist of HuM, he had joined Azhar and served as his bodyguard, developing close ties with al-Qaeda through Khalid Sheikh Mohammed, bin Laden's chief of operations. Farooqi was the key suspect in almost every terrorist attack in Pakistan after 9/11. One of the country's most wanted terrorists, he had a half-million-dollar price on his head. He was killed in a firefight with security forces in southern Pakistan in September 2004.

One of the suicide bombers involved in the Christmas Day attack on Musharraf was a young Islamic militant who had recently been freed from an Afghan prison. Twenty-three-year-old Muhammad Jamil had fought in Kashmir before moving to Afghanistan where he received guerrilla training at an al-Qaeda camp in Rishkor, south-east of Kabul. The sprawling compound, which now houses the Afghan army, had previously served as the main training centre for militants from Pakistan and other countries. The volunteers were given standard 40day or three-month guerrilla training here. Jamil was captured fighting for the Taliban regime by the opposition Northern Alliance forces in 2000. After spending some three years in an Afghan jail, he was finally released by President Hamid Karzai in April 2003. Pakistani intelligence agencies, with their long association with militant groups, cleared the young man of any anti-state activities and allowed him to rejoin the militant camp in his home town of Kotli in Pakistan's semi- autonomous state of Azad Kashmir.

Jamil's links with the ISI were revealed during his detention at Baharak jail in Afghanistan's Panjshir valley, where he told his captors that he was a Pakistani army officer. He repeated the claim when paraded before foreign journalists. Pakistani authorities rejected the statement saying it was extracted under duress. But there is no denying his contacts with the Pakistani spy agency, which had facilitated the recruitment of thousands of youths to fight in aid of the Taliban regime. Intriguingly, the Kotli camp, run by JeM, had continued to function under ISI supervision despite Musharraf's orders to close down all such facilities. (When Musharraf learned that it was still functioning, he sacked Major-General Khalid Mahmoud, then the director of the ISI's Kashmir cell.)

JeM had developed a substantial following among the soldiers and lower-ranking military officials. Those radical contacts were extremely useful in the December attacks on Musharraf. Some two dozen air force personnel were part of a clandestine JeM cell, which was involved in the 14 December attempt to blow up the presidential convoy. Members of the cell lived in a residential colony near the Chaklala air base right in the heart of the Rawalpindi garrison, and met regularly with jihadist leaders without being spotted by intelligence agencies. One was Mushtaq Ahmad, who was instructed to plant the explosives under the bridge over which Musharraf's cavalcade passed on 14 December. A high-tech jamming device fixed in the President's car delayed the detonation by a few crucial seconds that allowed the cavalcade to cross before the explosion. It was not clear whether it was inefficiency or a deliberate oversight on the part of the intelligence agencies that they did not notice such a large quantity of explosives tied to the bridge along the high-security presidential route. Ironically, it was Indian intelligence that had warned Musharraf of the first attempt to kill him by blowing up the bridge. Mushtaq was handed a death sentence in a secret trial in November 2004, but mysteriously escaped from the detention centre inside the top-security Chaklala air base. Some other Islamic militant groups that had earlier been aligned with the ISI also turned to jihad after being proscribed by the government. These included HuM and HJI, both of which had a long history of involvement in Afghanistan and were closely associated with al- Qaeda. They felt betrayed by Musharraf's U-turn.

A small ramshackle building in a crowded neighbourhood in Rawalpindi served as HuM's headquarters. Toting automatic rifles, a number of young bearded militants kept a close vigil on visitors. Inside, the walls were adorned with large propaganda posters carrying pictures of Islam's holy places, the Qur'an and Kalashnikovs. Sporting a white skull cap and a long beard, Khalil wondered why his group was pronounced terrorist. 'We have asked the Americans a number of times to tell us our crimes before announcing the punishment. There is no evidence against us.' He accused the Americans of pursuing a policy of intimidation. 'We don't understand the definition of terrorism. Those who are fighting with small rifles are terrorists and those who are dropping bombs are not.' Khalil spoke fondly about his association with bin Laden. 'He is a brother Muslim. I have known him since the days of the Afghan jihad when he was considered a friend, a mujahid and a hero by the Americans,' he smiled. 'Now the Americans have changed their glasses and call him a terrorist.'

Like hundreds and thousands of his peers, Khalil had fought against the Soviet forces in Afghanistan until he saw what he called the myth of Soviet power shatter before his eyes. Though the days of the Afghan struggle were over in 1989 for Khalil and hundreds like him, the jihad was not. The holy warriors, hardened on the battlefields of Afghanistan, found another cause to fight for – the cause of Kashmir's liberation from India. Following the collapse of the Soviet Union in 1990, which was seen by the Islamists as the 'triumph of jihad', hundreds of militants fanned out in 1990 to new destinations. Khalil was a student at a madrasa, Jamia Naumania, in Pakistan's North West Frontier Province when, at the age of 16, he was induced into jihad.

After the Soviet invasion of Afghanistan, the madrasa he attended had become the centre of jihadist activities by a fatwa calling Muslims to join the war against communism. Without telling his parents, Khalil left home in Dera Ismail Khan in 1981 to join the mujahidin in Afghanistan. For three years he had no contact with his family. He fought alongside an Afghan mujahidin group led by Younus Khalis and Commander Jalaluddin Haqani in the eastern Afghan provinces of Khost and Paktika. It was also the period when he first came into contact with bin Laden. Their relationship proved to be long lasting. In 1984 Khalil, along with another militant leader Saifullah Akhtar, founded Harkat-al-Jihad-al-Islami (HJI), the first Pakistani-based jihadist outfit. But just a few years later he broke away to form his own group, Harkat-ul-Ansar (HuA). By 1990, HuA had emerged as one of the most feared militant groups fighting in Kashmir. A large number of its cadres came from the Deobandi madrasa network in the North West Frontier Province. Espousing pan-Islamic ideology, the group believed in violent means to liberate Kashmir from India and make it a part of Pakistan.

About sixty per cent of HuA's initial 1,000 members came from northern Pakistan and Afghanistan. In later years, the ethnic composition of the organization changed with new recruits coming from Pakistani-controlled Azad Kashmir as well as Punjab and Karachi, many of them school drop-outs and jobless youths looking for some meaning in their lives. Many of them were inducted by roaming jihadist recruiting cells who, after delivering sermons in local mosques, invited the worshippers to join the jihad. Although HuA and later HuM, which it merged with, believed in Taliban-style fundamentalist Islam, it did not require its cadres to go through the same kind of religious training as conducted by LeT.

In its April 1995 report to Congress, 'Patterns of Global Terrorism', the US State Department associated HuA with terrorist activities for the first time. The report said that HuA had several thousand armed members, trained in the use of light and heavy machine guns, assault rifles, mortars, explosives and rockets. The same report also accused the group of having links with the hitherto little-known 'Al-Faran' organization which had captured western tourists in Kashmir in July 1995. One of the hostages was beheaded, another managed to escape, and the fate of the rest remains unknown. Kashmiri militants privately acknowledge that the hostages are no longer alive.

On 1 October 1997, the US Secretary of State, Madeleine Albright, submitted to the US Congress a list of 30 international terrorist organizations, which Washington had decided to bring under the purview of the Anti-Terrorism and Effective Death Penalty Act, 1997. HuA was one of the groups on the list. After being blacklisted by the US administration it resurfaced under a new banner, HuM. The new group was immediately put on the terrorist watch list by Washington. The State Department report for 1997, released in 1998, accused Pakistani officials of supporting Kashmiri militant groups, including HuM.

The rise of the Taliban gave a huge boost to Pakistani militant groups like HuM. Afghanistan became a base for their operations. Their leaders shared common origins, personnel and especially patrons. Most HuM activists came from the same seminaries in the Pakistani border region that the Taliban movement had emerged from. These groups were heavily backed by the ISI, which also patronized the Taliban. Both were important in furthering Pakistan's strategic interests – to extend Pakistani hegemony over the neighbouring state.

More than 10,000 Pakistani militants were believed to have received training in camps run by al-Qaeda and other jihadist groups during Taliban rule. The evidence of their close connection with bin Laden emerged in August 1998 when scores of Pakistani militants were killed in a US cruise missile attack on an al-Qaeda camp in the Afghan southeastern border town of Khost. A day after the attack, Khalil vowed to take revenge for the death of his activists. 'The US has struck us with Tomahawk cruise missiles at only two places, but we will hit back at them everywhere in the world, wherever we find them. We have started a holy war against the US and they will find no place to hide,' he declared.

Khalil was at the meeting in Afghanistan in February 1998 at which bin Laden announced the formation of an International Islamic Front against 'Jews and crusaders'. He was also a signatory of the ruling issued by the group which had stated that it was the duty of all Muslims to 'comply with God's order by killing Americans and their allies'. On 29 September 2001, Pakistan's government banned HuM, but its activists soon regrouped under new banners, Jamaat-al-Ansar and Harkat-ul-Mujahideen-al-Alami. They retained their links with the Taliban despite the shift in Pakistan's policy.

Khalil led hundreds of his fighters into war against the US forces. He returned home in January 2002, after the fall of the Taliban regime, and continued his jihadist activities despite the ban on his organization. HuM continued supporting the Taliban and al-Qaeda remnants operating from their bases on the Pakistan-Afghan border. Khalil was detained by Pakistani police in August 2002, only to be let out a few months later. He was arrested again in 2004 after HuM activists were found to be involved in a failed attempt to assassinate Musharraf. Pakistani security forces suspected that HuM activists operating in small cells were responsible for many terrorist attacks in the country after 9/11. HJI, led by Saifullah Akhtar, was another jihadist organization which had a vast network within the country and outside. The group constituted a significant part of the Taliban forces in Afghanistan and its fighters were known as Punjabi Taliban (because most of its fighters came from Punjab). HJI described itself as the second defence line of every Muslim country and claimed to have links with radical Islamic movements in around 24 countries including Chechnya, Britain and a number of Central Asian states.

Like most other Pakistani jihadist leaders, Akhtar was the product of an Islamic seminary. A Pashtun from the Waziristan tribal region, he received his elementary education at Darul Uloom, Wana before moving to Jamia Binoria in Karachi for higher Islamic education. He taught there briefly before joining the Afghan mujahidin in 1980. Akhtar spent a large part of his jihadist life in Afghanistan, first fighting the Soviet forces, then as a key commander of the Taliban forces. His headquarters in Kabul, known as Darul Irshad, became the main centre for Pakistani militants. More than 50 of his men were killed when American jets bombed it in November 2001.

The group's connection with Islamist elements in Pakistan's army was revealed in 1995, when Akhtar was implicated in a right-wing coup plot. It was late evening on 8 September 1995, when Pakistani customs guards stopped an army vehicle outside Kohat town in the North West Frontier Province for a routine check. The search found a huge cache of arms stored in the back cabin. Smuggled from the Dara Adam Khel tribal area, the weapons were ostensibly being supplied to Islamic militants fighting in Kashmir. The case was immediately reported to the army authorities.

The attempt initially looked like a maverick operation by some zealots in the army to support Kashmiri freedom fighters, but subsequent investigations led to startling revelations. The weapons were actually meant for a group of rebel army officers plotting an 'Islamic revolution' in the country with the help of some other Islamic militant groups.

At the centre of the coup plot were Major-General Zaheerul Islam Abbasi and Brigadier Mustansar Billah and a group of middle-ranking army officers. The rebels, who had close ties with some Islamic militant groups and hardline Muslim clerics, had conspired to eliminate the top military and civilian leadership and establish an 'Islamic dictatorship' in the country. They had planned to storm a corps commander meeting at Army General Headquarters in Rawalpindi and take over the military command. General Abbasi was to declare himself 'Amirul Mominin' (the supreme leader of the faithful) and turn Pakistan into a theocratic state. One of the main accomplices in the plot was Saifullah Akhtar. Major-General Abbasi, who was posted as Director Infantry at GHQ, had a controversial record. As a Brigadier he was posted in the late 1980s as Pakistan's military attache´ in Delhi from where he was expelled on espionage charges. The bearded General, who was known for his extremist religious views, was at the end of his career after having been overlooked for promotion. Brigadier Billah, who sported a long unruly beard, had more radical religious beliefs. He was never considered professionally sound and was consigned to an obscure post at GHQ. The conspirators were highly influenced by Lt.-General Ghulam Mohammed Malik, a former commander of the 10th corps in Rawalpindi who had retired just a few months earlier. Although the General did not have any direct role in the coup plot, most of the rebel officers idolized him because of his radical Islamic views.

A military court handed down jail sentences to General Abbasi and the other accused, but Akhtar was mysteriously freed and allowed to join the Taliban forces then closing in on Kabul. Akhtar's name resurfaced in 2004 when he was arrested in Dubai in connection with a plot to assassinate Musharraf.

There are differences between the various groups. Some, such as LeT, are more focused on India (though they all share the Kashmiri cause as a rallying point). Others, like HuM, are more involved in Afghanistan: some have closer links with transnational jihadists; others, such as JeM, are more concerned with purifying Pakistan itself. They share a common culture and anti-western world-view. They draw their footsoldiers from the ranks of the lower middle class, their ideology from radical clerics and their direction from a nuclei of battle hardened leaders with serious ISI connections.

As they evolve, regroup and reposition themselves in response to domestic and international pressures, one thing becomes clear: the more powerful groups, which are the more radical ones, have outgrown their handlers.

WHAT IS ISLAMISM? HISTORY AND DEFINITION OF A CONCEPT

Once, Jacques Delors, the former president of the EU Commission, defined the European Union (EU) as a UPO (Unidentified Political Object). By this definition, he of course wanted to emphasise the particularity and the uniqueness of the EU as a new and unprecedented political and economical construction. The UPO metaphor may also be applied to Islamism, as a URO (Unidentified Religious Object), since scholars have not yet reached a consensus about the definition and the meaning of this concept. Since the nineteenth century, the concept 'Islamism' has been used quite differently by western orientalists, islamologists and political scientists. The situation is not much clearer within the Muslim world. Muslims are using various names and appellations to define themselves and their coreligionists, '*Islamiyyûn*' [Islamists] being one of them.

It is almost certain that the etiquette of 'Islamism' was used for the first time by French writers at the end of the seventeenth century. *Le Petit Robert* gives 1697 as the first reference to the word. The Enlightenment philosopher Voltaire is one of the first writers to use the term: 'this religion is called *islamism*'. In a work from 1838, Tocqueville found the 'root of *islamism* in Judaism'. Caussin de Perceval, Comte de Gobineau, Ernest Renan and Baron Bernard Carra de Vaux equally make use of the term, the latter characterising 'Islamism' as a 'spent religion'.

The above-mentioned writers use 'Islamism' as part of the title of their respective works, either of a book or a chapter. Caussin de Perceval places it in the title of his book *Essai sur l'histoire des Arabes avant l'Islamisme, pendant l'époque de Mahomet* (3 vols, 1847–9). This title leaves no doubt that, in the mind of the author, 'Islamism' means 'Islam', e.g. the religion founded by Muhammad. Comte de Gobineau has devoted Chapter II of his book on *Religions et philosophies dans l'Asie Centrale* to the study of *l'Islamisme persan*. He considers Islamism as a camouflaged mixture of religions prior to Islam. After this very short remark, Gobineau continues his fascinating analysis on Iranian and central Asian societies, although he does not concern himself to engage in a further analysis of 'Islamism'. It is very clear that Gobineau uses the term 'Islamism' only in the sense of 'Islam' without any specific political or ideological connation. Some years later, Ernest Renan, a compatriot of Gobineau, used the term 'Islamism', especially at the famous conference he held at the Sorbonne (Paris) on 29 March 1883. This conference became very famous, and still is, because of its highly polemical aspect. At that time, an enigmatic Muslim personage named Sayyid Jamal al-Afghani (1838–97) was agitating in Egypt,

Persia and the Ottoman Turkey. He sojourned in Paris and engaged himself in a lively debate concerning the position of Islam towards modernity and science. It is in this context that Renan holds his speech on *Islamisme et la Science*. Renan, in perfect accordance with the intellectual context of his epoch, uses 'Islamism' as a parallel to 'Christianism' (the equivalent of 'Christianity' in English). By 'Islamism', Renan simply means 'Islam' as he uses 'Islam' and 'Islamism' as interchangeable terms.

'Islam' and 'Islamic' have become the most frequently used terms by western islamologists, orientalists and political scientists. This replacement is very clear indeed among a huge number of western writers of multiple disciplines, from Ignaz Goldziher (1850–1921), Arnold Toynbee (1852–83), Max Weber (1864–1920), Oswald Spengler (1880–1936), Fernand Braudel (1902–85), Claude Cahen (1909– 1991), Ann K.S. Lambton (b. 1912), Henri Laoust (d. 1976) and William Montgomery Watt (1909–2006) to contemporary scholars such as Samuel Huntington and Francis Fukuyama. We do not find the word 'Islamism' in the index of their works. Prior to the Islamist revolution in Iran in 1978–79, the terms 'Islamism' and 'Islamists' are also practically absent from the vocabulary of newspaper reporters.

The change in the vocabulary happened with the outbreak of the Islamic revolution under the leadership of Ayatollah Khomeini, who preached a political Islam and established the first '*Islamist* government' in the twentieth century. This religious revolution made it imperative to find a new vocabulary in order to outline the specificity of this new phenomenon. Suddenly, the world witnessed a multitude of terms and formal rules destined to grasp the 'novelty' of the new era in the history of Islam. By way of example, frequently used terms were 'Islamic fundamentalism', 'radical Islam', 'Islamic revival' and 'political Islam'. These terms, which became titles of numerous books and multiple articles, were clear and ambivalent at the same time. They indicated that this kind of 'Islam' is quite different from other versions of 'Islam'. However, what precisely does this 'new' form of 'Islam' contain? The ambiguity remains almost complete. Surely, it has become evident that this particular form of Islam was (more) political, often violent and severely critical towards the West, and, last but not least, determined in its hostility towards established regimes in the Muslim world. Nevertheless, this list determining the main characteristics of 'Islamic fundamentalism', 'political Islam', 'Islamic radicalism' or 'radical Islamism' does not bring about a clear conceptualisation of the phenomenon.

We had to wait until the tragic events of 9/11 to witness the rise of the need for conceptual clarification. It is a fact that, since 9/11, the use of the word 'Islamism' has increased among politicians and journalists worldwide. It is equally observable that scholars have progressively focused their attention on the ideological contients of Islamism.

Diverging from the nineteenth-century definition, 'Islamism' is no longer an emulation of '*christianisme*', but a rather new and independent concept. This change is observable in scholars' works, and particularly so in books and articles posterior to 9/11. For example, two eminent French islamologists, Olivier Roy and Gilles Kepel, previously used both 'political Islam' and 'fundamentalist Islam' extensively whereas they now tend to use 'Islamism' more and more often.

The term appears neither alone nor besides 'neofundamentalism' or 'political Islam'. Actually, the latter term is not equivalent to 'Islamism' in Olivier Roy's terminology. 'Political Islam' designates a failed project in his works, whereas 'Islamism' denominates the new form of activist Islam. Bruno Etienne, director of the *Observatoire du Religieux* at the Department of Political Science, University of Aix-en-Provence, has dedicated much of his time to the study of Islam and gives the following definition of 'radical Islamism': 'it proposes as a cure of all the evils of modernity/ modernisation the return to political Islam's roots: the ideal City State of the *Rashîdun*, (the 'rightly guided' four Caliphs: 632–61)'.

In general, 'Islamism' is abundantly present in many other articles and books. Malise Ruthven's new book on *Fundamentalism* is another example. Despite the title, she extensively uses 'Islamism' in her analysis. Parallel to 'Islamism', some authors are also using 'radical Islamism' (William E. Shepard), 'Islamic Activism' (Quintan Wiktorowicz) or 'Mobilizing Islam' (Carrie R. Wickham). The above examples are only representative, tracing the general trend on this issue without being exhaustive.

How do Muslim authors designate themselves and their coreligionists? In Arabic, Muslim/Muslims are called *Muslîm* (singular masculine), *Muslima* (singular feminine), *Muslimûn* (plural masculin) or *Muslimât* (plural feminine). However, the Muslim equivalent to Islamists is *Islamiyyûn;* it is used only in this form (plural masculine) and therefore with a significantly limited and restricted use.

The Qur'an uses the terms *Muslimûn* along with *Mu'minûn* [Believers], never *Islamiyyûn.* Islamic classical works generally respect the Qur'anic terminology. Theologians from the four prevailing schools (Hanafi, Mâliki, Shâfi'i and Hanbali) use *Muslimûn* and *Muslim*, not *Islamiyyûn.*

The same can be noticed in the works of great medieval historians, jurists and thinkers such as Ibn Ishâq (d. 768), Ibn Hishâm (753–5), Bukhari (810–70), Farâbi (870–950), Mas'udi (d. 958), Mawardi (972–1058), Avicena (980–1037), Ghazâli (1058–1111), Averroes (1126–98) and Ibn Khaldun (1332–1406). The same tradition is observed and followed in modern times among Muslim authors of the eighteenth, nineteenth and twentieth centuries.

This trend is observed with authors such as Muhammad Ibn Abd al-Wahhab (1703–92, the founder of Wahhabi sect), Sayyid Jamal al-Afghani (1838–97), Muhammad Abduh (1849–1905) and Rashid Rida (1865–1935). Continuing our route forward, we observe that Muslim leaders who played a crucial role in the twentieth century did not use 'Islamism' in their abundant works. Hasan al-Banna (1906–48), in his famous work *Rasâ'îl* [Tracts], extensively uses 'Muslims' and 'Muslim Brothers' especially when addressing his own disciples. When he investigated 'Islam', he sporadically used the term '*Islam al-shâmil*' [Self-sustained Islam] or '*Islam al-Hanif*' [the True Islam]. Neither the zealous ideologue of the Muslim Brotherhood Sayyid Qutb (1906–66) nor Mawdudi (1903–79), an eminent Islamist leader of Southwest Asia, used the term 'Islamism'. A last example would be Ayatollah Khomeini (1902–89), who brought political Islam from theory into reality. While being a Shi'a, he used the same terms as the Sunnis, e.g. '*Muslimîn*' or

'*Musalmanân*' (Persian version of Muslims). However, a number of Muslim authors actually have used 'Islamism' [*Islamiyyûn*]. The Sudanese Hasan al-Turabi (b. 1932) is one of them. When he discusses different fractions among Muslims in his book *Al-Islam wal Hukm* [Islam and Government], he uses *Islamiyyûn* to designate 'political Muslims for whom Islam is the solution, Islam is religion and government and Islam is the Constitution and the law'.

Some (Muslim) lay authors increasingly use *Islamiyyûn*, as for example the Tunisian Salwa al-Sharafi, author of *Al-Islamiyyûn wal-Dimuqrâtiyya* [Islamists and Democracy]. We find a thorough analysis of Islamism in Larbi Sadiki's book *The Search for Arab Democracy*, where he presents a critical analysis on Islamist discourse and ideas, although not as an independent study, but as an appendix to the main issue of his book (democracy). The problem is that Sadiki, like western authors, deals with the terms 'Islamism' and 'Islamists' without providing a clear definition of these concepts.

Aziz al-Azmeh, the author of *Islams and Modernities*, labels contemporary Islamic movements 'political Islamism' and not, for instance, 'Islamic fundamen-talism'. William Shepard uses 'Islamic totalism' to describe 'the tendency to view Islam not merely as a "religion" in the narrow sense of theological belief, private prayer and ritual worship, but also as a total way of life with guidance for political, economic, and social behaviour'. Commonly, this takes the form of the claim that Muslims should have an 'Islamic state', 'that is, a state in which all law is based on the *Shari'a*'.

This is, in our view, a fairly precise definition of what 'Islamism' is. However, it is difficult to understand why Shepard constructs a neologism 'Islamic totalism' different from 'Islamism', which in his view is 'the tendency to view Islam as an ideology'.

Unfortunately, he does not elaborate further on the reason for this distinction between the two terms 'Islamic totalism' and 'Islamism'. Shepard's merits lie essentially in his conscious academic *démarche*, where he acknowledges the necessity of defining concepts that a scholar has the intention to use in his/her works. He points out that labels such as 'fundamentalist', 'modernist' and 'secularist' have 'undoubtedly often functioned as obstacles to understanding the actual people and tendencies involved, in part because they are frequently used without explicit definition'. It is equally interesting to observe how various Muslim groups address each other, whether in a friendly or an unfriendly manner. Let us mention some of the most noticeable and politically significant groups. At the very beginning of Islam's history, the first group which was distinguished in a negative way from the community of Muslims is the *Munafiqûn* [Hypocrites]. At the time of Muhammad's rule in Medina, they expressed views that differed from and even contradicted Muhammad's world vision. They built a mosque without his authorisation, which led him to qualify their mosque as *Masjid al-Zirar* [The Mosque of Dissension].

The Qur'an is particularly severe vis-à-vis this particular group. The second group is the *Khawârij*, who, under the Caliphate of Ali (656–61), disapproved of his decision to accept the arbitration between him and his rival Mu'awiya. Later in history, the immense Muslim empire has witnessed the emergence of a variety of concurrent groups and sects: Sunni (various schools) vs Shi'a (different sects), *Mujâhid* [Combatant] vs *Munâfiq* [Hypocrite], *Khâriji,* ['Excommunicated'], *Mu'tazili* ['Rationalists'], *Usûli* [Theological Fundamentalist] vs *Akhbâri* [believing that the tradition of the prophet provides sufficient guidance], and finally, in the Iranian context, *Khodi* [Insider] vs *Nâ khodi* [Outsider]. In fact, Iranian 'Islamists' of our day call themselves *'Usul gara'*, which literally means 'fundamentalist', but in a positive sense. It designates a 'person of principles' who is the 'true Muslim'. These Muslim authorities who are against Islamists often call them *Irhâbiyyûn* [Terrorists] or *Mutatarrifûn* [Extremists].

In the light of these considerations, it seems necessary to present a definition of 'Islamism'. This definition must satisfy two demands. First, it must encompass all or at least the most significant elements that are normally attributed to 'Islamism'. Second, it must exclude attributes that are alien to 'Islamism'.

DEFINITION OF ISLAMISM

Having all these interrogations in mind, we propose a definition as follows: 'Islamism' is a religious ideology with a holistic interpretation of Islam whose final aim is the conquest of the world by all means. This definition is composed of four interrelated elements. The first is a *religious ideology*, the second a *holistic interpretation of Islam*, the third *conquest of the world*, and finally the fourth and the last element is the use of *all means* in the search for the final objective. Each of these four elements will be briefly examined in the following.

Islamism is a religious ideology

Among western thinkers and scholars, there has been a tendency to attribute a kind of religious aureole to non-religious ideologies. Jean-Jacques Rousseau calls what he regarded as the moral and spiritual foundation essential for any modern society 'civil religion'. To some authors, contemporary political ideologies such as communism, fascism and Nazism are considered as 'political religion'.

Compared with the above-mentioned, Islamism has a particularity: it is already a *religious* phenomenon, and labels like 'civil', 'secular' or 'political' religions do not apply to it. 'Clerical fascism' is perhaps the nearest concept which comes closest to Islamism.

The concept of 'Islamism' is composed of two elements: 'Islam' and 'ism'. The former stands for a religion and a civilisation with its specific history, and the latter indicates a non-Islamic suffix. The composition of these two elements refers to a bi-pillar construction, composed by religion and ideology. Islam is a religion with a long history and with different theological and juridical schools. The Qur'an is not really a coherent book able to provide Muslims with clear and unambiguous guidelines. Roughly speaking, it is divided into two very different and somewhat contradictory sets of statements, principles and commandments.

The *surats* [chapters] are divided into the Mecca period of 12 years' length (from 610 to 622), and the Medina period of ten years' length (from 622 to 632). The first and initial period is characterised by relative moderation, toleration and pluralism. You find this aspect of Islam in some verses in the Qur'an. For example the Qur'an states: 'You shall have your religion and I shall have my religion' (surat 109, verse 6).

We may call the Mecca period the moderate phase of Islam. In contrast, the Medina period is essentially characterised by politics, power and war. The moderate and open-minded language and behaviour give place to a power language. The following verse shows the change in the Qur'an's language when it states:

And slay them wherever ye find them, and drive them out of the places whence they drove you out, for persecution is worse than slaughter. And fight not with them at the Inviolable Place of Worship until they first attack you there, but if they attack you (there) then slay them. Such is the reward of disbelievers (s. 2, v. 191).

This example is an illustration of the Qur'an's ambiguous discourse and its ambivalence in recommended behaviour. The Medina period can be termed as the radical phase of Islam. The Qur'an also reflects this part of Islam. The fact is that some Muslims (known as 'cultural Muslims') refer to the Mecca period alone, and others (Islamists in particular) consider the Medina period as the achievement of Islam in its final shape. Then there is a third group (the overwhelming majority of Muslims) which refers to both periods. This consideration among many others demonstrates that it is practically impossible to identify the 'real message' of Islam. Therefore, the world is facing various manifestations of Islam at a time when no consensus exists among Muslims on fundamental aspects of their faith, except for two cardinal, and thus very general points: the acceptance of the unity of God (Allah), and the reliability of the prophecy of Muhammad as the last Prophet.

This means that if we take only the Qur'an, which is the main source of Islam and which should be the point of convergence between Muslims, it leads us to further confusion about Islam. If we add to the Qur'an other sources of Islamic creed as for example Sunna, Hadith, Rivaya, Fatwas and so on, we get more than one billion disoriented and confused persons, all Muslims of divergent articles of faith, all convinced that their own version and their own understanding of Islam represent the only truth. Yet, while 'Islam' is a general, elusive and ambiguous phenomenon, 'Islamism' as an ideology represents a coherent, specific and identifiable construction.

Ideology may be defined as: 'sets of ideas by which men explain and justify the ends and means of organised social action, with the aim of preserving or reconstructing a given reality'. In totalitarian systems ideologies are a powerful instrument for the mobilisation of the masses as well as sources of legitimacy, sources of the sense of mission of a leader or a ruling group. In this sense, Islamism is more than merely a 'religion' in the narrow sense of theological belief, private prayer and ritual worship, but also serves as a total way of life with guidance for political, economic and social behaviour. Selectively, Islamists pick up some elements in Islam and turn them into an ideological precept. Islamism indeed fulfils all requirements of an ideology, but it goes beyond the purely ideological dimension and sacralises the very essence of ideology. Therefore, Islamism differs on this point from other totalitarian ideologies as it takes its legitimacy from a *double* source: *ideology* and *religion*. Owing to its double character, actions undertaken by Islamists are seen by them as religious duties. Where a Nazi feels responsible to his Führer, an Islamist is responsible to his Leader *and* before Allah.

Islamism is also a regressive ideology which is oriented towards the past (*salaf*). Its ideal is the Medina model under Prophet Muhammad as well as the caliphate of the first four caliphs (*Khulafâ al-Râshidûn*). In this respect, Sayyid Qutb is explicit when he declares: 'If Islam is again to play the role of the leader of mankind, then it is necessary that the Muslim community be restored to its original form'.

The Holistic Interpretation of Islam

In the above discussion, we said that Islamists are selective when choosing religious principles from the original sources of Islam. How can a set of selective elements be holistic? There is no contradiction here. In the first place, Islamists argue that their set of selected elements is, in reality, the 'true' Islam and, in the second place, they are convinced that this 'true' Islam' is holistic and embraces all aspects of Muslims' life in eternity. The holism is based on the absolute indivisibility of the trinity *Dîn* [Religion], *Dunya* [Way of life] and *Dawla* [Government]. This indivisibility is supposed to be permanent and eternal. Its ultimate goal boils down to the fulfillment of this mentioned triad on a global scale. The triad's totalitarian character is confirmed by the writings of the main contemporary Islamist thinkers and leaders: Hasan al-Banna and Sayyid Qutb of Egypt, Ayatollah Khomeini of Iran and Abu Alâ Mawdudi of Pakistan.

Conquest of the World

To Islamists, the existing world is both wrong and repressive. It is wrong because the existing world does not correspond to Islamic principles. Islam as a political power is no longer as predominant as it used to be in the past. The world is also considered repressive because non-Muslims occupy what the Islamists consider to be Muslim territory (e.g. Palestine, Kashmir, Chechnya) or because Muslims live under severe repression from their own (anti-Islamic) governments.

In order to get rid of these conditions of repression and wrong-doing, the Islamists mainly propose two other 'ideal reference points'. The first is the 'Medina model', e.g. society as it was shaped by Muhammad himself. The second is the classical era of the Caliphate. The Caliphate is one of the longest political institutions in history. Its lifespan extended from the year 632, right after the death of Muhammad the Prophet, until its abolition by Mustafa Kemal in the year 1924. During this very long period of time, the Caliphate experiences were of course not all of the same nature, and not all the experiences were triumphant. The Caliphate was sometimes unified, strong and glorious, whereas at other times it was divided, in conflict, in crisis and weak. The first type of experiences was of incomparably shorter duration than the second. The second reservation concerns the non-Sunni Muslims, especially the Shi'a communities. According to the general position of Shi'a, the Imamate, not the Caliphate, is the rightful and legitimate institution. However, Shi'a Islamists like Ayatollah Khomeini, without hiding their preference for the Imamate, have moved slowly but consistently towards a more consensual attitude. Together with the Sunni Islamists, they share pride in, but also nostalgia for the disappeared past. Therefore, it is fair to say that the restoration of the Caliphate today represents a general claim of all Islamists, independently of their sectarian membership.

To the Islamists, the restoration of the Caliphate is the first step towards the 'Islamisation' of the world. From their perspective, Islam constitutes a universal religion whose aim is to rule over the entire world. After all, Allah promised the regency on the earth to His 'virtuous servants', as claimed in the Qur'an:

> the earth is Allah's, to give as a heritage to such of His servants as He please; and the end is (best) for the righteous. He said: 'It may be that your Lord will destroy your enemy and make you inheritors in the earth; that so He may try you by your deeds' (s.VII, v. 128–9).

Utopia? Perhaps. But a powerful one, capable of inspiring action and motivating people to sacrifice their lives.

By all means The Islamist

The Islamists' spectrum of means to reach the above mentioned goal is quite wide, expanding from propagation, peaceful indoctrination and political struggle to violent methods such as assassination, hostage taking, terrorist and suicide actions, and even massacre of civil populations. However, the use of violence is not systematic. All Islamists do not use violence all the time, but some have recourse to it sometimes and, since there are various Islamist groups of different obedience and with different affiliations and histories, the use of violence by Islamists remains non-concomitant.

It is possible that, simultaneously, some Islamists use extremely violent methods in one part of the world while other Islamists use non-violent methods in another part. This variation in patterns of action is determined by different factors. It can be the consequence of a strategic and deliberate choice by the leadership, as is the case for al-Qaeda.

It can also be the result of prudential considerations when a group of Islamists living in a particular situation prefer to follow a relatively quietist and hence pacifistic line for a while. This line of action was for example adopted by the Muslim Brotherhood in Jordan, and for certain periods of time in Egypt. In Europe, *Hizb al-Tahrir al-Islami* [the Islamic Liberation Party] is a good example of an Islamist movement which for the time being claims to be non-violent. The quietist attitude of some Islamists is an exception. In general, the use of violence is integral to their strategy for achieving their ends. Among the various violent methods, terror is proven to be the preferred one, and is indeed frequently used by Islamist groups. The use of terrorism by Islamists confirms a general rule that Hannah Arendt formulated in her study of totalitarianism: 'Total terrorism (is) the essence of totalitarian government ... guiding principles and criteria of action are, according to Montesquieu, *honor* in monarchy, *virtue* in a republic and *fear* in a tyranny'.Terrorism, and diffusion of fear in the civil population, is therefore the instrument of choice in the hands of Islamist groups.

ISLAMISM: A DIVIDED MOVEMENT

Islamism is a monist entity, but is far from being a monolithic movement. 'Despite the global aspirations of their ideologues, Islamists have no centre; there is no overall pan-Islamic radical leadership'. On this particular point, Islamism is similar to communism and fascism. Communism was divided between various tendencies which were sometimes antagonistic (Stalinism, Trotskyism, Maoism, Albanian and North Korean versions). There were also different variations within the fascism movements. For example, fascism in Italy was not identical with the *Action Française* or Falangism. Islamism is characterised by the same kinds of divisions; different sub-groups within the global movement promote divergent interpretations of the ideological creed. For the sake of clarity, it is convenient to summarize the division inside the universe of Islamism around two axial pillars: division determined by sub-religious affiliations, and division emanating from the diverse scope of claims and ambitions.

Sunni, Shi'a and Wahhabi

In the domain of sub-religious affiliations, Islamism is divided into three main branches: Sunni, Shi'a and Wahhabi. This classification is neither perfect nor exhaustive, but it is useful. For instance, Wahhabi is also a Sunni sub-sect, but it is so different from other Sunni sub-sects that it may be treated as an autonomous entity. Sunnism is divided into four theological and juridical schools: Hanafi, Mâleki, Shâfi'i and Hanbali. Wahhabi is a derivative of the Hanbali School with a particularly dogmatic interpretation of Islam.

The Sunni Islamists represent the vast majority of Islamists. Sunni movements embrace the geographical space reaching from Mali to Bali, from the Somalian desert to the Pakistani Himalayas. Chronologically, Sunni Islamism is older than both Shi'a and Wahhabi Islamism. Its origins may be traced back to Ibn Hanbal (780–855), then to the theologian al-Ghazali (1058–1111). Contemporary Islamism as a movement and as an organisation is a phenomenon of the twentieth century. It emerged with the creation of the Muslim Brotherhood by Hasan al Banna in Egypt in 1928. The Muslim Brotherhood is a mother association for sub-organisations such as *Tanzim al-Jihad* [Jihad Organisation] or *Al-Takfir val-Hijra* [Atonement and Emigration], the latter being responsible for the assassination of the president Anwar el-Sadat in 1981. People like Ayman al-Zawahiri (second to Usama Bin Laden) come from this type of organisation.

The Wahhabi branch of Islamism is found essentially in Saudi Arabia, to a lesser degree in different Emirates of the Persian Gulf, and finally in some parts of Caucasus (Chechnya in particular) and central Asia. The Wahhabi Islamism is rooted in the instructions of Muhammad 'Abd al-Wahhab' (1703–92), who was deeply influenced by Ibn Taymiyya (1268–1328), a Hanbali theologian of the Middle Ages. Compared with other Muslim sects, Wahhabis are generally known to be particularly intransigent and at times even violent. Unprecedented global and spectacular terrorist actions like the 9/11 operation have become a trademark of Wahhabi Islamism. It exercises brutality within Muslim societies too, as seen in the case of the assassination and beheading of hostages in Iraq, committed by al-Zarqawi's brigades. At the present time, frontiers between the Wahhabi and the non-Wahhabi are blurred, and sectarian differences have pratically disappeared. For example, al-Qaeda counts in its ranks a number of Sunni Muslims of different sectarian or theological orientation. Leading al-Qaeda personalities such as al-Zarqawi (killed in Iraq, 7 June 2006) and especially Ayman al-Zawahiri are Sunni, but not Wahhabi Muslims. Such a fact attests to the trans-sectarian character of this organisation, which is developing into an ecumenical global terrorist organisation.

Shi'a Islamism is represented mainly by the post-revolutionary Iran, a country where about 80% of the population is affiliated to Shi'a Islam. Following the Islamic revolution of 1979, Iran became an active centre of terrorist activities in the name of Islam. The initial event was the hostage affair of 4 November 1979, where 52 American diplomats and staff of the US embassy in Tehran were kept prisoners for 444 days. The Shi'a Islamist group Hezbollah from Lebanon was created under the auspice of the Islamic Republic of Iran in 1982 as a reaction against the Israeli occupation of South Lebanon. For years, the organisation committed violent actions against military and civilian persons in Israel, in the name of legitimate defence against the invader. In 2005 part of the organisation took part in the parliamentary elections in Lebanon by winning 14 seats in a parliament of 128 seats.

Historically, relations between Sunni and Shi'a have generally been conflictual, and the intensity of conflict has varied depending on political contexts. As an example, in recent times, Sunni–Shi'a relations have particularly deteriorated in Iraq and in Pakistan, resulting in sporadic mutual assassination and the burning of the other confession's mosques. Relations between the Wahhabi and the Shi'a have been even more critical and predominantly hostile. According to the Wahhabi traditional teaching, the Shi'a is a heretical sect and as such it is not recognised as Muslim. Owing to a range of crucial events such as the victory of the Islamist revolution in Iran in 1979, the assassination of the Egyptian president Anwar el-Sadat in 1981, the success of the Mujahidin in Afghanistan, when they pushed the Red Army out of country (in 1989), the rise of the Taliban, then of al-Qaeda, relations between the Sunni, the Shi'a and even the Wahhabi *Islamists* have seen a noticable amelioration. Shâfi'i Muslims like the Egyptian Zawahiri concluded an alliance with the Wahhabi Bin Laden; and the Iranian Shi'a Islamist regime supported Sunni groups like the Hamas in Palestine and the Algerian Islamist group (*Front Islamique du Salut*/ FIS). Furthermore, there has been no sign of hostility between the al-Qaeda or other jihadist Wahhabi groups and the Islamist Shi'a, neither with the Iranian government nor the *Hezbollah* in Lebanon. It is also a fact that, despite Ayatollah Khomeini's vehement criticism of the Saudi dynasty in the 1980s, the Iranian post-Khomeini government maintains very good relations with the Saudi government. On the Wahhabi side, Usama Bin Laden, following almost the same path, avoids appealing to sectarian feelings in his discourse.

The hostility between Shi'a and Wahhabi Islamists only surfaced after the Coalition Forces' invasion of Iraq in 2003. The Iraqi section of al-Qaeda, under the then leadership of the Jordanian al-Zarqawi, began an open and bloody war against the Iraqi Shi'a. In one of his taped declarations (14 September 2005), Zarqawi pronounced on behalf of the al-Qaeda organisation in the Land of Two Rivers [Iraq], and declared 'all-out war on the *Rafidha* [a pejorative term for Shi'a], wherever they are in Iraq'. Nevertheless, he exempted militant groups around Muqtada Sadr (an extremist Shi'a militant organisation) from being targets. In the same vein, it is interesting to mention a letter of Zawahiri (second to Bin Laden) to Zarqawi (the al-Qaeda commander in Iraq).

In this letter, released by the Americans on 13 October 2005, Zawahiri criticised attacks on the Shi'a in friendly albeit vigorous terms and called Zarqawi to reason and moderation. In the light of the ongoing events in Iraq (September 2006), it seems that Zawahiri's advice is being ignored by both the Sunni Islamists and other Sunni resurgents. The Lebanon crisis of July–August 2006 provides another interesting case for examination of Sunni–Shi'a Islamist relations. Roughly speaking, the Iranian Shi'a regime and the Alawi (a sub-sect of the Shi'a) Syrian government sided with the *Hezbollah* of Lebanon. Sunni and Wahhabi governments (e.g. Saudi Arabia and Egypt) chose a more balanced attitude, criticising implicitly the action of *Hezbollah* – kidnapping of two Israeli solders on the Israeli territory – while supporting the Lebanese government, while the Sunni Islamists have so far remained silent.

To sum up, it is no exaggeration to say that, despite some important differences and even reciprocal animosity among Sunni, Shi'a and Wahhabi Islamists, they have more in common than in opposition. They believe in the totalitarian character of Islam, and they strive towards the same ultimate goal (a global Umma). Moreover, they cultivate strong anti-western feelings as well as the use of violent methods of actions. They share the same ideals, practice the same methods and nourish the same patterns of solidarity and animosity towards the external world. All these elements point to the existence of a tacit strategic alliance of these three Islamist sectarian branches.

National and Global Islamism

The second criterion for differentiating one Islamist group or organisation from another is the scope of its goal. This criterion leads us to identify two categories of Islamists: the 'National Islamists' and the 'Global Islamists'. Both groups share the same ideology; but the scope of their goal is not the same.

National Islamism embraces movements whose claims are partly articulated by the modern concept of nation, especially in four geographical areas, Kashmir, Palestine, Lebanon and Chechnya. The geopolitical context of each area brings about different uses of nationalism by these Islamist groups.

Lashkar-e-Tayyiba [The Pure Army] wants Kashmir to be separated from India and integrated into Pakistan. The purpose of the Islamic Regiments who fight in Chechnya is to separate Chechnya from Russia in order for it to become an independent state.

Hamas claims independence for Palestine, but also insists on the obliteration of an already existing nation, Israel. Hezbollah, while supporting the idea of obliterating Israel, for the time being concentrates on extending its political and military domination within an already existing state: Lebanon.

What adds to the dynamic nature of the Islamist nationalist groups is that they very often evolve following a centrifugal or a centripetal scheme. A centrifugal force expands from a centre, whereas a centripetal force attracts other forces towards its centre.

The Palestinian Hamas is unique because of its strong emphasis on the centripetal aspect. Following the Hamas covenant, Palestine is 'the navel of the globe', as it is the homeland of central Muslim holy sites, like the al-Aqsa Mosque in Jerusalem, and was the first Muslim territorial conquest outside the Arabian Peninsula.

Therefore, following the *Mithâq* [Covenant], every Muslim in the world has the duty to fight for the elimination of Israel and the restoration of Palestine as a Muslim country [*Filastin al-Muslima*]. Hamas repeatedly demands military, social, educational and financial support from the other Islamic nations, openly inviting fighters from outside to present themselves in Palestine. Where more secular Palestinian movements like the Palestine Liberation Organization (PLO) and al-Fatah tend to present the conflict as being between Israelis and Palestinians, Hamas formulates it as an Islamic struggle against world Zionism. Article Six of the Hamas Charter stipulates that:

The Islamic Resistance Movement is a distinguished Palestinian movement, whose allegiance is to Allah, and whose way of life is Islam. It strives to raise the banner of Allah over every inch of Palestine' (article 6). Hamas explicitly defines its nationalism 'part of the religious creed. Nothing in nationalism is more significant or deeper than in the case where an enemy should tread Muslim land' (article 12).

The Covenant identifies World Zionism as Islam's enemy number one, and argues that this enemy uses Palestine as its basis for the destruction of the surrounding Muslim countries, and finally the conquest of the world. Therefore, Muslims have to converge their efforts on Palestine. Hamas does not explicitly advocate centrifugal expansion and world domination by Islam, but the nostalgia of the Caliphate is present as a background reference in the movement's Covenant. It should not be forgotten that Hamas is originally a branch of the Egyptian Muslim Brotherhood Association, to which the restoration of the Caliphate represents a necessity.

A neighbour to Hamas, the Shi'a-movement Hezbollah, has also occasionally invited foreign fighters to join the movement, but it is not at all a dominant feature of the movement's ideology as it is for Hamas. While being largely financed and supported by Iran, it insists on its authentic Lebanese character. Although most of Hezbollah's operational activities are limited to the

Lebanese and North Israeli area, its objectives include not only centrifugal expansion of the Shi'a-dominated territories within the Lebanese borders, but also ultimately the obliteration of the State of Israel and the elimination of western influence in the Middle East. Hezbollah explicitly states that it does not aim at fighting on a global level. This being said, the global dimension is still present, but as a very marginal and non-violent statement in a Hezbollah statement from 1998 where it calls for people all over the world to follow its Shi'a-muslim creed:

We understand Islam as a message that aims at establishing justice, security, peace and rights for all people no matter what nation, race or religion they belong to (Hezbollah Press Office, 20 March 1998).

The Kashmiri Wahabbi-inspired group *Lashkar-e-Tayyiba* (or *Taiba*) is an excellent example of a nationalist Islamist movement with a strongly centrifugal ideology. It concentrates most of its terrorist actions in one location, Kashmir, while cultivating a mindset that prepares for a global extension of its operational activities. In order to pursue this extension, the movement is developing linkages with other terrorist groups in various places, such as the Philippines, Nepal, Afghanistan, Palestine, Chechnya, Kosovo and Eritrea. To the *Lashkar-e-Tayyiba,* Kashmir's projected merger with Pakistan is only the first step towards the re-establishment of Islamic rule over India.

This step should be followed by the conquest of all other parts of the world that have been under a Muslim ruler at some stage in history, from Myanmar to Spain. The ultimate goal is to realise a global 'pure Islamic caliphate' that would reign even on the American continent. As *Lashkar-e Tayyiba* is affiliated with Usama Bin Laden's International Islamic Front for Jihad against the USA and Israel as well as with the United Jihad Council, it integrates both levels of the above-mentioned paradigm of 'nationalism' and 'globalism'.

Global Islamism embraces movements such as the Muslim Brotherhood in its various forms, Khomeinist movements in Iran, followers of Mawdudi in Pakistan and elsewhere, and of course the organisation al-Qaeda.

They all pursue the same goal, although at different paces and through different discourses. This goal is, in brief, the restoration of Islam's might and glory, to be achieved once all Muslim territories have been liberated from the yoke of non-Muslim occupants. The consistency and cumulative character of the discourse of global Islamists can be traced in the writings of the most influential leaders of this doctrine. The selection which follows is not exhaustive, though quite representative. It should be stressed that none of these leaders have ever pronounced a discourse which would indicate their opposition to the re-instauration of the Islamic empire and the conquest of the world by Islam. On the contrary, the same kind of discourse has been repeated by the same leaders in different occasions.

Hasan al-Banna is the first who pronounced his programme for reaching this goal. He said: If Islam is again to play the role of the leader of mankind, then it is necessary that the Muslim community be restored to its original form. It is necessary to revive that Muslim community which is buried under the debris of the man-made traditions of several generations, and which is crushed under the weight of those false laws and customs which are not even remotely related to the Islamic teachings, and which, in spite of all this, calls itself the 'world of Islam' (Introduction) – *Rasâ'îl*.

Sayyid Qutb is the second Islamist thinker and leader who has explicitly formulated the use of jihad for reaching the ultimate goal: the conquest of the world. In powerful terms, Qutb writes: Those who say that Islamic Jihad was merely for the defence of the 'homeland of Islam' diminish the greatness of the Islamic way of life and consider it less important than their 'homeland'. This is not the Islamic point of view, and their view is a creation of the modern age and is completely alien to Islamic consciousness. ... Of course, in that case the defence of the 'homeland of Islam' is the defence of the Islamic beliefs, the Islamic way of life, and the Islamic community.

However, its defence is not the ultimate objective of the Islamic movement of Jihad, but is a means of establishing the Divine authority within it so that it becomes the headquarters for the movement of Islam, which is then to be carried throughout the earth to the whole of mankind, as the object of this religion is all humanity and its sphere of action is the whole earth.

The Pakistani theologian Mawdudi explains in his work *Islam Today* how success can be obtained by following Muhammad's example. In the chapter 'The real cause of success', Mawdudi outlines how the first Muslims were a 'small but devoted group of courageous and selfless people', who succeeded in creating a city state in which the Islamic principles 'no longer remained mere theoretical expressions, they became a living reality in individual and social life'. The Medina model is the 'Ideal period', as Mawdudi titles one of his chapters. From this model, Mawdudi explains how Islam is spread throughout the world with means including the use of violence. To Mawdudi, the experience of Muhammad and his immediate successors must serve as a model for Muslims today.

Despite the fact that Ayatollah Khomeini represents the Shi'a minority, which has been the victim of the Sunni caliphate throughout history, he is convinced of the necessity of worldwide Islamic power. He said: This is a duty that all Muslims must fulfill, in every one of the Muslim countries, in order to achieve the triumphant political revolution of Islam. We see, too, that together, the imperialists and the tyrannical self-seeking rulers have divided the Islamic homeland. They have separated the various segments of the Islamic *umma* from each other and artificially created separate nations.

In order to assure the unity of the Islamic *umma*, in order to liberate the Islamic homeland from occupation and penetration by the imperialists and their puppet governments, it is imperative that we establish a government. ... The formation of such a government will serve to preserve the disciplined unity of the Muslims (*Islamic Government*).

Last but not least, one of the most important letters of Zawahiri (second leader of al-Qaeda after Bin Laden) to Zarqawi (former al-Qaeda's commander in Iraq, killed on 8 June 2006) very clearly expresses the author's intentions concerning the future of the world. This letter, which was intercepted by the Americans on 13

October 2005, states: 'It has always been my belief that the victory of Islam will never take place until a Muslim state is established in the manner of the Prophet in the heart of the Islamic world, specifically in the Levant, Egypt.' To realise this plan, Zawahiri outlines a four-stage plan, as follows:

First, expel American forces from Iraq. Second, establish a caliphate over as much of Iraq as possible. Third, extend the jihad to secular neighboring countries, with specific reference to Egypt and the Levant – a term that describes Syria and Lebanon. And finally, war against Israel.

In this statement, Bin Laden's deputy frames the broad plans for the al-Qaeda movement. Moreover, in a book smuggled out of Afghanistan in December 2001, Zawahiri said that the goal of jihad is to establish a religious state throughout the Islamic world and 'reinstate its fallen caliphate and regain its lost glory'.

Concluding Remarks

In the present study we have limited our investigation to tracing the evolution of Islamism as a *concept* through history. Then, we tried to highlight the constituent elements of Islamism, which introduced a broader discussion about the very definition of Islamism itself. We have demonstrated that the concept of 'Islamism' has been transformed throughout the nineteenth and twentieth centuries from designating a religion (Islam) to defining a particular ideology which is rooted in Islam. Labelling the groups of Muslims who make an ideological interpretation of Islam with the purpose of justifying their militarism has not been an easy task. Contemporary western authors have used different names reaching from 'fundamentalism' and 'extremism' to 'radical Islam' and 'Jihadism'.

Broadly speaking, Muslim authors have followed a similar pattern, as they have begun to use the term 'Islam-ism' only recently, probably inspired by western writings. The new tendency – within both the Muslim and the western worlds – points towards a consensus around the term of Islamism. This new 'Islamism' is very different from what the classical western authors had in mind. The new Islamism is understood as an equivalent to totalitarian ideologies like Nazism and communism. Thus, as a new concept, Islamism needs to be defined to avoid ambiguity. We have proposed a new definition which embraces important characteristics of Islamism as a phenomenon.

The rest of the study was devoted to identifying different types of Islamist groupings, in terms of their sectarian characteristics and according to their national or global goal. In this respect, we came to the conclusion that, despite sectarian and other differences among various Islamist groups, their final objective remains the same. They all aim at the re-instauration of the Islamic might in the world: to achieve this goal, the use of violence is not rejected, or is explicitly advocated.

However, the expression of this same goal does find some variation among Islamists. In general, leaders and thinkers of the Muslim brotherhood, such as Hasan al-Banna and Sayyid Qutb, as well as some post-Qutbian leaders of the 1980s, e.g. Shukri Mustafa, are explicit about the global issue.

Islamists such as Khomeini and even Mawdudi have, in practice, been more preoccupied with the establishment of an Islamic government in their respective home-countries, Pakistan and Iran. Nonetheless, the idea of establishing an Islamic world government and a world *Umma* is present in their discourse and action, although, in a less elaborate theoretical form than in the case of al-Banna and Qutb.

JIHADISM, QUTBISM AND WAHHABISM

Islamic extremism is interesting to study from a criminological or criminal justice perspective, but far too often scholars and experts have put it off out of charitable deference to the sensitivities of Muslims or a simple desire to leave well enough alone. It is difficult, but not impossible, to conduct such analysis and be charitable too. An objective, balanced approach is probably most needed, as are more nuanced distinctions among types of adherents to the Muslim faith. This lecture intends to talk about some basic distinctions between Muslim extremists and Muslim moderates, setting the groundwork for more in-depth analysis. It must be quickly noted that once we do this (distinguish extremists and moderates), we are immediately setting up straw man arguments for the extremists to use — enabling moderates to be perceived as compromisers with the West, and saying there are distinctions to be made when Islamic doctrine holds there are no distinctions. There is danger in choosing the words to use since careless terminology unintentionally winds up promoting the ideology of extremists (Streusand & Tunnell 2006).

For example, the term "jihad" simply does NOT have negative connotations for most Muslims, even when used in the context of describing terrorist purpose or action. Although it is true Muslims have debated the meaning of the term for centuries, any Westerner who uses the term to describe a jihadist (or mujahidin) in a negative way makes himself the enemy of all Muslims. Similarly, anyone who says that Muslims worship the same God (emphasizing the God of Abraham as the common heritage of Judaism, Christianity and Islam) simply does NOT understand that Muslims regard their God as different, with Abraham as the first Muslim, with Moses and Jesus having it wrong, and with Mohammad bringing it down perfectly.

However, some basic distinctions can be made. First of all, anyone labeled an "extremist" generally resorts to (or thinks in terms of) a militant solution first and finds justification for it in faith or the literal meaning of text (e.g., "when texts have spoken, reason must be silent"). It is this silencing of reason which characterizes an extremist. A moderate is inclined to supplement their faith with reason, the power of mind, and freedom of thought, before considering a militant solution. The whole "faith then reason" versus "reason then faith" juxtaposition is, of course, quite familiar as a Western dichotomy derived from the Augustine/Aquinas debates , but it should be noted many intellectual forms of Islam go far back before then, to philosophical differences with the ancient greeks and/or the reception of Aristotle (Bertolacci 2006). Militancy is also a word we should define.

A militant solution usually means an irregular fighting force is put together of some kind, which is a common denominator with insurgency, insurrection, armed resistance, and (quite often) terrorism. An inclination to use force or at least to count on it during protest and demonstration characterizes a militant. It is probably the case that extremists and militants outnumber moderates in the Muslim world, but differences of opinion (among world leaders) lead to consideration of at least "some" militancy and extremism as not always breeding terrorism. Many Muslim countries (Pakistan, for example) tolerate some forms of militancy and extremism because they don't see it as always breeding terrorism. The analysis contained herein only examines a limited number of extremist and moderate types (a Part II of Islamist Extremism is in the works). Calling upon academic free inquiry, one can also urgently demand that an examination of what seems to be recurrent problems with Islam be conducted, and toward that end, two hypotheses about the religion are usually considered good starting points — (1) that Islam is inherently violent - and (2) that Islam is susceptible to hijacking or distortion which promotes violence. These hypothesis seem to organize the literature fairly well, and their examination is followed by some in-depth analysis of many specific issues. Westerners, especially Americans, are curious. What is it about those militant strands of Islam that seem to spawn so much bloodshed in the world?

Much of what is to be discussed here will seem foreign and incomprehensible from a Western viewpoint. Therefore, some practical conceptual framework might be useful at the outset, especially when discussing terrorism which is apparently driven by deep religious conviction. The Lecture on Religious Terrorism only touched on this — and it is the rare secular mind that can comprehend the depth of religious passion within Islamist extremism (perhaps fanaticism is a better term). Readers might find useful the framework provided by Cooper (2004) which draws upon the concepts of "political religion" (from the philosopher Eric Voegelin) and "pneumopathology" (from the philosopher Friedrich Schelling). In the fields of political science and sociology, the term "political religion" usually refers to an ideology where the goal is to create a form of politics with the same power as religion.

Totalitarianism and theocracy are terms often associated with this, but are not absolutely necessary conditions, as even democracies can develop things like "civil religions" around events like SuperBowl Sunday (the favorite example of sociologists who study such things). There is some debate among scholars about the exact role of the cult of personality in political religions, and Cooper (2004) is illustrative of modern debates over whether such phenomena are really forward-looking (modernist) or backward-looking (fundamentalist). The term "pneumopathology" refers to a disease of the spirit, an imaginative second reality (being deranged by one's own beliefs) which explains the world in different terms than what common sense would provide. In short, it refers to a religious conviction so strong and intoxicating that it blinds a person to common sense and makes it impossible for anyone to reason with them. As Cooper (2004:40) puts it: "there is an inherent friction between commonsense reality and the occult reality within which the terrorist lives imaginatively, an imaginary reality where killing the innocent to impress others is understood to be heroic, altruistic, and self-sacrificing." As a leader of Hezbollah put it: "we are not fighting so that the enemy recognizes us and offers us something. We are fighting to wipe out and annihilate the enemy."

Armed with frameworks and terminologies, it can be seen that the war on terrorism (as war on Islamist extremism) is, in some sense, a contest of souls (a spiritual war and more than an ideological or conceptual war, if you will) where the order of battle involves who has the strongest belief system regarding the best system of interrelationships between worlds (i.e., the spiritual, secular, religious, commercial worlds, etc). Within the predominantly spiritual universe that is Islamist extremism, terrorists guided by it genuinely believe they are heroic, more heroic and successful than any soldier or businessman could ever be. The hero fantasy consumes their imagination. Extremists are, after all, defending their god, and coming closer to their god. The acts of destruction that they engage in (*any* destruction being a victory) bring value to the cause and are a vivid proof of faith.

The act of terrorism might be publicly condemned but secretly admired by most Muslims, even moderates. Any terrorist acting in the name of Allah (particularly within the Wahhabi view that *the world ought to be Muslim*) is to be revered and admired. Such terrorists are the Middle East's longed-for superhero, and seek to be the next best thing to the Mahdi or the Twelfth Imam. They are not deterred by weapons, for they know that weapons will not destroy their cause. The terrorist longing for union with god thru carnage is inseparable from the impulse toward annihilation. Their goals and ambitions soar above logic, and they have created a fantasy world (a second reality) in their minds about an angry god who wants to pat them on the back for slaughtering apostates or nonbelievers (shunning the usual religious response to apostasy as not being good enough). America is hated precisely because its power and the Western viewpoint threatens much that is central in the promises of their faith.

THE HYPOTHESIS THAT ISLAM IS INHERENTLY VIOLENT

At the outset, it must be noted, as Khan (2006) does, that this particular hypothesis — that puritan Islam is inherently violent and Muslim militants are addicted to carnage — has had a counterproductive effect in promulgating an ontology where significant negative changes are taking place in international law, such as expansion of preemptive war doctrine and other reactionary practices are ascendant (e.g., declining civil liberties, prescribed extra-judicial killings, torture, renditions, indefinite detentions, and numerous other human rights violations). There are as many evil necessities in counterterrorism as there are in terrorism. There are also many ways Islam easily serves as a mantle or cover for terrorism, although I wouldn't go so far as to say Islam always and inevitably leads to terrorism, as some have said who advocate this hypothesis (Wright 2001; Lewis 2003), and do so on the basis that the only sense in which Islam is a religion of peace is when all nonbelievers are converted and there is no occasion for war; i.e., the final command of Mohammed in the Quran is carried out — to conquer the world in the name of Islam (9:29).

Islam is not a pacifist religion which values passive witnessing, but in all fairness, other religions have promoted violence or been quite pushy about how they go about witnessing their faith. Islam, however, seems to have particularly assembled all the right ingredients for being violent-prone or at least non-democratic in its method of conflict resolution. From most interpretations, warfare of some kind is always mandated against nonbelievers. Twenty-six (26) chapters of the Quran deal with *jihad*, a fight able-bodied believers are obligated to join (Surah 2:216), and the text orders Muslims to "instill terror into the hearts of the unbeliever" and to "smite above their necks" (8:12). Further, the "test" of loyalty to Allah is not good acts or faith (as is common in Christian religion), but martyrdom which results from fighting unbelievers to the death (47:4), fighting the good fight being the only assurance of salvation in Islam (4:74; 9:111).

Much of this is, of course, subject to scholarly debate (the most frequent grounds for such debate being that passages are takenout of context, but that is something all religious doctrines are subject to). Yet, just by looking at certain passages, one can easily find support for the "violent Islam" hypothesis — passages such as the following: the sins of any Muslim who becomes a martyr are forgiven by the very act of being slain while slaying unbelievers (4:96), and those who are unable to do jihad, such as women or the elderly, are required to give "asylum and aid" to those who do fight unbelievers in the cause of Allah (8:74). Then, of course, there is the so-called X-rated vision of Paradise, to wit: martyrs are rewarded with virgins, among other carnal delights, in Paradise (38:51, 55:56; 55:76; 56:22). Regarding asylum privileges, it is unknown why the Muslim practice of asylum never developed along the forty-day rule of medieval Western common law, yet seems to have evolved into some sort of lenient, international law approach to political asylum.

Fifty-seven (57) nations in the world support Islam as part of their dictatorship or theocracy, and it is the world's second-largest (20%) and fastest-growing religion among the oppressed and disenfranchised. There are no formal denominations to speak of (other than Shiite and Sunni, but all mosques are ostensibly non-denominational), and it is perhaps more accurate to talk about *schools of thought*, sects, or cults. Even then, those terms don't fully capture the richness and depth of Islamic variation since there are "religious" schools of thought (Sunni and Shiite), "political" schools of thought (chronological and geographical Renaissance periods), "legal" schools of thought (Islamic jurisprudence about Qur'anic interpretation), and the traditional distinctions between sect (offshoots such as Salifism) and cult (breakaways such as Qutbism) don't apply all that well. There are strange offshoots of Islam, some of which seem to "insulate" societies from terrorism, or at least produce a different variety. Such is the case, for example, with the peculiar religion of the Omanis, who are followers of Abdallah ibn Ibadah al-Maqdisi's branch of Islam, a breakaway from the Khariji ("quietist") movement in Basra in 650 AD.

Some experts suggest that the movement is an offshoot of a dissident Shiite sect hailing originally from Ibadh in Saudi Arabia, which was introduced to Oman in the eighth century. Experts also believe Oman (a 25% Sunni society that is fairly open to Israel) has been relatively free from terrorism precisely because of its religion, with Janardhan (2006) explaining this as follows: Oman is the only Ibadhi country in the world, with its tenets closely linked to the Maliki Sunni school, and Ibadhism rejects primogeniture succession and asserts that the leadership of Islam should be designated by an imam who is capable and elected by the people, where both political and religious leadership are vested in an imam. What little terrorism exists in Oman is usually seeded from the ideology of imama ("rule of the imam") and its values, and most dissidents typically argue that their intention is not to overthrow the regime, but to spread the Madhab ("Islamic jurisprudence") of Ibadhi. Jails and pardons are the typical punishments. Many Muslims consider the Ibadhi orientation unorthodox, but it has conditioned the society in such a fashion that it is extremely conscious of sectarian affiliations and avoids things along divisive lines.

In one respect, it seems that the ascetic monotheism in Islam insists that the religion be defined more by opposition than affirmation. As such, *Islam and Islamic extremism are undeniable social movements to be reckoned with*, as believers think their prophet being the last to appear in the Holy Days makes Him the real messenger of God, and that anyone believing otherwise is an "infidel" or apostate deserving of less-than-human dignity and worth. There is a strong anti-secular thrust in Islam along with a belligerent superiority that make it dangerous, but perhaps no more than certain puritanical or reconstructionist strains in other religions. What Islam needs is a Reformation period like the Protestant Reformation that occurred in Christianity (An-Na'-Im 1996), but it has only had a Renaissance period with Ba'athism — that fascist, pan-Arabic, secular movement which started in Syria during the 1950's - Ba'ath meaning "renaissance" or "rebirth" in Arabic. However, far more important in Muslim history was the Mongol destruction of Baghdad in 1258 and killing of the last Caliph. Muslims believe this historical event brought down God's scourge upon them, and the appropriate response is to recover the purity of the early companions [Salafs] of the Prophet, called Salafism after the term for "venerable forefathers" or "early companions." A central component of this response is the notion of jihad, but far more important for Westerners to try to understand is the fairly-complicated concept of "caliph" which is, again, a term Muslims would prefer non-Muslims try not to meddle with.

With respect to political correctness over issues and terms like Islamofascism, it may or may not be useful to sort out which things Muslims find insulting and which things they just need to get over about. Cartoons are but one example, but nonetheless, it is important to be sensitive to genuine socio-cultural differences. There are twenty-one (21) nations where some form of Arabic is the national language, and although not all Arabs are Muslims, the notion of an "Arab world" or "Muslim world" has great appeal to believers. This is because they see themselves as belonging to a super-nationality that goes beyond traditional nation-state boundaries (it's called the Muslim *umma* or *Ummah*, the community of believers). It's not that they aren't patriotic to their native country; it's that their allegiance to this super-nationality is greater.

Collectivity arguments aside, much of this is because they desperately want a counterpart to the Jewish notion of Zionism. *It's almost impossible to understand the Arab or Muslim mindset without reference to an intense hatred of most Jews and all of Zionism.* Even if the Jews were to leave the Middle East, Muslims would still feel threatened by Zionist conspiracies because many Arabs see Jews as subhuman criminals who hide behind democracy and work in the shadows. Christians are seen as a more insidious threat - an irredeemable, immoral, corrupt, greedy, selfish, sinful, crusading people who hide behind the name of capitalism. America is seen as the second Israel, because it supports the Zionist entity. In the Muslim mindset, concepts like tolerance, democracy, pluralism, and freedom are meaningless when spoken by a Westerner because Arab trust, as among many in the Third World, has been broken by years of colonialism, imperialism, capitalism, and globalism. Most Muslims see the noble intentions of the West as mere slogans that disguise the true goals of political domination, religious conversion, and economic exploitation.

Sociologically, most Muslims function under a rather unique patriarchal, extended family system, unlike other extended family systems that might be found around the world. In a traditional extended family system, aunts, uncles, cousins, grandparents, etc. are treated as immediate family, but a Muslim household or co-joint household might be larger, the defining attribute being that there can only be one breadwinner. Patriarchy is evident in name-giving. All Arabs have at least three names, and they keep their father's last name for life. Cultural prescriptions and prohibitions abound. For example, standing close to one another, extended handshakes, feeling a person's breath, and looking deeply in the eyes is approved of for men, but not for women. The oppression of women in Islamic society has been extensively studied by many and has basically reached no significant conclusions nor good recommendations for reform (Ahmed 1993; Haddad & Esposito 1997).

Local customs continually perplex Western visitors. Some Arab nonverbal gestures are the complete opposite of those in the West. For example, shaking your head up and down means "No" instead of Yes. Muslims are extremely sensitive to insult by word and gesture, and probably more so with words (some common English words are considered profanity). They believe words have power. Like any converted religion, Islam tends to look backward for inspiration, but Muslims scholars seem to systematically neglect any liberal, progressive, or Western-friendly scholarship from their own history, such as the work of Ibn Khaldoun and numerous writers during the Arab Golden Age (A.D. 750-1400). We shall see later than most Islamic extremists want to go back *before* the Golden Age. It may not be impossible for Islam to coexist peacefully in the modern world, but there are utilitarian and practical problems in marshaling the best resources to find a suitable reform strategy that benefits the most Muslims and non-Muslims alike.

THE THESIS THAT EXTREMISTS HAVE HIJACKED MAINSTREAM ISLAM

Interviewing and negotiating with terrorists (ideally, ex-terrorists) are probably the only ways to prove at least some of the many forms of this hypothesis — that radical extremists have "brainwashed" the Muslim population in some way. It is also true that increased American understanding is vital for any improved understanding of the religious underpinnings of Islamic extremism of most relevance or interest, and for that, a delineation of the scope of concerns is needed. As anyone on the receiving end of terrorism has the right to be, victims are deservingly concerned with understanding at least the following: (1) how easy it seems for some Islamic extremists to justify the senseless slaughter of innocents in the name of religion; (2) how blowing yourself up with as many other people around you can possibly be seen as religious obligation or martyrdom; and (3) like El Fadl (2002) asks, how can a morality be so blindly convinced it's the only way of life that it tramples all over the rights of others.

The following extremist movements are all currently active in the Muslim world, and it is the thesis of writers like Esposito (1999) and others that these movements have all engaged in hijacking mainstream Islam, much as Elijah Muhammad hijacked it to claim whites were a race created by an ancient evil scientist, although America has less to fear from the Black Muslim movement than from more dangerous splinter groups like the five percenters (an ideology popular with hip hop and rap musicians) or Jamaat al-Fuqra (a Pakistani-American terrorist cult). Discussion of any extremism, of course, begs the question "extreme to what?" and one would be hard pressed to define "mainstream" Islam in any case. Sunni Islam and Salafism (explained below) are the most likely "mainstream" contenders, but Islam is essentially an open religion that sees itself as a complete code of life. All it takes to become a Muslim is to believe in the Six Beliefs, practice the Five Pillars, and take an oath. How mainstream or orthodox a believer is depends upon how fervently they practice their religion, and it is the translation of belief into practice that has produced the most opportunities for extremists to hijack mainstream Islam.

- *Islamism* is a term describing the worldwide puritanical Islamic revival movement that seeks to replace secular governments with Shari'a law and establish theocracies throughout the world via relatively peaceful means; it's not exactly a Muslim version of Zionism, but a throwback to the ideas of the 1928 Muslim Brotherhood that created an Islamic version of communism
- *Islamofascism* is a rather uncomplimentary term used to describe certain extremists with political agendas who happen to be Muslims or use the cover of Islam to seek an end to democracy, capitalism, individuality, human rights, and modernization within a particular nationality and ultimately on the global stage; with few exceptions which make something out of the fact that Yassar Arafat's uncle worked for the Nazis (Trifkovic 2002), most experts believe there are no meaningful historical connections between Islam and fascism
- *Jihad* is a controversial term in Islamic thought which technically refers to any kind of struggle in the name of Islam, the means for spreading Islam and truth, and fighting for what is right and condemning what is wrong; Muhammad said there were two types of jihad, "little jihad" or battle with one's attackers in holy war, and "greater jihad" or purification of self by fighting a battle for what is right; Koranic interpretation says jihad is of three kinds: against a visible enemy, the devil, and one's self; depending upon context, jihad can mean good deeds, personal struggle, armed defense, or holy war
- *Jihadism,* which might be called the religion of Jahiliya (a term referring to the pre-Islamic era in Arabia, literally

meaning ignorance), is a backward-looking strand of Islamic extremism developed by the Pakistanis and Taliban which considers itself the true Islam and sees a war of Armageddon or Plague of God coming in which all non-Jihadists deserve to be killed and the Jihadists themselves will benefit from rewards in both this life and heaven, but mostly in heaven

- *Qutbism* is a radical form of conservative Islam developed in Egypt that advocates armed struggle against any government which usurps God's authority; many experts assume this to be Usama bin Laden's personal belief or part of his twisted distortion of Islam
- *Salafism* is a mainstream type of Sunni Islam and fairly moderate belief about being on the right path and the addition of analogue reasoning to a literal interpretation of text, but it is quick to condemn those who innovate too much from doctrinal interpretation; it considers the right path straight and fixed, to be always followed, no matter how much much this trumps the rights, well-being, laws, values, or morality of others, especially infidels; it maintain control over believers, in part, by borrowing from Wahhabism, a denying of the right for believers to contemplate any of the Divine attributes of God or what He looks like
- *Sufism* is a rather mystical, esoteric sect of Islam which consists of a combination of moderate and extreme beliefs, for example, that God dwells in the hearts of men, texts have hidden messages, and a personal means of worship without public prayer is possible; other less commonly held beliefs include faith in divine manifestations, the existence of invisible beings such as a genie, certain magical practices, and an anti-technology bias; Sufis have historically been the most common victims of Muslim genocide; i.e. fundamentalists regard Sufism as a type of heretical pseudo-Islam; and although much of Sufism is about love, spiritual journey, and having keen insight, militant versions of it have been known to exist

- *Wahhabism* is a rather totalitarian-oriented form of Sunni fundamentalism practiced mostly in Saudi Arabia and among many American Muslims (Malcolm X 1987) and European immigrants which calls for a purification of Islam by returning to basics, enforcing the women's dress code, removing corruption from politics, restoring a Golden Age, and engaging in jihad as an obligation when it comes to protecting Islamic interests or promoting the true purpose of Islam; like the Shiite denomination and other sects, it relies upon the *fatwa*, or point of law by a recognized authority, as a binding obligation of all Muslims, and since the Rushdie affair, a fatwa has become associated with ordering a death sentence

THE BACKGROUND OF ISLAMIC EXTREMISM

These have been rather complex characterizations of complex movements, so perhaps some further background is in order to understand them better. For centuries, young Muslim men have gathered at neighborhood *madrasas* (religious schools), run by headmasters and *mullahs* (religious teachers) to study Islamic holy works and receive free meals. The free meals really draw people out, even when they are offered to celebrate some terrorist act of matyrdom, the latter being also rewarded by financial gifts to families. However, sometime around 1979 (the date of the Iranian revolution), the content of teaching at the madrasas took a violent turn. It was the purpose of the Iranian revolution to spread Shiite fundamentalism throughout the world, and the first enemy was the Sunni ruling parties in most Arab countries (hence the 1980-1989 Iran-Iraq war since Iraq was ruled by Saddam Hussein, a Sunni socialist).

Iranian-style Shiite fundamentalism is characterized by dominance of the clergy (mullahs) in all sectors of life, the eradication of all voices of opposition, and a kind of mindless fanaticism to follow the orders of the Shiite leader - in this case Ayatollah Khomeini, who represented what all Shiites believe - that there are twelve descendants of Muhammad's cousin Ali who were handpicked to lead the Muslim world in *jihad*, or holy war

(Sunnis, by contrast, believe leaders should rise up from among the people). Khomeini had long been preaching the virtues of suicide bombing (heavenly rewarded terrorism) to terrorist groups like Hezbollah and Hamas in his pre-1979 exile days. Anyway, Shiite fundamentalism spread throughout Asia and Africa like wildfire, especially in places like Pakistan and Afghanistan where Mullah Omar (a Shiite madrasas dropout) created the Taliban in 1995. Usama bin Laden joined Mullah Omar and based his al-Qa'ida organization in Afghanistan during 1996. Usama bin Laden masterminded the September 11, 2001 attacks on America, and the next month (October 2001), the U.S. invaded Afghanistan. Later, in March of 2003, the U.S. invaded Iraq, partly on suspicion that the Iraqi regime supported al-Qa'ida.

While the Shiite branch of Islam experienced a revival as early as 1979, the Sunni branch of Islam started experiencing it's own revival of fundamentalism around 2001, and an interest developed in ideas that had been around a long time, like Wahhabism, which in many respects is the official ideology of university professors in much of the Middle East. Recently, *Sunni extremism has increased while Shiite extremism has declined*. Usama bin-Laden was raised a Sunni, and even though the Taliban rode the coattails of the Shiite revolution, the Taliban also executed many Shiite citizens and diplomats on soccer fields. To reconcile the tendency for Shiite extremism to result in so many dead Shiites, people like Usama bin Laden embraced another ideology, Qutbism, which allowed for a complimentary Sunni extremism which justifies a lot of dead Sunnis.

Egypt and Saudi Arabia are the most well-known Sunni nations, and Sunnis in general are sometimes considered more "reasonable" and moderate than the fanatical Shiites. Fascination with martyrdom defines Shiites. Their central holiday remembers the martyrdom of Hussein, one of Muhammad's descendents, and Shiites commemorate by flagellating themselves with whips, a ceremony that some experts say spawns suicide bombers (at least according to Jewish sources). Egyptian- and Saudi-style Sunni fundamentalism is quite different, more rational, and more homicidal than suicidal. To be sure, it, too, celebrates the idea of martyrdom, but Sunni fundamentalism is more like a warrior religion that glorifies violence, brute force, or what Muslims call the "greater jihad" — a purification of self by fighting a battle for what is right.

AN IN-DEPTH ANALYSIS OF JIHADISM

Jihad is an Arabic word that literally means "combat" or "striving" and jihad is sometimes regarded along with allegiance to the Iman as the violent Sixth Pillar of Islam, although orthodox Islam only recognizes Five Pillars. The idea of jihad being the violent Sixth Pillar comes from the Khawarij sect, which was part of the fundamentalist Islamism movement that started in the early 20th Century. The Khawarij sect is named after Dhul-Khuwaysarah, a man that Muhammad prophesied would have an overprotective love of religion. The Khawariji interpretation of the role of excommunication is completely the opposite of the Salafist interpretation of excommunication (*takfir*). Salafism is rather restricted about who should be declared an infidel and therefore excommunicated. Followers of the Khawariji interpretation, or Jihadists, see few if any restrictions on who can be declared an infidel, and therefore justify unrestricted warfare or terrorism against infidels. Even traditional Qur'anic interpretations hold that those who reject Islam reject God, and one of the principal characteristics of rejecting God (*kufr*) is the inclination toward violence and oppression, encapsulated by the broad concept *zulm*, which means transgression against one's own soul or human nature. Now, many if not most Muslims reject the duty to propagate Islam by force and limit jihad to self-defense (Hashmi 2006), but then again, there is no such thing as a pacifist movement in Islam, and most Muslims respect the necessity of a continuous tension between incessant warfare and peace.

There is some controversy in Islamic thought as to whether jihad can be declared before or after an enemy attacks, or in other words, in a pre-emptive strike or in self-defense. A strict and literal reading of the Qur'an says self-defense only, but Islamic law has always justified a first-strike position. Just saying that women ought to have a right to vote is a crime of violence against all of

Islam, and this can trigger a Jihadist reaction against not only the person who said that, but against whomever they got that idea from — a kind of scorched earth policy or nipping things in the bud. The basis for most anti-Americanism among Muslim extremists is part of the notion that any country that would give women the right to vote, or all minorities equal rights, is probably a country populated by infidels who are attacking Islam with crimes of violence. It may be important to note the quite popular opinion in the Muslim world that it was under attack by America first.

Jihad is also part of the name in at least two terrorist groups that make up the shadowy umbrella group called Islamic Jihad, which has millions of supporters throughout the Islamic world because these supporters agree with militaristic interpretations of jihad. The two main groups are the Egyptian Islamic Jihad and the Palestinian Islamic Jihad, both formed in the mid-1970s with origins going back to the 1928 Muslim Brotherhood.

Egyptian Islamic Jihad: This is the Cairo-based group that assassinated Egyptian President Anwar Sadat in 1981, and is responsible for a number of other assassination attempts inside of Egypt up to 1993. Since then, it has targeted American and Israeli interests around the world, and has a well-funded network operating out of Egypt, Yemen, Afghanistan, Pakistan, Sudan, Lebanon, and the United Kingdom. They succeeded in bombing one embassy in Pakistan during 1995, and the CIA thwarted another embassy bombing attempt in Albania during 1998. They are involved in a number of criminal activities, besides terrorism, around the world.

Palestinian Islamic Jihad: This is a relatively small group that operates out of Syria and is fanatically dedicated to the killing of Jews and total destruction of the state of Israel. By comparison, Hamas is a more moderate group. Formed in the Gaza Strip during the mid-1970s, it has been the consistent target of Israeli counterterrorism raids. They regularly conduct suicide bombing infiltrations into Israel, but are also known to target other Arabs seen as too moderate or too Western, having carried out attacks as far away as Malta and in Jordan and Lebanon. In February, 2003, the FBI arrested their alleged North American leader, a Univ. of South Florida professor, but in December, 2005, the trial resulted in acquittal.

Suicide bombings (a tactic that came into popularity around 1983) are a trademark of jihadists. The religious element involved is that believers think they will attain a heavenly reward for their sacrifice. The political element involved is that it sends a message of how desperate and passionate the believers are. Expert opinion is mixed on the effectiveness of suicide bombing as a strategy of asymmetric warfare. Experts also agree that it is difficult if not impossible to profile a suicide bomber. Some say it ultimately backfires by turning public opinion against the bombers and those who support them. Support often comes in the form of charitable donations to the family of suicide bombers. Many poor parents in the Arab world may be inclined to encourage their children to become suicide bombers. For its photogenic value in a globalized world of mass communication, suicide bombing is a weapon of genius.

The Guarantee of Heaven for Islamic Martyrs

Suicide, under orthodox Islam, is a sin. However, Jihadists consider the circumstances to cleanse the sin, making it the act of a holy martyr, not a suicide. The actual percentage of Muslims who agree with this interpretation is hotly disputed, as is the concept of martyrdom. A martyr is technically someone who dies for their religious faith, but the outcome also matters, in terms of who gets to write history. Martyrdom, therefore, is intimately tied up with Islamic arrogance that their goal of religious domination will be victorious in the end. The study of all things in the end is known by the religious term *eschatology*, and Islam contains strong elements of Zoroastrianism, the world's first religion to have a full-blown eschatology. Many experts believe that Zoroastrianism, a religion that existed from 1500 BC to 700 AD in Persia and still popular in parts of Iran and India, had a significant impact on Islam. In a nutshell, the basic idea that Zoraster had is that earth is a battlefield between good and evil, and that good is destined to win out over evil, and anyone who allies themselves with good is guaranteed to be part of this destiny. What Mohammed took from this is the idea that whoever martyrs themselves for the sake of good goes directly to a special place in heaven, or in a worst case scenario, goes to hell for a short time and then goes to heaven. Satan, as the embodiment of evil, also plays a big role, as a real entity who tempts people to renounce their faith, and the martyr with the most guarantee of a special place in heaven is the one who fights Satan.

Demonizing America as the "Great Satan" makes it a fitting opponent in the predestined war between good and evil. Heaven is more than a transcendental place to Muslims. Orthodox Islamic eschatology holds that the afterlife is physical; people are said to have bodies, and they will experience material pleasures, including unlimited food, drink and sex. Heaven is known to some Muslims as the Gardens of Paradise where unimaginable spiritual and sensual pleasures await. To other Muslims, the rewards are quite imaginable, such as the 72 virgins waiting to have sex with each martyr every day (their hymens miraculously regrow the next day). This account was popularized by the media in 2001 when a CBS reporter interviewed a Hamas recruiter who talked about it. According to one translation, the Koran 78:31 reads "*As for the righteous, they shall surely triumph. Theirs shall be gardens and vineyards, and high-bosomed virgins for companions.*" Some Islamic scholars argue this is a false translation, and that passages like that are referring to angels or heavenly beings. Other Islamic scholars argue it's only 70 virgins instead of 72, and that your wife is always one of them. Yet other Islamic scholars say the whole thing is intended to be taken in a transcendental way, the pleasures of heaven being so great it's like having an eternal erection or first-time sex all the time.

AN IN-DEPTH ANALYSIS OF QUTBISM

Qutbism is named for the Egyptian radical Sayyid Qutb (pronounced SIGH-yid KUH –taab) (1906-1966) who himself was a protégé of the Pakistani journalist Abul Ala Maudoodi, and their collective ideas are sometimes called Maudoodi-Qutbism. It is difficult to categorize their ideas collectively, as some scholars regard them as romantic idealists longing for a return to a "purer" form of Islam, and others regard them as the architects of all militant fundamentalism in Islam (Ruthven 2002). To be sure, both men at first experimented with ways to incorporate Western thought into Muslim philosophy, but ended up creating the Muslim equivalent of a Christian holy war crusade. Qutb was radicalized sometime around 1949 after visiting the United States where all he found was crass materialism, greed, and unbridled sexuality. Upon his return to Egypt, Qutb joined the Muslim Brotherhood and wrote radical books denouncing all things materialistic, modern, and Western. His ideas would become the theoretical basis for many radical Islamic groups of today — including al Qaeda.

Qutb feared that decadent American influences, like jazz and dance, would invade Egypt and all the Arab world unless something was done to stop it. It didn't help that America was starting to support Israel around 1951. From a Qutbist viewpoint, the U.S. replaces colonial Europe as the embodiment of evil, and the U.S. is the source of all the ills and misfortunes in the Arab world. This radically changed the Muslim Brotherhood, which was originally set up to hate communism, but gradually came to hate America. To get some idea of how mainstream these ideas are, ask any Arab or Muslim if the U.S. somehow tipped the balance of power in the Middle East to favor Israel at the expense of Arab well-being, and you'll get a resounding "Yes" that this is exactly the case, and that idea is Qutbism. Ask any Arab or Muslim if they think American fads and fashions in music and dress are corrupting the morals of Muslim youth, and you'll also get a "Yes" and that idea is Qutbism.

America is not only seen as decadent according to Qutbism, but as a pagan state. American religious denominations are regarded as nothing more than providing entertainment ceremonies. According to most mainstream Muslims, America is not a religious society that takes God seriously. Americans commercialize religion and worship material things like prosperity instead of God. Perhaps worst of all, America has no sense of justice. A popular Muslim story goes like this: a couple once approached Mohammed to ask for forgiveness in the eyes of Allah. Mohammed asked them "forgiveness for what," and the couple said adultery. Mohammed asked if they were drunk at the time, and the couple said no. So, Mohammed order them stoned to death. The moral of the story is that Mohammed at least inquired about drunkenness as a possible excuse for the crime, but even though the couple were surprised by the stoning, they went to their death knowing that they carried no sins with them as they met Allah.

Qutb is also famous for being an outspoken critic of secular Islamic governments (empty shells with an Islamic flag, he called them). Arrested for treason in 1954, Qutb was tortured and imprisoned for the rest of his life until executed by Egyptian President Nasser in the Sixties. He felt that most Muslim societies including Egypt were lost in an Age of Ignorance, and the solution was for the faithful to emigrate away from this ignorance and form a new Islamic society. He also predicted a great battle would ensue between the Muslim nations. Qutb did not go so far as to declare his fellow Egyptians apostates (a word describing those who have denounced their faith), but he did call them sinners. It can be seen, then, how important and pivotal a figure he was in getting Muslims to call other Muslims the equivalent of infidels (apostates). He did this by creating a whole new revolutionary ideology of takfir (excommunication).

Qutbism is the primary ideology of Dr. Ayman Zawahiri, Bin Laden's "number two", and widely regarded as the mastermind behind the September 11, 2001 attacks on the United States, and the connections are quite complicated. While in Egypt before meeting Bin Laden, Dr. Zawahiri founded the At-Takfir w'al-Hijra movement which declared that most Muslims are apostates because of their sins. By the late 1970s, Dr. Zawahiri founded another group called Al-Jihad, also based on Qutbism, which reached out to Palestinians, such as Abdullah Azzam, who served as Bin Laden's teacher and mentor. By this time, the ideology had evolved into a conception of all Muslim governments as illegitimate and needing to be replaced by terrorism to restore the essential nature of Islam. Qutbism is also the primary ideology of Omar Abdel-Rahman, leader of an Egyptian terrorist group who assisted Bin Laden in Afghanistan.

Abdullah Azzam, had originally been a member of the Palestine Liberation Organization, but became disillusioned with its secularism. Azzam studied law and the ideas of Sayyid Qutb to become a teacher in Saudi Arabia. There, one of his students was Osama Bin Laden, and this teacher and student both came up with the idea to move to Afghanistan to fight the Soviets. Dr. Zawahiri joined them a bit later, and al-Qaeda was born. They rallied troops and supplies, using Bin Laden's money and ironically enough, CIA support, and defeated the Soviets, with Azzam dying in battle during 1989. Then, al-Qaeda set up shop in Sudan, but were expelled from there, so they set up training camps back in Afghanistan for exporting terrorism. The ideology at this time was that the "forces of ignorance" against Islam had to be fought militarily anywhere in the world. Jihad in the al-Qaeda conception is that all jihad is military, and all Islam is jihad. Anyone considered an apostate would be put to death by al-Qaeda. Dr. Zawahiri became adept at using false passports, masquerading in disguise around the world, and placed sleeper cells all over Europe and the U.S. The following is a quote by Dr. Zawahiri in 1997:

al-Qaeda: "A conflict between the Muslim nation and the United States is unavoidable. Israel is only the American spearhead in the war against Islam. The forthcoming terrorist Jihad will not be limited to strikes against Israel. With Allah's help, we know the United States well, and we also know its weaknesses. The most vulnerable spot of the United States is to send them the bodies of their sons. Therefore, we should throw in their faces the flesh of their sons, minced and grilled. The United States must pay the price, and it must pay dearly." (Ayman al-Zawahiri)

Note: The al-Qaeda organization is "base" for a number of Sunni extremist groups who are the direct beneficiaries of Osama Bin Laden's resources and leadership. The most well-known member groups of al-Qaeda are: the al-Zarqawi network and Ansar al-Islam movement in Iraq (the link between Saddam Hussein and al-Qaeda); the Libyan Islamic Fighting Group, Jemaah Islamiyad in Asia, and the Islamic Movement of Uzbekistan.

al-Zarqawi network (aka al-Tawhid): With bin Laden and his deputy, al-Zawahiri, on the run, a new group has emerged, which operates separately but in the name of al-Qaeda. Led by a one-legged Jordanian named Abu Musab Zarqawi (real name Ahmed Fadil Nazzal al-Khalayleh), the al-Zarqawi network has bombed synagogues throughout Europe, plotted to use biological weapons in Britain, and beheaded an American in Iraq.

Zarqawi is sometimes called the "second bin Laden," and is committed to the demise of the West. While fighting in Afghanistan, Zarqawi lost a leg, and was treated for it in Iraq, where he resumed operations by merging with the Kurdish Islamic terror group, Ansar al-Islam, in Northern Iraq. He has clearly been an active terrorist second-in-command.

AN IN-DEPTH ANALYSIS OF WAHHABISM

Wahhabism is named for Muhammad ibn 'Abd al-Wahhab (1703-1791), leader of a movement to bring back the sternness and austerity that once existed in Islam before the Arab Golden Age. Wahhabism is also the official religion of Saudi Arabia.

In the late 18th-century, Muhammad ibn 'Abd al-Wahhab joined forces with those who would become rulers of Saudi Arabia (especially Muhammad bin Saud), and together they conquered the Arab peninsula in what historians have called the Wahhabi-Saudi alliance, wiping out thousands of people because they loosely interpreted the Koran.

This alliance (and the Saudi royal family) attempted to take control of the whole Persian Gulf, but met with British resistance in 1865. The alliance managed to increase its territory in 1915, and in 1917 forced the British to pay them five thousand pounds a month to cease their expansionism.

The next significant date was 1932 (when the state of Saudi Arabia got its name; also called the second Wahhabi conquest), and the Saudis rounded up 400,000 people and carried out mass executions and amputations (resurrecting the old *lex talionis* law of "an eye for an eye").

The regime invented petrodollars during the 1960s with newfound wealth from oil, and by this time, Wahhabism became associated with Salafism, making it appear less like a warrior ideology and more like mainstream Islam. Theologically, Wahhabism is similar to Hanbalism (based on the ideas of Ibn Hanbal), who argued with the Shiites and the Khawarij sect about the Sixth Pillar of Islam among other things (Lang 2003). Wahhabism has been the inspiration for Islamic reform movements around the world, from Indonesia to Africa, and, of course, with the Taliban of Afghanistan. Some 80% of mosques that exist in the United States are funded by Saudi money, but most American Muslims practice a more peaceable and tolerant version of Sunni Islam that, in most cases, is opposed to militant Wahhabism.

Wahhabists do not like being called by that name, as they prefer to think of themselves as a Sunni or Salifi sect and be called "servers of the divine unity" or unitarians.

The Wahhabi-Saudi movement is a simplified and conservative form of Sunni Islam that aims to cut down on luxurious living habits. Accordingly, Wahhabi-oriented mosques are simple and without minarets. Adherents dress plainly and do not smoke tobacco or use drugs.

Television and photography are also looked down upon as artificial two-dimensional representations of human beings (Algar 2002). It should be noted that *the so-called "Wahhabi lobby" is quite powerful and wealthy*.

Wahhabi activists in Washington D.C. pose as workers for lobby groups such as the American Muslim Council and American Muslim Foundation and contribute thousands of dollars every year to the campaigns of American politicians in hopes of getting American counterterrorism laws, like the Patriot Act, reversed. As examples of this powerful influence, the Bush administration regularly orders the redaction (classification) of intelligence reports linking Saudi wealth to the financing of terror, and the FBI has faced numerous setbacks in the war on terror because the Wahhabi lobby persuaded Congress to force FBI agents through sensitivity training (read news story).

Wahhabism is an extreme form of Islamic fundamentalism that is undeniably violent, intolerant, and fanatical beyond measure. The Wahhabi mindset does not allow for any conception of *jihad* other than "death to infidels" (they particularly dislike the United States and regularly call it the "Great Satan") and Wahhabism doesn't conform to any conception of *fatwa* that allows debate or argument. All who do not accept the Wahhabi way must suffer the consequences. For example, strict punishment is prescribed for those who listen to music other than the drum, or don't pay attention to the precise details of their facial hair. The death sentence is given out for drinking or sexual transgressions.

Their goal is to take over the Muslim world and be the only voice of Islam.

They have many schools and organizations for teaching the Wahhabi way, such as the Muslim Student Association, the World Assembly of Muslim Youth, and the Islamic Assembly of North America, some of which have been investigated by the FBI for suspicion of terrorist financing (read news story), and they seem to support crimes other than terror. The following excerpt is from a typical fatwa issued by a untypically radical Wahhabi cleric, which gives you some idea of the level of fanaticism:

Wahhabism: "People should know that Jews are backed by Christians, and the battle that we are in is not with Jews only, but also with those who believe that Jesus is the son of Allah. I am against America until this life ends, until the Day of Judgment. I am against America even if the stone liquefies.

My hatred of America is so strong, if part of it was contained in the universe, it would collapse. She is the root of all evil and wickedness on earth. Who else implanted the tyrants in our land, and who else nurtured oppression? Make no allies, and show no mercy or compassion toward them. Their women are yours to take, legitimately. God made them yours. Why don't you enslave their women? Why don't you wage jihad? Why don't you pillage them?" (Shaikh Saad Al-Buraik, April 2002)

The worst sin in Islam, according to Wahhabism, is "shirk" and the meaning is exactly as it is in English - when one avoids doing their duty, work, responsibility, or fighting.

Shirk is conceived of as similar to associating partners with Allah, or polytheism. Wahhabism maintains that there are three kinds of shirk: (1) major shirk, which relates to aspects of worship, intention, obedience and fidelity; (2) minor shirk, which relates to the act of showing off, even in a minor way; and (3) hidden shirk, in which a believer might fall into inadvertently. Penalties for the third kind, which could happen to you even without your knowing it, in your dreams, for example, including killing you and everyone around you. That's a rather extreme way of enforcing discipline, and it's more than the political purpose of making an example out of someone; it's justified by religious underpinnings.

What do Islamic Extremists Need Or Want?

The Muslim world or religious universe is in serious need of self-restraint and internal reform. The voices of moderate Muslims, who wish to live modern lives, unencumbered by burqas, fatwas, and jihad, need to be heard, but they are on the defensive. Moderates cannot compete with the roar of militant Islam's determination, money, and violence. As a result, Islamic extremism, with its hatred of the West and goal of world domination will probably continue to appear to many as the only kind of Islam.

Islamic extremism justifies terrorism, in the form of extermination of civilians (infidels) and suicide bombing (in pursuit of martyrdom). Such extremists drape their language in the context of enemies - *enemies of God* or *enemies of Islam* - and have no problem recruiting large numbers of *mujahideen* (holy warriors).

The Muslim world of popular thought is in need of a sense of humor, or at least some type of cultural sarcasm. Intellectual appeals won't do; it probably has to be at some other level. To be sure, there are TV shows, movies, and music in America that seem so real, it's hard to tell the difference between reality and fantasy. In America, sometimes you hear of an American child imitating violence in movies, or a child who takes devil worship themes in rock and roll seriously.

But, imagine 98% of a population who sees and hears these kind of "hidden meanings" everywhere, and you've got a good description of Muslim popular thought. *Conspiracy theories* abound. In the West, we think of them as bad jokes, silly urban legends, or the kinds of things only an idiot would believe. In the Muslim world, people are deadly serious about conspiracy theories, and everything from litter on the streets to dogs that roam the West Bank are all part of a Jewish plot to humiliate Palestinians (Davis 2003). Muslims seriously believe President Bush started a war to avenge the assassination plot against his father, and after 9/11, Muslims seriously denied any Arabs were involved, and that the attacks were part of a joint CIA and Israeli plot, and photos were doctored by Hollywood special effects technicians.

Try as you will, there's no way to convince Muslims that their beloved conspiracies are something otherwise. The Pew Global Attitudes Project (at right) shows the level of mistrust.

Speaking of humor, one of the best weapons of counterterrorism is *ridicule* since terrorists fear that more than death. They fear losing at psychological warfare, at having their leaders appear as bumbling idiots.

Even dictators cannot survive a climate of free speech characterized by satire and ridicule. One of the first things Fidel Castro did, for example, after taking power was to put up signs saying "No counterrevolutionary jokes here." In the Muslim world, pride, honor and shame are profoundly important, so ridicule as a weapon might have some effect, although backlash can be expected. Mike Waller's Fourth World Blog has long advocated the weapon of ridicule. So, what do the extremists want? If it were possible to list the "demands" of Muslim extremists, and from a hostage negotiation point of view, it should always be possible to list some rational demands, then this would be the list:

- A complete pull-out of all American and Western (infidel) soldiers from the sacred territories of Islam (this would mean most of the Middle East, not just Saudi Arabia)
- An end to any and all American and Western support for Israel (so that Israel can wither away and die; or better yet, just disappear off the face of the earth)
- A change in the way international political and economic organizations, like the U.N., treat the Muslim world (instead of tying financial aid to socio-political reform, just send money with no strings attached)

- A pan-Islamic super-state consisting of many nations and territories (large enough to encompass all of the Middle East, parts of Africa, and most of Eurasia)
- A purging of all Western-style influence and a hands-off policy by the rest of the world (to be accompanied by a mutual respect for cultural differences in regard to freedom, rights, democracy, education, medicine, social services, clothing, and thought)

Among the list of things that most of the Western world finds unacceptable is the implied superiority and effectiveness of Islamic justice. It is difficult to overstate how harsh and backward most conceptions of Islamic justice look in practice.

Death is pretty much proscribed as a penalty for all sorts of offenses, including "thought crimes," manner of dress, and careless speech; definitely not things associated with progressive regimes, but certainly "effective" in the extreme sense of a totalitarian-style deterrence.

Islamic conceptions of just war are likely to be unfamiliar to most Westerners. Khadduri (1984) provides a neat little description of the Islamic approach as follows:

Islamic Conceptions of Just (Jihad) and Unjust War

1. Just wars are wars in the defense of cities against foreign attacks
2. Just wars assert valid claims against a foreign people who fail to honor a city's (or community of believers) rights
3. Just wars are against foreign people who refuse to accept a public order considered to be the best and most suitable for them
4. Just wars are against a foreign people whose place in the world is considered to be that of servitude as the best and most suitable for them
   1. Unjust wars are motivated by the Ruler's personal advantage such as lust for power, honor, or glory
   2. Unjust wars are wars of conquest waged by the Ruler for the subordination of peoples other than the people of the city (or community) over which he presides

3. Unjust wars seek retribution, the object of which can be achieved by means other than force
4. Unjust wars lead to the killing of innocent men for no reason other than the Ruler's propensity or pleasure for killing

It is also true that in jurisprudence, Islam makes no distinction between civil society and the state, that the individual is considered a limb of the collectivity, that Muslims have duties vis-a-vis the community (umma), and that no individual rights exist in the sense of entitlements. Many scholars have criticized Islam in terms of over-emphasizing duties, not rights, which takes the form of a certain anti-individualism which runs contrary to the idea of human rights.

3

Terrorism

INTRODUCTION

The history of mankind is replete with tales of horror of some power-wielding humans going mad, while others have been the victims of their unimaginable brutalities. The perpetrators have ranged from individuals to armed groups to states. The systematic use of terror as a means to attain political objectives exists all over the world.

The attention we give to terrorism often seems disproportionate to its real importance. Terrorism incidents make superb copy for journalists, but kill and maim fewer people than road accidents. Nor is terrorism politically effective. Empires rise and fall according to the real determinants of politics – namely overwhelming force or strong popular support – not according to the bit of mayhem and pandemonium caused by isolated fanatics whom one would take seriously enough to vote for it. Indeed, the very variety of incidents that might be described as Terrorism has been such as to lead critics to suggest that no single subject for investigation exists at all. Might we not regard terrorism as a king of minor blotch on the skin of an industrial civilization whose very heart is filled with violent dreams and aspirations. Who would call in the dermatologist when the heart itself is sick?

But popular opinion takes Terrorism very seriously indeed and popular opinion is probably right. For the significance of Terrorism lies not only in the grotesque nastiness of terrorist outrages but also in the moral claims they imply. Terrorism is the most dramatic exemplification of the moral fault of blind willfulness. Terrorism is a solipsistic denial of the obligation of self-control we all must recognize when we lived in civilized communities.

Certainly the sovereign high road to misunderstanding Terrorism is the pseudo-scientific project of attempting to discover its causes. Terrorists themselves talk of the frustrations, which have supposedly necessitated their actions, but to transform these facile justifications into scientific hypothesis is to succumb to the terrorists' own fantasies. To kill and main people is a choice people make, and glib invocations of necessity are baseless. Other people living in the same situation see no such necessity at all.

History of Terrorism

Terrorism is not a recent phenomenon. The Zealots employed it against the Roman occupation in Palestine. The Assassins used it in eleventh and twelfth centuries in Persia and Syria. The Thugs in India used it for many centuries against innocent travelers to appease the bloodthirsty goddess Kali. Terrorism became an important feature of European politics during and after the French Revolution as different political groups comprising anarchists, nationalists and social revolutionaries practiced assassinations, bombings and various forms of violent seizure and destruction of property.

Terrorism has become the greatest evil in our worlds today. It is perpetrated by fanatics who are utterly indifferent to the sanctity of human life. Although the international community remains divided a universal definition of what is meant by terrorism, yet it remains committed to confront it through a variety of means.

What Is Terrorism?

In the present scenario, the terrorism is being successfully tackled by the United States and its allies who have declared War on Terrorism. If we ponder upon the word Terrorism, it's a relative term, which takes on a different meaning if we change its context. Terrorism has no absolute and globally accepted definition and its interpretation can easily be used or abused to suite particular needs. The adage that "one man's terrorist is another's freedom fighter" reveals the wide range of variations in its interpretation but, if simply stated, terror is extreme or intense fear. It is a psychological state, which combines the physical and mental efforts to create dread and insecurity. The matter of terrorism is complicated. The terrorist of yesterday is the hero of today and the hero of yesterday is the terrorist of today. This is serious matter of constantly changing world in which we have to keep our heads straight to know what is terrorism and what is not. But most importantly to know what causes it and how to stop it. The present terrorism scenario is very closely related with Islam.

Globally Accepted Definitions

On December 6, 2001, Justice Ministers of the 25-member European Union adopted a new common definition of terrorism. It defined terrorism as: "Acts committed with the aim of seriously intimidating a population, forcing a government or international organization to abstain from performing any act, or seriously destabilizing or destroying the fundamental political, constitutional, economic or social structures of a country or an international organization."

Bruce Hoffman, an expert on terrorism, defined it as: "Ineluctably political aims and motives, violent, or equally important, threatening violence, designed to have far-reaching psychological repercussions beyond the immediate victim or target, conducted by an organization with an identifiable chain of command."

International Summit on Democracy, Terrorism and security held in Madrid on March 10, 2005. The panel calls for a definition, which would make it clear: "Any action constitutes terrorism if it is intended to cause death or serious bodily harm to civilians with the purpose of intimidating a population or compelling a government or an international organization to do or abstain from doing any act."

THE RISE OF TERRORISM

"Most Muslims are not fundamentalists, and more fundamentalists are not terrorists, but more present day terrorists are Muslims and proudly identify themselves as such.", writes Bernard Lewis in 'The Crisis of Islam'. Thanks to the rapid development of the media, and especially of television, the more recent forms of terrorism are aimed not at specific and limited enemy objectives but at world opinion. Their primary purpose is not to defeat or even to weaken the enemy militarily but not to gain publicity and to inspire fear – a psychological victory. The same kind of terrorism was practiced by a number of European groups, notably in Germany, Italy, Spain, and Ireland. Among the most successful and most enduring in this exercise has been the Palestine Liberation Organization (PLO).

The PLO was founded in 1964 but became important in the 1967, after the defeat of the combined Arab armies in the Six-Day War. Regular warfare had failed; it was time to try other methods. The targets in this form of armed struggle were not military or other government establishments, which are usually too well guarded, but public places and gatherings of any kind, which are overwhelmingly civilian and in which the victims do not necessarily have a connection to the declared enemy. Examples of this tactic include, in 1970, the hijacking of three aircrafts – one Swiss, one British, and one American – which were all taken to Amman. These and other operations by the PLO were remarkably successful in attaining their immediate objectives – the capture of the newspaper headlines and television screens. They also drew a great deal of support in sometimes-unexpected places, and raised their perpetrators to staring roles in the drama of international relations. Small wonder that others were encouraged to follow their example.

For a while freedom and independence were used as synonymous and interchangeable terms. The early experience of independence, however, revealed that this was a sad error. Independence and freedom are very different, and all too often the attainment of one meant the and of the other, and the replacement of foreign overlords by domestic tyrants, more adept, more intimate, and less constrained in their tyranny.

A new phase in religious mobilization began with the movement known in western languages as pan-Islamism. Launched in the 1860s and 1870s, it probably owed something to the examples of the Germans and the Italians in their successful struggles for national unification in those years. Their Muslim contemporaries and imitators inevitably identified their objectives in religious and communal rather than nationalist or patriotic terms, which at that time were still alien and unfamiliar. But with the spread of European influence and education, these ideas took root and for a while dominated both discourse and struggle in the Muslim lands. Yet the religious identity and loyalty were still deeply felt, and they found expression in several religious movements, notably the Muslim Brothers. With the resounding failure of secular ideologies, they acquired a new importance, and these movements took over the fight – and many of the fighters – from the failed nationalists.

A letter to America published in November 2002, and attributed to Usama Bin Ladin, enumerates in some detail various offences committed not just by the government but also by the people of the US and set forth, under seven headings, "what we are calling you to do, and what we want from you." The first is to embrace Islam; the second is to stop your oppressions, lies, immorality, and debauchery; the third, to discover and admit that America is a nation without principles or manners; the fourth, to stop supporting Israel in Palestine, the Indians in Kashmir, the Russians against the Chechens, and the Manila government against the Muslims in the southern Philippines; the fifth, to pack your luggage and get out of our lands.

This is offered as advice for America's own goods, so do not force us to send you back as cargo in coffins. The sixth, to end your support of the corrupt leaders in our countries. Do not interfere in our politics and method of education. Leave us alone, or else expect us in New York and Washington; seventh, to deal and interact with the Muslims on the basis of mutual interests and benefits, rather than the policies of subjugation, theft and occupation. The document ends by telling the Americans that, if they reject this advice, they will be defeated like all the previous Crusaders, and their fate will be that of the Soviets who fled from Afghanistan to deal with their military defeat, political breakup, ideological downfall, and economic bankruptcy.

"If freedom fails and terror triumphs, the peoples of Islam will be the first and greatest victims. They will not be alone, and many others will suffer with them."

THE TROUBLE WITH TERRORISM

Charles Townshend writes in "Terrorism": "Terrorism upsets people. It does so deliberately. That is its point, and that is why it has engrossed so mush of our attention in the early years of the 21st century.

Insecurity can take many forms, but nothing else pays quite so sharply on our sense of vulnerability. After September 11 we found ourselves in an apparently open-ended and permanent state of emergency, a "war against terrorism", whose ramifications are as inscrutable as terrorism itself.

Terrorism is never easy to understand, and least of all in the aftermath of a terrorist attack. When society feels under threat, attempts at rational analysis are often openly resisted as giving aid and comfort to, or even sympathizing with, the enemy. Yet without such analysis, combating Terrorism seems a baffling contest against an indefinite threat. Although Terrorism can sometimes took rational, more often it seems to go straight off the chart of common sense – to be not only unjustifiable, but atrocious, mad or mindless."

The Problem of Definition

"Both political and academic efforts to get to grips with terrorism have repeatedly been hung up on the issue of definition, of distinguishing terrorism from criminal violence or military action. In a word it is labeling because terrorist is a description that has almost never been voluntarily adopted by any individual group. It is applied to them by others, first and foremost by the governments of the states they attack. States have not been slow to brand violent opponents with this title, with its clear implications of inhumanity, criminality, and – perhaps most crucially – lack of real political support. Equally, states find it quite easy to produce definitions of Terrorism. The USA, for instance, defines it as ' the calculated use or threat of violence to inculcate fear, intended to coerce or intimidate governments or societies'; the UK as 'the use or threat, for the purpose of advancing a political, religious, or ideological course of action, of serious violence against any person or property'." "In the states view, only the state has the right to use force – it has, as academics tend to say, a monopoly on the legitimate use of violence. But outsiders may wonder whether all use of violence by non-state actors is equally unjustifiable, even it is formally illegal. The very first revolutionary terrorists in the modern sense believed themselves justified in opposing with violence a repressive regime in which no freedom of political expression or organization was permitted."

"Thus arose a notorious adage that one person's terrorist is another's freedom fighter. This relativism is central to the impossibly of finding an uncontentious definition of Terrorism."

"Terrorism is a distinctive form of modern political agency, intended to threaten the ability of a state to ensure the security of its members' – and thus its claim to legitimacy. To get closer to a definition of Terrorism we need to unpick its political logic. For the core of nearly all definitions of Terrorism – the use of violence for the political ends – is too similar to the definition of war to be much of use."

Terrorism & War

"Clearly war and terrorism are intimately related. It is hard to imagine a war that did not generate extreme fear amongst many people, and sometimes this is more than a by-product of violence – it is a primary objective."

"The essence of Terrorism, by contrast, is surely the negation of combat. Its targets are attacked in a way that inhibits self-defence. But, of course, what marks Terrorism out in the public mind is its readiness to attack not just selected but also random targets; in the indiscriminate bombings of a street market, a store, or a bar, we see a deliberate flouting of the international law of war, and a refusal to accept as binding the prevailing moral distinctions – b/w belligerents and illegitimate targets. So the vital part of the US definition is the non-combatant targets against whom violence is perpetrated."

The Terror Process

I. Seizing attention: shock, horror, fear, or revulsion: this is certainly the most straightforward stage. The thirst for order and security impels societies to establish conventions and boundaries to regulate violent coercion: when these are transgressed, shock is generated.

II. Getting the message: what do terrorists want: by no means all-terrorist groups rush to claim responsibility for their actions, or if they do so, deliver a comprehensible rationale or demand. When terrorist acts are left unsigned - like 9/11 attacks – it is up to the onlookers to fill in the blanks. The results can be varied. George W. Bush assured his citizens that the 9/11 attacks were 'intended to frighten our nation into chaos and retreat'. But retreat from what, or where? American commentators, both official and unofficial, showed a marked reluctance to accept a surely well-established view that Usama bin Laden's primary motive against the US was the defilement of Saudi Arabia by the presence of US troops. Instead they preferred more abstract explanations of the attacks rooted in envy or hostility towards American prosperity and democracy.

III. Fight or flight? – The response: partly because the assessment of motives can be quirky, responses can be unpredictable or contradictory. If the demands are comprehensible and fulfillable, fear may drive people to comply. It is easy enough for people to fulfill minimal demands – to keep quiet and defuse to help the police, for instance; but bigger political demands can't usually be delivered directly. The people who are most likely to be intimidated or alarmed are the people who in most political structures are outside the decision-making sphere.

Strategies of Terror

T. P. Thornton proposed two basic varieties: enforcement and agitational terror. The function of the enforcement terror is likely to be limited, aimed at preserving the security of the rebel organization by deterring the public from giving information to the security forces. To succeed in this, the organization needs a sufficiently extensive surveillance system to persuade people that assisting the authorities will be detected: most terrorist groups are simply too small for this. Agitational terror is likely to grasp at mush extensive, longer-term goals: revolution of some kind, or 'national liberation'. Some of these goals are more feasible than others.

"Terrorist action may be auxiliary -one element of a larger military or guerilla strategy; it may be confined to limited goals; or it may be absolute – the pursuit of political goals through the systematic use of terror alone. It is this absolute, independent terror strategy, rather than terrorist action per se, that should properly be labeled terrorism. "Thus Terrorism properly so-called is not just the use of violence for political ends; not just outrageous violence; not just violence by the armed against the unarmed; it is conceived as a free-standing, sufficient, and decisive political strategy."

Terror & Politics

"Thinking about the terror process leads to the conclusion that the essential distinction b/w war and terrorism lies in their operational logic: war is ultimately coercive, terrorism is impressive. War is physical, terrorism is mental. Terrorism operates, therefore, through subjective psychological pressure.

Women & Terrorism

From Vera Zasulish, who carried out the first Narodnik armed attack when she shot the governor of St. Petersburg in 1878, to Waffa al-Edress, the first female Arab suicide bomber in Israel in January 2002, women have been frontline actors and, consequently, pioneer recasters of gender roles.

Crusaders & Conspirators

The Good Terrorist

Good terrorist are those whose actions are justified by the oppressiveness of the system they oppose.

Who becomes a terrorist? The answer is likely to be that it depends on the circumstances. Terrorist organizations differ markedly in how they recruit their members. Some will indeed require fanatics, ideologies, dreamers; others may be so embedded in their communities that recruitment resembles a rite of passage.

Freedom Fighters: that one man's terrorist is another man's freedom fighter – or one man's freedom fighter is another man's terrorist – is surely a commonplace of our times. There are some obvious grounds for relativism. Terrorism as a distinctive political concept got its name from the actions of the holders of the state power, perhaps the first modern regime – the French Convention of Year II of the French Revolution (1793-4). Since then, governments have been on any quantitative measure the most prolific users of terroristic violence. Yet there is not hint of this in the dominant official discourse, terrorism is used by extremists – rebels – against the established order – the state.

International Terrorism

"Communist states, especially Soviet Union and their surrogates, as well as other militant totalitarian regimes like Iran, Libya and Syria, are actively exporting terrorist and terror techniques into other countries. Their activity is a manifestation of transnational state-sponsored terrorism. They indoctrinate, fund, train, arm sub-state groups of diverse national origins to at as their tools, using psychological warfare and propaganda to create severe psycho-social conflict in contemporary life."

US insistence on the central role of state-sponsorship has survived such cautionary advice, however; and several of the old 'rogue states' have been recently re-identified by President Bush as part of an axis of evil.

Super Terror

It has become clear over the last decade that we need to look into the future, to access the possibility of terrorists acquiring and using so-called 'WMDs' – chemical, biological and nuclear weapons. Although they did not involved such weapons, the unprecedented scale of 9/11 attacks seemed to bring the exponential expansion of destruction a big step closer.

THE REIGN OF TERROR

"Virtue without Terror is Powerless"

The French Revolution's ruthless and systematic use of violence created a model for the application of terrorizing force by the holders of state power over the next couple of centuries. A recent college textbook on terrorism identifies three functional levels of state terrorism: intimidation, coerced conversion; genocide – deliberate extermination of an entire class. Ethnic, or religious group. Although the prime exponents of terrorism from above were overtly repressive autocracies and despotisms, or radical revolutionary regimes like the Bolsheviks during the Russian civil war. The USA tolerated the persistent, systematic terrorization of the Southern Black community by the Ku Klux Klan, as well as the less dramatic use of intimidatory violence by employers against labour organizations.

Nationalism & Terror

We need to understand the way in which different societies maintain their vision of their collective selves, and so produce different terrorisms and different terrorists. In other words, the framework for much modern terrorist action is ethnic or nationalist. Indeed, the emblematic terrorist act of the early 20th century – the assassination of Archduke Ferdinand, heir to the throne of Austria-hungry, at Sarajevo in June 1914 – was carried out by a Serbian nationalist. Nationalist movements have shown mush greater resilience and destructive capacity than the small and fissiparous left-wing revolutionary groups. They tend to be significantly bigger, for one thing, and to draw on a broader pool of recruitment; and though their cause – freeing or uniting the nation – is not necessarily more practicable than the revolutionary dream of total social transformation, nationalism has dominated modern politics precisely because it connects with a visceral, apparently natural force.

Terrorism may play a leading part in the attempt to preserve or reawaken the national spirit, and also in the accompanying struggle against a foreign or imperial government. But there is another and possibly more intractable problem: what all too often stands in the way of national liberation movements is not only the foreign government, but the fact that people of other ethnic groups live within the presumed national territory.

Religious Terror

"The fight in defence of religion and belief is a collective duty; there is no other duty after belief than fighting the enemy who is corrupting our life and our religion." At the end of the 20th century the world faced a revival of religious fundamentalism, quite puzzling to many people who has assumed that the process of secularization was, although perhaps erratic, an irreversible one. The long standing liberal assumption that the rise of modern society and the decay of religion were two sides of the same coin was suddenly thrown into doubt; and the shock effect of this was soon registered in writing on terrorism, where religion has confidently been consigned to the margins of terrorist motivation.

One of the leading surveys in the late 1990s asserted that 'the religion imperatives for terrorism is the most important defining characteristic of terrorism today.' While the author of an American college textbook on terrorism put 'religious fanaticism' top of her list of terrorist motives. Official assessments reflect this too; for instance, the Canadian Security intelligence Service 2000 Public Report states that 'one of the prime motivators of contemporary terrorism is Islamic religious extremism'.

SUICIDAL TERRORIS]M

Suicidal terrorism, sometimes called suicide terrorism, is a form of organized urban terrorism that goes by a variety of other names, such as "new" or "next generation" terrorism. It is NOT that form of urban terrorism which refers to inner-city, door-to-door combat like Marighella's idea of urban guerrillas winning by losing via authorities exposed as counterreactive and repressive, NOR is it usually enough to meet the definition of insurgency. Instead, it's referring to what some experts call *"postmodern" terrorism* (Laqueur 1996) or *"new school" terrorism* (James Woolsey once said old school terrorists use violence to get a seat at the table while new school terrorists want to blow up the table). This type of terrorism is not designed to be pragmatic or realistic, but symbolic and an effective media ploy. A not uncommon part of the pattern of this behavior is for one segment of the terrorist group (the "political wing") to engage in fake diplomacy, token social services and education, business fronts, and the contesting of elections, while another segment of the terrorist group (the "military wing") engages in ambushes, assassinations, kidnappings, and suicide bombings. There is usually a lot of propaganda and window-dressing surrounding this form of terrorism, but all of it is false. Suicidal terrorism can occur in a number of settings, both indoor and outdoor. It is also not confined to the Middle East, serves numerous terrorist purposes, and may very well be the kind of terrorism we'll see more of in the future (Bloom 2005).

Traditional approaches to countering urban terrorism, to be sure, have always involved indoor "structure clearing." Small units go building-by-building in what is called a MOUT (Military Operations in Urban Terrain) operation. A significant difference between this kind of operation and others is the attention that must be paid to *avoiding casualties*.

Counterterrorism in an urban environment requires knowing the terrain and knowing the enemy. The terrain will mostly determine positions and movements (such as whether a top down or bottom up assault is called for), as well as where safe footholds (consolidation points) can be gained. The terrain, also to some degree, determines the method of entry or breach, and sometimes this is subdued (rather than the more typical explosive, dynamic, "flooding" entry).

The counterterrorist response to urban terrorism requires *avoiding predictable patterns* at all costs. Far more important, however, is knowing the enemy, and being able to distinguish between those who wish to die (the martyrs or suicidal terrorists) and those who do not wish to die (the guerrillas or ordinary terrorists). While some level of advance intelligence may be helpful in making these distinctions (perhaps a sociology of place, or ecology), distinctions are often made in split seconds at the tactical level. Guerrillas normally evade attack, while martyrs typically do not, preferring instead to die in place. Martyrs also generally have better, fortified positions, but both types will likely use booby traps. The time and place of the firefight may very well be the best indicator of whether suicidal terrorism is involved.

Suicidal terrorism is mostly terrorism without a cause or conscience, or if there is a cause, it's overly blinded by hate and rage, and the behavior logically runs contrary to the idea of terrorism itself (it's more akin to mass murder or certain hostage-taking incidents). It used to be that terrorists played by some rules, practiced guerrilla hit-and-run tactics, conducted surgical strikes, and at least had some moral scruples over the killing of innocent noncombatants, or a plan to defeat the enemy. Not any more. The traditional higher callings among terrorists, like ideology, religion, and homeland seem to be less and less relevant, and are used only today as a subterfuge for popular support and media exposure. In many ways, we are entering the Rebellious Era of terrorism, where any target is fair game, collateral damage is not in its lexicon, every terrorist wants to cultivate a Robin Hood image, and every motive or cause becomes politicized by the media reaction to it. The "new" terrorists seem to be engaging in terrorism for the fun, or "hell" of it. This lecture attempts to spell out the vision of destruction that these kind of terrorists have.

THE SYMBOLISM OF THE ACT

The geographic location, or place, of the suicidal terrorist event is of some importance. There are many reasons why urban areas, capitol cities, and places where innocent people congregate are the new playgrounds for terrorists. One is the fact there are more human shields for the handlers of the suicidal terrorist to hide behind, although nothing prohibits handlers from manipulating their proxies at a distance. It's easier, however, for the related parties to escape and hide in overcrowded, urban areas. There is also an abundance of targets in urban areas. Cities are a target-rich environment. The anonymity of city life lends itself to false or fake identification. Authorities will have a hard time maneuvering in urban areas. Terrorists know that the real reason why the military stays out of cities is not because of some agreement to respect police turf, but because you can't maneuver tanks and military equipment easily there. They also know that most city services are woefully under-prepared for terrorist attack.

They also know that most democratic governments have something like a Posse Comitatus Act which prohibits the military from being used as a domestic police force. When selecting a target, terrorists usually seek out the one that is: (a) most high up in vital importance; (b) softest in terms of being unprotected; and (c) most significant or symbolic to their cause. What's new about suicidal terrorism is the symbolism behind the desperation of the act.

Some of the new RULES that terrorists play by include the following. (1) Indiscriminate, arbitrary, and unpredictable killing of noncombatants. The idea that there are no innocent bystanders is not new to the theory of terrorism. What's new is the desire to kill or maim as many of the general public as possible. (2) Lone wolves or beserkers. These are individuals who constitute a terrorist cell unto themselves. Terrorists have moved beyond the principle of leaderless resistance (not knowing who's in charge) to an organizational model that makes room for "covert" or "sleeper" cells. These individuals go off unpredictably and at times and places of their own choosing. (3) Faith in victory. Suicidal terrorism never gives up, it never surrenders or quits, and it never compromises anything in vain. This is what makes it different from religious terrorism which wants to lose, achieve martyrdom and go to heaven, and this is what distinguishes it from nationalistic terrorism, which seeks government concessions regarding a homeland. (4) Cherished symbols as targets. What gives a target symbolic value is if large numbers of a population group regard it affectionately. Suicidal terrorists never attack anything citizens regarded as a monstrosity. (5) Internecine conflict. Not only do the new terrorists seek mutually assured destruction, they often want the conflict to spill over onto as many foreign shores as possible. (6) Technology. Classic terrorism had strong ties to anarchism and the shunning of technology. The new terrorism embraces technology, and manifests a desire to be as advanced and exotic as possible. They are not technocrats, but they have a proclivity toward modern consumerism. (7) Weapons of mass destruction. Suicidal terrorists admire chemical, biological, and nuclear weapons, and want to get their hands on them. Laqueur (1999) makes an interesting point that as the intelligence level of a terrorist goes down, the desire to obtain weapons of mass destruction goes up.

THE END OF IDEOLOGY

Most of what Daniel Bell (1960) predicted in his book, *The End of Ideology,* came true. We are living in un-heroic times of free-floating aggression, angst, and self-delusion. Less than one half of one percent of the population would commit to an ideology, yet all of us want some sort of adventure or passion out of life. IDEOLOGY is defined as *a form of social or political philosophy in which practical elements are as prominent as theoretical ones. It is a system of ideas that aspires both to explain the world and to change it* (Encyclopedia Brittanica 2002). With the fall of the Berlin Wall, more than the Cold War ended. So did our desire to do any hard thinking about the global economy, culture clashes, mass immigration, ethnic hatred, how to end human suffering, and how to guard against government bureaucratization. Today, everyone is a populist (populism is the cause that champions the plight of the average, ordinary person). Further, it's an anti-intellectual climate, both for the terrorists and counter-terrorists. Most of the current War on Terrorism can be seen as a cleansing or mopping-up operation for the remaining few "pockets" of intellectual revolutionary terrorism. Let's analyze this connection more fully.

Leftist (radical, Marxist, revolutionary) terrorism has always been the domain of intellectuals who consider themselves a vanguard elite. The notion of a vanguard strategy has been around since Lenin and the Bolsheviks (a word meaning majoritarianism) who believed that hard-core Communist Party followers should consider themselves the "vanguard of the proletariat" (the working class). The Trotskyites (followers of Leon Trotsky) rejected the idea of a worker's state in one country (Russia), and believed in a worldwide vanguard which would enable a permanent, global Socialist revolution. Castroism is a variety of Trotskyism, and Maoism is closer to Leninism (although the peasant class is championed under Maoism). Che Guevara toyed with the idea of "consciousness raising" in the Americas, but rejected it in favor of the Maoist idea that happiness is a warm gun.

True-cause revolutionary and liberationist ideologies faded away precisely because the struggle was taken inward - psychologically. The workers of the world never united, and it was an American, Abbie Hoffman, who declared in 1968 that the movement was all about "Revolution for the Hell of It." More intellectually significant were the existential philosophers, Jean-Paul Sartre and Herbert Marcuse, especially Marcuse's (1964) book *One-Dimensional Man*.

HERBERT MARCUSE: German-American existential/ phenomenological philosopher, Father of the New Left, Leader of the radical intelligensia, and Celebrator of the Hippies who argued that well-off, middle-class college students should throw off their "manacles" of unearned privilege and fight in common cause with the poor and downtrodden to destroy the welfare/warfare state. Liberation from affluence is the only thing worth liberating. Mass media, oppressive culture, advertising, management, and most contemporary modes of thought are the enemies and appropriate targets for liberators.

Now, within Frazier's hierarchy, you'll recall, is an organizational level called the active cadre. This is the vanguard of a terrorist group. They have been indoctrinated or led to believe that terrorist violence is absolutely necessary on their part as righteous champions of whatever poor and downtrodden group they are fighting for. Cooper's (1977) doctrine of necessity is applicable. It says that a person becomes a terrorist not because they enjoy violence, but because they are forced toward it. They come to believe that continuance of the status quo is worse than the violence caused by terrorism. They may come from backgrounds where they were raised to detest violence, but their utter hatred of the status quo helps them overcome any feelings of guilt about killing innocent people. Notice it's not the cause or ideology that drives the terrorist. Instead, it's an internalization of other people's problems and the desire to be heroic. If anything, it's an ideology of violence. It would be immoral not to be violent.

The idea that there should be no scruples of conscience when it comes to blowing things up can be traced to the 1848/1849 German activist Karl Heinzen. The Communists, especially Engels, tried to shut him up, but Heinzen proclaimed the first terrorist philosophy of mass destruction. Heinzen's beliefs are known as the doctrine of unjustified means.

KARL HEINZEN: Nineteenth-century German radical freethinker who resurrected Gracchus Babeuf's (1792) philosophy that "All means are legitimate in the fight against tyrants." In his essay *Der Mord* (Murder) he proclaimed that all means were valid to hasten the advent of democracy. As a radical democrat, Heinzen wrote: "If you have to blow up half a continent and cause a bloodbath to destroy the party of barbarism, you should have no scruples of conscience. Anyone who would not joyously sacrifice his life for the satisfaction of exterminating a million barbarians is not a true republican."

Suicidal terrorists frequently want little by way of practical or political gain. In the words of a Hizbollah leader, "We are not fighting so that the enemy recognizes us and offers us something. We are fighting to wipe out the enemy." New terrorism appears to be motivated by little more than a desire to bomb the hell out of one's evil enemies, or as one contemporary philosopher of terrorism, Ken Wilber calls it, "first-tier, blue thinking."

The notion that terrorism is a kind of spiritual quest, sojourn, or state of consciousness can be attributed to *Ken Wilber*, who is probably best known for his 2001 book, *A Brief History of Everything*, his extensive website, and his opposition to the war in Iraq.

Wilber's theory of terrorism is called AQAL (All-Quadrants, All-Levels) theory, and although it's a little complicated (and explained in numerous places elsewhere), I'll try to summarize AQAL theory.

The Four Quadrants are similar to my own (O'Connor 1994) neo-functionalist approach to explaining how the four parts of society are affected by terrorism, but Wilber uses them as representative of segments of society that must all be attended to equally in order to prevent pathological personalities or societies from developing. The Quadrants consist of:

- The upper right quadrant - atoms, molecules, cells, organs, neural systems and brains

- The upper left quadrant - intent, consciousness, maturity, the mind, sensations, perception, impulse, concepts, and aesthetic taste
- The lower right quadrant - groups, families, tribes, villages, and nations
- The lower left quadrant - the cultural, world views, cultural perspectives, values, and morals

The Levels are more extensive, color-coded, and reference a worldview or state of consciousness, and their essential characteristic is that each one thinks of itself as the only way to see things:

- *Beige*: Archaic-Instinctual. The level of basic survival
- *Purple*: Magical-Animistic. The level of gangs, corporate tribes, athletic teams, etc.
- *Red*: Power Gods. The level of self; powerful, impulsive, egocentric, heroic, e.g. the "terrible twos," rebellious youth, frontier mentalities, soldiers of fortune, wild rock stars
- *Blue*: Conformist Rule. The level of life as having meaning, direction, and purpose, with outcomes determined by an all-powerful Other. Rigid social hierarchies; paternalistic; one right way and only one right way to think about everything. Law and order, impulsivity controlled through guilt; fundamentalist belief; obedience to rule of Order; e.g. Puritan America, Confucian China, Islamic fundamentalism
- *Orange*: Scientific Achievement. The level that escapes from 'herd mentality' and seeks truth and meaning in achievement, materialistic gains, and the laws of science rule
- *Green*: Sensitive Self. The level of community, human bonding, ecological sensitivity, networking, and a human spirit freed from greed, dogma, and divisiveness
- *Yellow*: Integrative. The level of life as a kaleidoscope of natural hierarchies, systems, and forms, subject to flexibility and spontaneity, with differences and pluralities integrated into interdependent, natural flows

- *Turquoise*: Holistic. The level of Universal holistic system, uniting feeling with knowledge; multiple levels interwoven into one conscious system
- *Coral*: An indefinable level that may well be the realm of saints and mystics

Wilber's AQAL theory of terrorism is that far too little social resources have been directed toward the Left Quadrants, and that far too many societies have looked for natural hierarchies in the Right Quadrants, when the only natural hierarchies are atomic and in the Upper Right. Also, far too much Blue, first-tier, thinking is encouraged. Fear, loathing, and disrespect must give way to Orange thinking (which may imply the need for a World Police Corps). In short, terrorism should be conceived of as a form of self-doubt, breed from fear, and caused by the absence of genuine opportunities for respect, dignity, and self-development in the world today.

CRIMINAL TERRORISM

Postmodern terrorists have given up on revolution and liberation, and instead pursue what can only be described as organized criminal activity where it's "just business as usual." Narco-terrorism is one such variety, but many terrorist groups raise money through criminal activity, and to be sure, a few terrorists started out as street thugs or had a proclivity for such things as vehicle theft.

The so-called "true criminal" terrorist is rare, however. For one thing, the mentality is different between a criminal and a terrorist. Mental disorders abound among the criminal population — antisocial personality disorder, psychopathy, sociopathy, etc. The worst that can be said about terrorists is that they suffer from delusions of grandeur and a strong paranoid streak (Laqueur 1999). This is just the opposite of what most people think. They think that terrorists have to be crazy to kill so many innocent people, but they're "crazy like a fox." Criminals, on the other hand, are the crazies, suffering from anxieties, depressions, psychoses, neuroses, and personality disorders. Terrorists sleep very well at night, thank you.

On the other hand, there are similarities between some terrorism/insurgency situations and certain criminal patterns of group behavior, most notably gang war. The U.S. Army War College has a recently published (2005) document entitled "Street Gangs: The New Urban Insurgency" which compares mutated forms of terrorist-insurgents to criminal street gangs. We normally think of insurgents as military actors or as some form of nonstate terrorists, but in a complex situation, it's hard to separate those with political motivations from those with criminal motivations. It may very well be that the political insurgents pay criminals to do "political" work, but it's just as likely that in such situations, the criminals are more than happy to engage in terrorist-like action for the hell of it. If the latter is the case, then you got what Hobsbawm (1965) once called "primitive rebels" or banditry.

The question then becomes to what extent terrorism, or terrorist ideology, is a cover-up for criminality, or psychopathology? The literature on the forensic psychology of terrorism is enormous (Taylor 1991; Reich 1998; Robins, R. & J. Post 1997; Taylor & Horgan 2000), and there is no one, neat answer to the question. Some experts argue that the psychological mechanism that allows terrorists to do what they do is a process of moral disengagement. Others say it's a coping strategy for stress. Some would argue that terrorist motives are driven by such things as boredom and the need for a sense of adventure. A few claim it's the case of a massive inferiority complex, brought on by a strong sense of humiliation (Lindner 2001). Nobody argues that terrorism is psychopathy. It's apparent that most suicidal terrorists are well-read, educated, intelligent, thoughtful, reflective, rational people with common sense. They also just happen to be people you can't reason with, because they fervently hold fanatical or extremist beliefs deep in their heart and soul. They have what Voltaire called an incurable disease of the spirit, a fixation, if you will, with seeing no harm, no foul play, no bad intent, and no negative impact in what they do. They possess a dehumanized, emotionless attitude toward others, regarding most people as "the walking dead".

The motivations for becoming a terrorism are diverse, and they depend not just upon applied political psychology (Robins

& Post 1997) but the socio-historical context of the time and place (Crenshaw 2001). There are regions of the world where long-standing grievances are part of the local culture. There are times when the apocalyptic visions of fundamentalist religions take hold. There are places of higher learning which steer intellectual thought in the direction of justifying terrorism. One thing is clear – to become a terrorist, you need to be exposed to like-minded others. It's easy to sympathize with terrorists, but another thing to excuse their actions.

The profiling of terrorists is no easy task, and profiling the new, modern terrorists tends to baffle experts. CIA profiling tends to be more clinical and psychodynamic than FBI profiling. Criminal profiling uses a combination of psychology, observation, deduction and forensics. Terrorist profiling uses a combination of political psychology, sociology, psychoanalysis, and psychiatry. The closest thing to a composite of a "perfect" terrorist is a person with extreme hatred in their soul and an extreme sense of self-righteousness. They feel they have been left with no choice in a world which moves in the diametrically opposite direction of their convictions. They see their enemies in the world as evil – and evil must be destroyed, root and branch. In drawing up profiles, it's important not to make too much of national origin. That would be pretty much the same as racial profiling. It is helpful to consider social class background. Most suicidal terrorists tend to come from the elite, educated, upper social classes. Revolutionary terrorists are drawn from two extremes: the most upper and most lower classes. Nationalist and separatist movements produce terrorists from the lower classes. Religious terrorists come from all social classes. In the Muslim world, terrorists come from the ranks of the unemployed, and in the United States, from the middle class. Social psychological models are also helpful, as in Jeffrey Ian Ross' (1999) attempt to tie together structural factors about socio-cultural conditions with psychological facilitating traits. Here's a paraphrasing of those facilitating factors:

- a strong ego, need for excitement, and a feeling of being lost
- disorders along the paranoid-narcissistic spectrum

- drive to belong, join, or be part of a group
- an intellectually enriching learning environment or opportunities to learn new things
- a tendency to make cost-benefit calculations that exaggerate benefits and minimize costs

THE READINESS TO KILL AND DIE

It's true that some terrorist behavior is less than rational. Suicide, for example, is not normally the act of a rational person. Many experts (Ganor 2000; Schweitzer 2000) have commented on the tendency for modern terrorists to use suicide attacks. In fact, the Islamic Jihad (there are several Islamic Jihads started in the 1980s, all stemming from inside the Muslim Brotherhood movement started in the 1920s) have specialized in the use of suicide bombers, which involve a person wearing explosives or detonating a driven vehicle packed with explosives. Other groups have also embraced suicide terrorism.

The Tamil Tigers of Sri Lanka proudly wear cyanide necklaces as a sign of commitment to their cause, saying "We are married to our cyanide; it makes us clear-headed and purposeful." IRA terrorists have starved themselves to death; Russian revolutionaries have blown themselves up; and fascist movements have a distinct tendency toward a mystique of death. The Japanese kamikaze tradition best exemplifies this warrior mentality or mystique, which is characterized as a honor to be permitted to die. The Islamic tradition adds an element of "deluxe martyrdom" (Laqueur 1999), in which surviving family members are well taken care of.

CASE STUDY: *Islamic Jihad,* a shadowy, non-hierarchical collection of leaderless groups that evolved from the Muslim Brotherhood in Egypt about 1925. They seek to purify and unite the Arab world, and operated as an evangelical group within the mosques and universities for many years. They formed connections with Hizbollah and Hamas in the 1980s, and later with al-Qaeda, having been fighting an undeclared "holy" war against Israel, the United States, and anything Western for the last several years. Hostage taking (and eventual murder of hostages) and suicide bombing are their trademarks. They believe it is the religious duty of every Muslim to fight in the jihad, and in (bin Laden's fatwa) 1998, called for the killing of Americans anywhere in the world.

ADDENDUM: *Jihad* is a word with two meanings. It means holy war by means of the sword, but it also means struggle for one's soul against baser instincts. Muslim clerics, militants, and fundamentalists all reject the second definition as dangerous heresy. "Strict" interpretation of the Koran is used to support the holy war definition, which also brands as cowards those who turn away from their sacred duty to fight in the name of Allah. The holy war needs to be fought until all infidels, or nonbelievers, are driven from the Arab world and/or there are no competing religions in the world.

While some suicidal terrorism is probably done out of fatalism, the terrorist thinking they are going to die living under present conditions, or die if captured (the death penalty not being a deterrent here), deluxe martyrdom is a radically new phenomenon. For Muslims, suicide is not a mortal sin, as it is in Catholicism. The Koran does not permit suicide in principle, but religious leaders say it is allowed under special circumstances. The Koran does preach that it is a religious duty to fight and die for Allah and Islam. Martyrdom in the name of Allah carries the following benefits:

- eternal life in paradise
- permission to see the face of Allah
- the loving kindness of 72 virgins
- the promise of heaven for 70 relatives
- family financial rewards of thousands of dollars
- family increase in social status.

The perpetrator of a suicide attack is not considered to have committed suicide. Rather, they are perceived as a "shahid" or martyr fulfilling a religious command. They are not permitted to volunteer for suicide missions, but are instead selected by religious teachers, and undergo a series of training or indoctrination sessions. Part of this indoctrination may involve attempts at being buried alive to overcome the fear of death. Candidates come from a cross-section of society, and occasional use seems to be made of young females between the ages of 16 and 28. The role of women in suicidal terrorism is a matter of speculation, as is the degree to which suicidal attacks trigger more "copycat" suicidal attacks. Perpetrators are trained to use a "belt bomb" containing 15-30 pounds of explosives. Besides being a cheap and easy method of terrorism, it's the most accurate guidance system available in the world today. They can pretend to be a pregnant woman, and pause at precise moments when a crowd congregates around a target. The method attracts media coverage, and no escape plan is usually needed except for any handlers, supervisors, or back-up personnel in the area.

Istishad: The Islamist Word for "Suicide Bomber"

Islamists and Jihadists become quite angry when the media and the West refer to those who blow themselves up as engaging in suicide bombing. A typical angry reaction would go as follows: "This is not suicide. Suicide is weak, selfish, and mentally disturbed. This is 'istishad' which consists of martyrdom or self-sacrifice in the service of Allah. A martyrdom operation is the highest level of jihad. Nor is the action murder. A murderer is someone with a psychological problem. It's not murder because we're not bloodthirsty people. We don't like to kill. We don't do it because we like to kill civilians, but that is a fact of life because the jihad must go on."

THE INFORMAL PROCESS OF RECUITMENT

Postmodern terrorism relies upon informal means of recruitment. Certainly, some groups (Hezbollah is one) have formal indoctrination and allegiance ceremonies, but the vast majority of terrorist organizations rely upon schools, religious institutions, families, and word-of-mouth to get new members to join. Once the terrorist group has succeeded in getting one family member to join (and die), it is a simple matter to get the remaining members of that family to believe it is a "given" for the surviving members of that family to join. Another tactic is for the terrorist recruiter to set up someone as responsible for a criminal offense because the terrorists know that a prison experience will radicalize that person. Different recruiters from different terrorist groups may even threaten to report the person as a "collaborator with the enemy" to another group if they don't join the group the recruiter represents.

In the recruitment process, it's important to remove any sense of the recruit's self-identity. *There is no room for individuality in a terrorist organization.*

Success or failure (pride or shame) regarding the terrorist organization becomes an individual matter, and terrorist groups often compete with other terrorist groups over who has the most dramatic and violent operations.

It's also important for recruits to renounce any sense of hesitation, guilt, or remorse they may have. *There's no room for moral considerations within a terrorist organization.*

This objective is normally accomplished by demonizing the enemy; e.g. "anything which helps defeat the enemy" or "the more dead, the better." Nothing is illegitimate (although the Koran speaks of not poisoning the well) in the cause of defeating an enemy. No distinctions are made between the enemy's soldiers, civilians, women, or children.

After recruitment, there is a need to provide a mechanism for granting social status to the new recruit. They must receive respect from their acquaintances and be a source of awe and inspiration to the young. By intent, the whole process of recruitment is designed to make it look like it is a natural step to join a terrorist organization, much like the armed forces of a country would like it to look like it's a natural step to serve your nation.

THE AMATEURIZATION OF TERRORISM

When teenagers get involved in terrorism, they can hardly be considered professionals. It's not that all teenagers are immature; it's just that they rarely have the resources - financial or otherwise - to carry out much more than suicide, homemade, script-kiddie attacks. More than a lowering of the average age is the cause of amateurization, which is also synonymous with splinter groups that break off with a better-equipped main group. The growing trend toward more secretive and shadowy forms of organization contributes toward amateurization. In such organizations, there is less training, command, control, and leadership. Combined with no ideology or cause to believe in, amateur terrorism may turn out to be the real threat in the future.

Amateur terrorists can be defined as part-timers who work with homemade equipment, are only indirectly or remotely controlled by a leadership entity, operate in idiosyncratic fashion, and are just as likely to hurt themselves in the process of attempting to harm or shock others. Arquilla & Ronfeldt (2001) conceptualize this new era of terrorism as "netwar", a non-hierarchical organizational form that is designed for all sorts of doctrine - terror, crime, militancy, or vandalism. Under this conceptualization, jihad will take the form of cyber-jihad, and the "swarm" tactic this entails means allowing amateurs to do what they will. Rebel groups without a cause (clue) will simply take the path of least resistance - and may use technology as a force multiplier - to have an impact. Let's examine one such group, often looked at as the world's first post-communist, postmodern insurgency - the Zapatistas.

CASE STUDY: *the Zapatistas,* or Zapatista National Liberation Front (*Ejercito Zapatista de Liberacion Nacional* - EZLN), were Leftist rebels who championed the cause of Indians native to Mexico's Chiapas province. In 1994, the Zapatistas began killing Mexican soldiers and policemen. By 2001, the Zapatistas emerged as an above-ground "Robin Hood" group for the civil rights of oppressed people everywhere.

The Zapatistas started out without any computer technology, but they soon realized that transnational organizations and non-governmental organizations (NGOs) had computers and websites, so they started a propaganda campaign on the Internet by tailoring their terrorist attacks to what was newsworthy for the NGOs. Their Internet proficiencies progressed to the point of web hacks and cyber-crime. In the late 1990s, they were the world's first information guerrilla movement. When the Zapatistas launch a web attack, their "network" of supporters, sympathizers, and loosely-affiliated movements all launch web attacks too. The effect of this, as it is for suicidal and amateurish terrorism, is often more overwhelming than traditional terrorism.

HUMILIATION AS A CAUSE OF MODERN TERRORISM

The humiliation paradigm is most associated with the work of Straub (1990) on bystander intervention and Lindner (2001) on gendercide. Evelin Lindner is a psychological counselor with extensive private practice experience in the Middle East. She has developed a paradigm that draws heavily upon the psychological notion of empathy, and the viewpoint that all human beings yearn for recognition and respect, and that the withdrawal or denial of recognition and respect, experienced as humiliation, is the strongest force that creates rifts between people and breaks down relationships. Humiliation is defined as a personal feeling where respect and recognition are lacking, and it is not due to ethnic, religious, or cultural differences (which create rifts by themselves or are used as fronts for the deeper humiliation rift). Nor is humiliation the same as feeling like a victim (which generally results in either depression or lashing out in rage). Instead, humiliation is the feeling of being helpless, pinned down, held down, or kept passive (and unable to control world events). Criminologically, humiliation is quite different from deprivation, the standard concept in criminology to explain these kinds of things. Lindner's (2001) research involved years of trying to understand things like why some Palestinian mothers would want to have more babies so their children could grow up to become suicide bombers, or why successful businessmen (like Osami bin Laden) would abandon wealth and promising careers to become terrorists. The answer, it seems, is a sense of felt humiliation and helplessness about being unable to contribute effectively to the "global village" or one's notion of global responsibilities. Two points can be made about this explanation — one, that suicidal terrorists are deeply sincere and selfless about their motives for terrorism— and two, that the world's movement toward globalization or a "global village" has negative side effects that create terrorism (*even humanitarian aid can be humiliating*).

Apparently, the postmodern terrorist cannot sit passively by and watch world events run their course without some personal commitment. Terrorism is then, like an eating disorder or alcoholism, where the person tries to "drown" their sorrow or humiliation, and further, will "manufacture" a series of humiliations (when there is none in their lives) by over-empathizing (sincerely and deeply) with the problem of others' suffering. Likewise, there will be those who are perceived (or misperceived) as the "humiliators" in all this, and above all, those most likely to be perceived as the humiliators are those who point out the inequalities and deprivations in the world (human rights violations) that were once taken for granted or just accepted. Perhaps this paradigm has some validity. It may very well be that some people turn to terrorism precisely because they feel deeply humiliated by the arrogant, self-congratulating style in which the leading nations of the world are constantly pressuring for greater human rights. It remains to be seen, however, if empirical research validates the hypothesis that empathy for suffering is a cause of terrorism. It may very well be that this line of explanation simply involves some twisted sense of heroism or bystander intervention gone horribly wrong.

SUICIDE BOMBINGS & TERRORISM

The suicide bombing in Iraq, Afghanistan, Palestine even in London and other parts of the world including the Muslim countries as well is also referred by many philosophers, leaders etc. in the ambit of terrorism.

Recently, Robert Pape wrote a book "Dying to win: the Logic of Suicide Terrorism". Pape is an assistant professor at the university of Chicago. He had collected a storehouse of information on 462 suicide bombers who made headlines by their successful missions from 1980 to 2004. By analyzing demographic data, the psychology of the terrorists and their ideological and political motives, Pape had drawn interesting and valid conclusions.

The most important point stressed by the Pape is that "Islamic fundamentalism is not a closely associated with suicide terrorism as many people think."

In the Bruce Hoffman's Inside Terrorism, most of the part is devoted to religion. Pointing out that none of the identifiable terrorist groups that had been operating in 1968 could be classified as religion, Hoffman notes that the first modern religious terrorist groups did not appear until around 1980. By 1994, however, fully a third (16 out of 49) of known terrorist groups 'could be classified as religious in character and motivation', and thus proportion leapt again the following year to almost half (26 out of 56).

Countering Terrorism Through Terrorism

Although terrorism is an inevitable reality in the present scenario, when the whole world is in the cruel jaws of it, but this ineluctable reality cannot be curtailed through the more terrorism or on the same pace; as many countries of the present world are trying to do it in this way.

The obvious example of Kashmir and Palestine tells otherwise. The relative term 'one man's terrorist is another man's freedom fighter' is also fully involved here. The freedom movements of Palestinians, Kashmiris and the Chechens have been branded through the Western media and also through diplomatic efforts the specific countries are doing on their best.

In the present scenario, countering terrorism has become more difficult for the countries in order to establish peace and stability in the world.

The definition of terrorism is still under the fog, and it would be under the fog until and unless the member countries of UNO would not adopt a universal definition of it; or until the US and its allies would not get their hidden motives under the umbrella of their 'war on terrorism'.

In order to counter terrorism countries are unilaterally adopting the same attitude (definition), which the US has set for them – pose the opposition as terrorists in front of the world and attack them unilaterally. Israel as well as India's state-terrorism falls in this scenario. As in the current imbroglio of Middle East Crisis, Israel's unilateral attack over Lebanon – just to search its two beloved and loyal soldiers – has further not only deteriorated the situation but also tell the whole world that "if you want to wipe off the terrorist from the surface of the world then kill the innocent civilians and change the cities into the graveyards", then you might be able to curtail terrorism and then peace, harmony and security can be established.

State-terrorism has become the order of the day. It is evident not only from Israel's unilateral attack over Lebanon but also in the case of India and Russia in Kashmir and Chechnya respectively.

COUNTERTERRORISM & DEMOCRACY

A world in which 80 per cent of terrorists were not Marxists but Muslims might present a totally different kind of issue. But the American response to September 11 showed that little had changed, except the roster of usual suspects: Afghanistan, Iraq and Sudan in place of the rogue states of the 1980s, Libya, Syria and Iran. The theory of state-sponsorship may be weakly developed but its practical significance is immense: it validates the direct retaliation, which has become an established American policy preference. A belief in the American deterrent effect of smart munitions has survived a surprising amount of contrary evidence.

Democracy against Terrorism

There can be no dispute that terrorism s undemocratic in that it ignores all conventional processes of representative politics. But does it go further than this? Is it inherently antidemocratic? And are democracies uniquely vulnerable to terrorism? We have already noted that democratic states may be more sensitive to the threat that terrorism is seen to present to public safety.

AMERICA'S 'WAR ON TERRORISM'

Prior to 9\11, whether this terrorism existed in this shape or not. Noam Chomsky, a Noble prizewinner, of USA defined terrorism: "Its calculated use of violence or threat of violence to attain goals that are political, religious or ideological in nature through intimidation, coercion or instilling fear."

On Jan 2001, President Bush declared Iran, North Korea and Iraq-the axis of Evil. 9\11 provided them perfect logic. After 17th September 2002, USA sums up with her national security strategy. USA possesses the right of pre-emption strike.

The United States has right for preemption strike against any measures that can crop up with fear. USA has attained unlimited military superiority of the world and there is no enemy of the

United States except Terrorism. After 9\11, war started against the Muslims on the name of terrorism.

FBI defines terrorism, "The unlawful use of force or violence against persons or property to intimidate or coerce a government, the civilian population, or any segment thereof, in furtherance of political or social objectives."

Department of Defence (DoD), "The calculated use of violence or the threat of violence to inculcate fear, intended to coerce or intimidate governments or societies as to the pursuit of goals that are generally political, religious or ideological."

Department of State (DoS), "Premeditated, politically motivated violence perpetrated against noncombatant targets by subnational or clandestine agents, usually intended to influence an audience."

If we take a look of the above-mentioned definition, the following steps can be derived:

I. For political stability

II. Dialogue

III. Involvement of other forces as UNO etc.

IV. War

Interior Motives of US War on Terrorism

If we take a look of Political disputes like Bosnia, Iraq, Chechnya etc the Interior motives of war on terrorism are:

I. To get hold of world's natural resources to ensure sustained supply. This is the foremost motive of Europe and America. After the first Arab war, Europeans did not want the cut off the oil from Arab. They directed against those countries, which possess natural resources. If this is not the case, why this war on terrorism is in the Middle East.

II. To malign Muslim freedom struggles. Wherever in the world, there is bloody freedom movement going on such as in Kashmir, Xing yang, Chechnya, Palestine. It is not in the best interest of America that these would be successful. Because according to Domino theory, a movement leads to another movement.

III. To damage the ideologies of Islam specially Jihad. They are against the Jihadees not against the independence of practicing Muslims. For that purpose, they have started reforms in the Madressahs in Pakistan providing them computers etc.

IV. To stop the rise of orthodox Muslim governments. They are doing it in the name of democracy. They are changing the elected governments. e.g.; in Taliban's case. In Iran. It is being isolated. They are there to protect monarchies in Gulf States. These changes are just to protect Israel.

V. To spread its own culture. If a nation dies it's a national death but if a nation dies of cultural death, it's all over. The United States is permeated its culture in the countries on the name of terrorism. As in Iraq, they made dance clubs in the Green Zone. The uniform of new force of Iraq i.e. identical as it matched with USA.

Causes Of Terrorism

I. Unresolved political disputes: In the hot disputes of the world, Muslims are involved. No effort has been made to resolve these issues. The cause is inherent in the disputes of one religion against the other politically. E.g.; Kashmir, Palestine, Chechnya.

II. Ineffectiveness of UNO: The world bode formed after the Second World War. "To avert any other international war. But it utterly fails in going that. The disputes if resolved in UNO, the terrorism was not prevailed as it is.

III. Globalization: It is suited to Western interests than the third world countries. It seeks the occupation of countries by multinational corporations (MNC's). This is spreading poverty and unemployment in the third world countries.

IV. Universal law of cause-and-effect: "like cause will produce like effects". If the go about combating terrorism with terrorism, it will produce obviously terrorism.

V. Double standards of the West: On one hand, previously when Afghan Jihad was going on- they were projected as heroes and then became terrorists. These are the pure double standards towards democracy. They are motivating the third world or least developed countries to increase their defence budget. As Pakistan is buying 75 Jets at the cost of $ 3.2 billion from America. Debt traps have been orchestrated.

What Terrorism Has Done?

It started after 9\11. Bush administration had got chance "to become world more safer". But it did in opposite manner;

I. Unilateralist approach of USA. It gave up the approach of bilateralism and multilateralism. "This terrorism is a threat to entire world community". The United States has decided to go it alone to combat terrorism.

II. The United Nations was sidelined. The prestige attached to UNO was ended.

III. The Muslim country's nuclear ambitions were strictly checked. As in Iran. As in Dr. AQ Khan's case.

IV. Calls were being made to challenge American superiority. No matter how we dislike this sole super power element. It does not have any vested interest.

V. Huntington's Clash of the Civilizations. This theory came to be true. " The battle line would be drawn on tenets lines of civilization." There is going to be war wherever a civilization ended. As Jews v/s Muslims, Hindus v/s Muslims, Islam and the West etc.

Effects On Pakistan

Pakistan has adversely affected by terrorism than any other country of the world. No country in the world has suffered in wake of terrorism than Pakistan. Although, Pakistan is a victim of terrorism is being labeled as a state sponsoring terrorism. The emergence of terrorism in Pakistan was the consequence of its direct involvement in Afghanistan war. Pakistan has learned the lesson "the hard way" but it is imperative that we must not forget it. Lot of time and energy of Pakistan is being consumed to make world understand that Pakistan is not the sponsor of terrorism but it's a victim, and while doing so it is being forced to make compromises on its vital interests. Even the friendly countries like China, Iran, Indonesia started looking towards Pakistan with suspicion. In a nutshell, terrorism has formed Pakistan to go on a back foot and became more defensive on this issue. It has become more important for Pakistan to clean its image tinted with terrorism and take rightful place amongst the community of nations.

Steps Taken By Pakistan:

I. Intimation of war on terrorism: First motive was to clean its image in the eyes of international community.

   President Musharraf took various steps to clean it. He visited many countries of the world, which were never being visited by any leader of Pakistan.

II. U-turn on its foreign policy: Pakistan had taken drastic u-turn after 9\11. It wanted to show international community that we are not fundamentalists. Pakistan took u-turn on its Kashmir and Afghan policy.

III. Ban on Jihadee organizations: Government of Pakistan banned almost all Jihadee organizations on 12th January 2002.

Counterterrorism Strategy By Dr Maleeha Lodhi

"There is no silver bullet that can address global terrorism in all its complexity," writes Dr Maleeha Lodhi in "The Threats of all Threats". "In a globalised world of interconnected threats and challenges," she further writes, "terrorism poses a clear and present danger to peace and security, more menacing than ever in the past. This threat has grown more urgent since 9/11; the attacks on the United States dramatised the increased lethality of terrorism and marked a watershed in the history of terrorism. Every continent has seen acts of terrorism. Perpetrators belong to diverse backgrounds, ethnicities and faiths. Since 1968, there have been at least 8,000 serious incidents of terrorism across the world. About 70 countries have been affected by the activities of as many as an estimated 100 terrorist entities.

She proposed a broad-gauge counter-terrorism strategy based on nine 'Cs':

(1) Comprehensiveness: A comprehensive, multifaceted strategy is needed that encompasses law enforcement, political, social, cultural, financial and diplomatic measures.

(2) Consensus at the global level is required on a strategy incorporating both short- and long-term measures that work in tandem.

(3) Causes and conditions that breed, encourage and contribute to terrorism must be objectively identified and addressed.

(4) Confusion between explanation and justification must be removed. Trying to understand a phenomenon does not mean giving in to terrorism.

(5) Capabilities must be improved and national capacities strengthened across the spectrum to pursue terrorists and prevent terrorist activities.

(6) Cooperative rather than coercive national and international strategies should be pursued so that the reaction to counter-terrorism measures does not compound the problem.

(7) Civil liberties and principles of good governance must be upheld in the fight against terror, because real security can only be achieved through respect for human rights.

(8) Civilisational and cultural: dialogue and understanding including engaging in the battle for the hearts and minds, must become an integral part of global consensus-building to evolve a joint strategy. Such a dialogue must be premised on the understanding that the root cause of friction between civilisations are not primarily religious differences, but mainly issues of power, competing political and economic interests, policies and misunderstandings.

(9) Conference at the summit level must be called to craft and coordinate an approach based on these elements.

Concluding Remarks

- Today terrorism is hybrid and complex in nature and scope, even across the continents by non-state actors. Countering this multi-headed phenomenon requires a multi-pronged, multinational, and sustained policy by the governments across the globe.

- One of the characteristics of the prevailing environment is that deprivation and an unjust political and socio-economic dispensation rapidly give rise to frustration. The consequent perception of helplessness is sufficient to motivate individuals and groups to adopt violence as an expression of their anger.
- Many decades ago, Dr. Martin Luther King Jr. said: "Injustice anywhere is a threat to justice everywhere." And time has proved how much right he was.
- The remedy lies in a tolerant and democratic society. Man's capacity for justice makes democracy possible but man's inclination to injustice makes democracy absolutely necessary. However to enable the United Nations to evolve an effective strategy for this purpose it is imperative to define terrorism that may be acceptable globally. Also make a distinction between terrorism and legitimate struggle for freedom and right of self-determination, the denial of which can breed terrorism and a threat to "peaceful co-existence".

4

Post-Modern Terrorism

World War IV is total war on a global scale. While numerous nations are arrayed against a myriad of terrorist organizations, the United States is at war with al Qaeda, a terrorist network that traces its origins to the Soviet invasion of Afghanistan over a quarter century ago. In Iraq, US and coalition forces face not only al Qaeda terrorists but also Hezbollah fighters, a group supported by Iran. Israel, meanwhile, battles Hamas and Hezbollah along with the al-Aqsa Martyr's Brigade and other groups associated with Yasir Arafat's Palestinian Authority.

World War IV seems complex but keep in mind during World War III (the Cold War) while American forces fought North Vietnamese regulars and National Liberation Front (Viet Cong) guerrillas in South Vietnam, we also fought the Pathet Lao in Laos and Khmer Rouge in Cambodia. From Greece and Yugoslavia to Korea and Vietnam and the Caribbean and jungles of Central America, the Cold War involved a large number of nations and groups. Nevertheless, it all came together as part of a struggle between competing worldviews.

The "War on Terror" is no less complicated and similarly encompassing. Since it is an Information Age war in which knowledge is power, it is essential to understand who we fight and what they aim to achieve. Our enemies are more than savage barbarians with a penchant for decapitating the innocent. They are integral to a concerted effort to redefine the world order. Al Qaeda presents the most expansive and acute threat to the United States.

As a part of its global threat, al Qaeda fighters oppose US troops in Iraq and Afghanistan. Additionally, al Qaeda poses an immediate threat to the stability of pro-Western and traditional Moslem regimes like Saudi Arabia. Its ultimate strategic goal is to establish a radical Islamic world order.

Al Qaeda uses terror as its primary tactic in achieving its goals. All terrorists employ violence against the innocent but different organizations use it in specific ways. Among the many terrorist organizations world wide, al Qaeda and, to a lesser extent Hezbollah, are most expansive in their uses of terror if only because their strategic goal of affecting a world Islamic revolution is more encompassing. In this regard, al Qaeda and Hezbollah are post-modern terrorist groups.

What's the difference? Hamas and the al Aqsa Martyr's Brigade are focused on Israel. While Arafat has no reservations against sending suicide bombers to blow themselves apart among Israeli soldiers and civilians alike, he is less likely to use chemical and biological or radiological weapons (even if he could get them) since these weapons of mass destruction cannot distinguish between Jews and Palestinians. Ultimately, since Arafat wants to turn all of Israel into a Palestinian state, he probably would avoid making it uninhabitable. Al Qaeda, in its global jihad, is not so constrained. Just as post-modern philosophers seek to redefine moral reality, post-modern terrorists want to redefine political reality with a similar radical totality.

The ultimate goal of al Qaeda, Hezbollah and associated organizations like the Abu Sayyaf Group in the Philippines, is to redefine the global political landscape with a world-wide Islamic revolution. Theirs is a holy war against the Judeo-Christian West, not just Israel. They are confident Israel will fall like a ripe olive once the United States is run out of the Middle East. Then Arafat will create a Jew-free Palestine from Gaza in the South to a "liberated" Jerusalem in the west to Haifa in the north. Religious diversity will not be a feature of the Islamic world order.

Ultimately, superior strategy wins wars. Osama bin Laden has a three-stage strategy designed to achieve Islamic world domination.

Stage One: Take control of the Middle East. Most immediately prevent a US-backed democratic Moslem regime from succeeding in Iraq. Then take power in a destabilized Saudi Arabia. A dominant Iran will then bring the Gulf States and North African Moslem regimes into a radical Islamic fold. The end result may resemble Armageddon if Israel squares off in a nuclear war against an Iranian-led Arab coalition.

Stage Two: Take control of secondary Moslem countries starting with Turkey and Pakistan. Bosnia, the Islamic republics of the former Soviet Union, Indonesia, Singapore and the Philippines will fall along with parts of China.

Stage Three: Isolate, dominate and then destroy the Judeo-Christian countries of Western Europe, South and North America—including the Great Satan itself, the United States. By 2100, al Qaeda will have its Islamic world order.

This is World War IV. Forget the sleazy sickness of Abu Ghraib. Stop mouthing meaningless slogans like, "Bush lied, soldiers died." Steel yourselves for a long, bloody fight. This is a war we must not lose.

USE OF VIOLENCE AND MASS PSYCHOLOGY IN POST-MODERN TERRORISM

Terrorism is the art of manipulating political opinions and decisions by the use of violence and mass psychology, specially in a democracy - in dictatorships, carefully targeted assassinations would be more efficient. There are basically two strategies:

1) collective blackmail;

2) provocations.

In the former, the enemy is forced to pay such a high price for peace and security, that compromises or appeasement will get wide support. This is clearly the intention of the IRA against the United Kingdom, or the ETA against Spain. In some cases, the enemy may become a political pariah, shunned by potential allies. This is the case of various terrorist groups operating against Turkey (to prevent EU membership), Israel, and the USA. The latter method was used for the "Bulgarian agitation" in 1876, and became the favourite strategy of Russian secret services throughout the 20th century. Provocations aim at compromising the "ordinary" suspects. Even the German National Socialists were tempted to use Jews as scapegoats for staged acts of terrorism.

Both traditional terrorist strategies are, however, messy and risky. Terrorists have learned, that the victims tend to react unexpectedly, by rallying around their political leaders and accepting tougher counter-terrorist policies. Many good men (from the terrorist perspective) have to risk their lives for committing terrorist acts, and even the most fanatic groups have a limited supply of voluntary suicide-bombers. In the case of provocations, on the other hand, terrorists may save man-power, but they have to sacrifice women and children in an attempt to earn sympathy and accuse their enemies for brutality. Would it not be possible to achieve the same results by less actual blood-shedding?

Terrorism needs media attention like plants need sunshine. If an airplane is destroyed, but everybody assumes it an accident by technical failure, terrorism gained nothing. If the reason of an air crash remains unsolved or doubted, a terrorist group may claim responsibility and celebrate it as their achievement. Why do the hard work of actually planting bombs in airplanes, if the most important factor is, to what and whom the media subscribes the incident?

Terrorists need journalists, but journalists too live of bad news and threats. Terrorists and journalists live in a symbiosis, mutually profitable relationship. Ideally, journalists provide terrorists with headlines and resulting public outcry, while terrorists provide journalists with the evidence required for verification. A maximal sensationalist "yellow press" needs a minimum of real bodies. If public hysteria can be created bloodlessly, just by media reports and threats, why fill the mortuaries?

In Iraq, coalition soldiers and civilians are killed almost daily. This has been chosen instead of open resistance, because killing 30 men in a battle once a month would, paradoxically, not produce the same net result. The ultimate aim is not to destroy the occupying military forces (Americans could easily afford to loose a thousand men in the whole war), but to keep the media occupied, and to make the "home front" tired of the whole issue. Killing military personnel would not be terrorism as such, but when the aim is to frighten the great public by continuous media attention, it could be classified as terrorism.

The remnants of the former Iraqi government and security forces are not the only people to have learned the might of the media, and how to influence it effectively. Terrorism is spreading all over the world as a substitute for old-fashioned fighting. High-profile kidnapping cases provide similar publicity, without body counts. During the Anthrax letter scare and SARS epidemics, ordinary people felt the temptation of jokes that could paralyze air traffic, mailing, private and public businesses. The media can be held hostage by so many different ways.

In long term, virtual terrorism may become a business-conscious enterprise. Advertisement and campaign bureaus, consults and lobbyists, belong to the 20th century, while the 21st century will see the privatization of full-service secret agencies with their trusted professional terrorists, provocateurs, media connections, stock exchange experts, life guards, arms merchants, human rights lawyers, and documentation centres. Disinformation is not even illegal.

Although this development may clean up terrorism somewhat, and save lives and limbs, there will follow the same problems that plague every expanding organization. Some terrorists become common criminals, but others may find the manipulation of financial markets more interesting. Airlines and insurance companies react to terrorist acts, and threats of such. There will be rivalries, and some terrorist organizations may turn into honest protection business.

Terrorism is a globally unevenly distributed phenomena. The natural objects are free and democratic societies, where the media is not censored, justice is clement, and the decision-making process is open and predictable. The most successful organizers and sponsors, however, are internationally protected dictatorships with closed borders, secretive administration, hierarchical power structures, and cheap work force. This inequality determinates that terrorists will be harboured by dictatorships against democracies, until the latter make serious counter-threats of promoting democracy by force, which will prevent dictatorships of exploiting their natural advantage too far.

Countries like Turkmenistan and North Korea know, that their real or supposed capability to retaliate are their best guarantees against foreign demands of liberalization, but the recent fate of Afghanistan and Iraq warn them of testing the patience of democracies beyond all limits. Peaceful coexistence of dictatorships and democracies is possible only in a state of mutual balance of terror. Russia has by far the longest tradition of state terrorism, global network of agents, propaganda machinery through international front organizations, and all kind of subversive tactics.

The restoration of Soviet-style centralization, and the possession of destructive potential, accompanied with continuing economical and demographical problems, make terrorism a temptation hard to resist. What would Russia have to loose by protecting terrorist groups and regimes?

In a postmodern world, Russia will cultivate and export the know-how and techniques it knows best. This will not necessarily mean, that Russia would sell too much nuclear technology to Iran, because it prefers to keep a monopoly.

Russia will not need to harbour Usama bin Ladin or Saddam Hussein in Moscow, because there are enough client states and nominally independent military bases to store them outside its borders. Most likely, postmodern Russian terrorism will appeal to the media, and avoid unnecessary brutality. Why blow up innocent people, when all critical opposition by democratic societies can be paralyzed and eliminated by the mere threat of risking world peace?

Who would seriously oppose bold demands of further credits, or the extradition of individual terrorists, if Russia would fully use all its potential?

Journalists, researchers, and politicians could be relieved by the prospect of saving lives - perhaps even their own - through appeasement at the cost of taxpayers. Nevertheless, this would be the end of democracy.

RELIGION, TERROR AND THE END OF THE POSTMODERN: RETHINKING THE RESPONSES

... a roaring motorcar, which runs like a machine gun, is more beautiful than the *Winged Victory of Samothrace*....We will glorify war – the only true hygiene of the world – militarism, patriotism, the destructive gesture of the anarchist, the beautiful ideas which kill... We will destroy museums, libraries, and fight against...feminism, and all utilitarian cowardice. The oldest among us are thirty; we have thus ten years in which to accomplish out task. When we are forty, let others, younger and more daring men – throw us into the wastepaper basket like useless manuscripts.

The architecture of... Adolf Loos epitomised the new spirit which rejected decorative excess. The functionalism and simplicity of the buildings contrasted strikingly with the highly ornamented façades of nineteenth century Vienna. Loos's Michaelerplatz Haus was erected opposite Emperor Franz Josef's ornate residence. So unimpressed was the Emperor by the stark rigour of Loos's shop building, that he is said to have closed the curtains in the Hofburg to keep it out of sight.

The assassins of September 11th made no demands. Fundamentalism is a symptomatic form of rejection, refusal; its adherents didn't want to accomplish anything concrete, they simply rise up wildly against that which they perceive as a threat to their own identity.

What is to be done, at present? The question is on everybody's lips and, in a certain way, it is the question people today always have lying in wait for any passing philosopher. Not: What is to be thought? But indeed: What is to be done?

Three moments in twentieth century thought which help us to rethink the relationship between religion and terror are Adolf Loos' proclamation that to be modern is to be unornamented; Filippo Marinetti's call for the purity and modernity of speed, and Jean Baudrillard's understanding that the "uncertainty principle does not belong to physics alone; it is at the heart of all our actions, at the heart of 'reality'". All three came together as the expression of a *religare* (a binding together) with the attack of September 11,

2001 when postmodernity ended with an act aiming for the return of an alternative modernity, obsessed with purity and the speed of destruction, and signaled by the symbolic destruction of the twin towers.

Terrorism is a self-expression of modernity and the rejection of that which is unnecessarily ornamented. The modernity of terrorism is expressed in its obsession with purity, destruction and speed, and involves the symbolic destruction of that, which it believes, is threatening. Terrorism is the articulation of alternative "modernities" – not, as is often mistakenly believed, that "so many radical Muslims [want] to fight to return to the seventh century". These acts of destruction are similar to that which demolished the Pruitt-Igoe housing schemes – an attack from *within that* which has created modernity so as to clear the space to create an alternative.

The central problem facing any response is therefore to acknowledge that terrorism is itself a symptom of modernity and in fact is more likely to be carried out by those who have been "modernized" and "westernized" – and who often reject Western modernity in favour of an alternative one. To eradicate terror would entail the eradication of modernity itself. Indeed, as Baudrillard points out, the attackers of September 11, 2001 were masters of modern systems and technology:

> ...a new terrorism has come into being, a new form of action which plays the game, and lays hold of the rules of the game, solely with the aim of disrupting it.... they have taken over all the weapons of the dominant power. Money and stock-market speculation, computer technology and aeronautics, spectacle and the media networks – they have assimilated everything of modernity and globalism, without changing their goal, which is to destroy that power....Suicidal terrorism was a terrorism of the poor. This is a terrorism of the rich. This is what particularly frightens us: the fact that they have become rich (they have all the necessary resources) without ceasing to wish to destroy us.

What should also be remembered is that the fact of this chapter (and of so many others), all the media discussion, books, articles and debate, are but a confirmation of the success of terrorism. This is because we have actually redirected our energies, interests and resources to inversely "legitimate" and "authenticate" what *has* occurred – and that we live in "terror" of what *may* eventuate.

In order to expand the dialogue on terrorism we can look to the theories of Loos and Marinetti and the ways in which they may have – perhaps unwittingly – driven the link between religion and terror. As part of this discussion these theories must also engage the radically different approach to terrorism by Jean Baudrillard and those, like Georges Bataille, who have influenced his work. It is out of this confluence of theory that we may perhaps begin to rethink religion and terror. This will lead us to ask if it is still possible to articulate responses in secular western democracies such as New Zealand, or can the West now respond only by "terrorizing itself". Baudrillard problematized the very possibility of this choice some time before the events of September 11, 2001:

> Islamic fundamentalism – a providential target for a system which no longer knows what values to subscribe to – has a pendant in Western integrism, the integrism of the universal and of forced democracy, which is equally intolerant, since it, too, doesn't grant the other the moral and political right to exist. This is free-market fanaticism, the fanaticism of indifference to its own values and, for that very reason, total intolerance towards those who differ by any passion whatsoever. The New World Order implies the extermination of everything different to integrate it into an indifferent world order. Is there still room between these two fanaticisms for a non-believer to exercise his liberty?

This chapter argues that terrorism is a form of *religare* (a binding together) occasioned and encouraged by modernity. Terror is in fact a form of religious impulse and belief that arises out of the Purist and Futurist roots of modernity. I begin with a discussion of the Purist and Futurist debates and the associated work of Adolf Loos in order to highlight the fundamentalism [the literal reading and assertion of "the fundamentals"] that informed modernism from the beginning. I then assess religion in modernity and modern religious fundamentalism's attack on secular modernity. This is followed by a discussion of terror, religion and modernity wherein terror is itself understood as a form of modern *religare*, involving symbolic acts to which our response validates. Terrorism is understood here as the embodiment of a modern religion of fear. This leads us to understand terrorism as the response within modernity to competing claims of the real; which raises the question of the possibility of disenchanting symbolic action. Such would seem to be a necessary path for a country like New Zealand. But as Baudrillard points out: "The revolution of our time is the uncertainty revolution" and this makes the outcome a very undecided one for the West.

MODERATE ISLAM-IN OTHER WORDS, TRUE ISLAM

For half a century after the first verse was revealed to the Prophet Muhammad (may God bless him and grant him peace), Islam underwent such an expansion as has seldom been seen. It spread from the Arabian Peninsula to the whole of the Middle East, North Africa and even Spain, drawing the attention of many in the West. In the words of the famous Islamic expert John L. Esposito, "What is most striking about the early expansion of Islam is its rapidity and success.

Western scholars have marveled at it."12 Over the next centuries, Islam reached all corners of the world, from Indonesia to Latin America. Today, Islam is accepted as the fastest growing religion, and its roughly one billion followers represent about one-fifth of the world's population. Interest in Islam particularly increased after the terrorist attacks of September 11, 2001.

Looking at today's Islamic world today, we see a wide range of religious practices, depending on societies' different customs and traditions, their cultural heritage, and world views. This has led some individuals researching or trying to understand Islam to form mistaken impressions. Those differences may symbolize only the traditional values of the society under examination, but Islam itself. The only way of arriving at an accurate opinion of Islam is to put aside these differences and turn to the Qur'an, where the essence of Islamic morality is set out, and to the actions of our Prophet (may God bless him and grant him peace).

Even if Muslims comprise the majority in a community, that does not mean that community's behavior, views and judgments will necessarily be Islamic, nor that they need be defended in the name of Islam. When evaluating an individual's—or community's—view of Islam, that must always be borne in mind. Differences may stem from prevailing conditions. The only way to ascertain whether those views are correct is by turning to the Qur'an, the most accurate source of truth about Islam, and to the actions of our Prophet (may God bless him and grant him peace). It is most unfair to pass judgment on Islam and Muslims without studying the Qur'an to learn whether a particular practice appears in it. Examining the lifestyle of a single community only can seriously mislead anyone who tries to understand Islam and form opinions about it. First, what needs to be done is to learn about Islam from its true source. Then, once the various models in different parts of the world are considered in the light of those criteria, many who only imagined they knew about Islam will actually come to do so for the first time; and can free themselves from the errors they have been laboring under so far.

Morality of Islam

Every Muslim has the duty to call others to the morality of Islam, to inform them of the existence of God and the proofs of His creation. God Himself has revealed that responsibility in Verse 3: 104: "Let there be a community among you who call to the good, and enjoin the right, and forbid the wrong. They are the ones who have success." He also reveals how that invitation is to be made:

> *Call [them] to the way of your Lord with wisdom and fair admonition, and argue with them in the kindest way. Your Lord knows best who is misguided from His way, and He knows best who are guided. (16:125)*
>
> *Correct and courteous words accompanied by forgiveness are better than charity followed by insulting words. God is Rich Beyond Need, All-Forbearing. (2:263)*

True believers know the importance of this responsibility, described in Verse 3:114: "They believe in God and the Last Day, and enjoin the right and forbid the wrong, and compete in doing good. They are among the righteous." Therefore, they call on all those around them—friends, relatives, everyone they can reach—to believe in God, fear Him, and display a proper morality. This pleasing characteristic of Muslims is described in Verse 9:71:

The men and women of the believers are friends of one another. They command what is right and forbid what is wrong, and perform prayer and pay charity tax, and obey God and His Messenger. They are the people on whom God will have mercy. God is Almighty, All-Wise.

From this verse, it's clear that all believers, throughout the course of their lives, are charged with explaining that proper morality, living by it themselves, recommending good deeds to others and advising them to avoid evil. God commands believers to use soft words, "Say to My servants that they should only say the best…" (17:53)

God describes good words and bad in this analogy in the Qur'an (14:24-27):

Do you do not see how God makes a metaphor of a good word: a good tree whose roots are firm and whose branches are in heaven? It bears fruit regularly by its Lord's permission. God makes metaphors for people so that hopefully they will be reminded. The metaphor of a corrupt word is that of a rotten tree, uprooted on the surface of the earth. It has no staying-power. God makes those who believe firm with the Firm Word in the life of this world and the hereafter. But God misguides the wrongdoers. God does whatever He wills.

Anyone who wishes to lead a virtuous life should encourage others toward virtue.

Anyone who wants to see good should make an effort to help spread it. Anyone who wants to see others behave according to their conscience should encourage them to do so, and anyone who opposes cruelty should warn those who engage in it. In short, anyone who wants right to prevail should call on all others to abide by it.

When issuing that call, however, it's most important to keep in mind that only God can inspire people to become Muslims, and cause words pleasing to them to have any effect. God has revealed that our Prophet (may God bless him and grant him peace), as a result of his noble character and superior morality, always treated people well—and has recommended him as a role model for all mankind.

Islam Commands

In the Qur'an (5:2), God has issued this command:

> *... help each other to goodness and godliness. Do not help each other to wrongdoing and enmity. Have fear of God. God is severe in retribution.*

As that verse makes clear, the faithful struggle only for what is good. They consider the words of God in Verse 4:127 of the Qur'an: "Whatever good you do, God knows it."

They never forget that they will be recompensed for all they do in the sight of our Lord, but God reveals that pleasing mutual aid needs to be in a framework of "good and godliness." The meaning of goodness is also explained in Verse 2:177:

> *It is not devoutness to turn your faces to the East or to the West. Rather, those with true devoutness are those who believe in God and the Last Day, the Angels, the Book and the Prophets, and who, despite their love for it, give away their wealth to their relatives and to orphans and the very poor, and to travelers and beggars, and to set slaves free, and who perform prayer and pay charity tax; those who honor their contracts when they make them, and are steadfast in poverty and illness and in battle. Those are the people who act loyal. They are the people who guard against evil.*

True goodness, therefore, is rather different from the way society in general perceives it. Those who do not live by the morality of the Qur'an view good deeds as favors they confer, whenever they happen to feel like it. Usually they restrict such good deeds to giving money to a beggar, or giving up their seat on the bus to an elderly person.

Yet as we have seen from the above verse, the Qur'an describes goodness as a concept encompassing the whole of a believer's life, as an obligation that must be fulfilled throughout the course of his life, not only when he feels like it or happens to remember it.

As a servant, any Muslim possesses true sincerity and helps the poor and needy, even if he himself is in need, even giving up the things he loves (Qur'an, 76:8).

In Verse 51:19, which reads, "And beggars and the destitute received a due share of their wealth," God has revealed that rendering assistance, helping others, and doing good are all incumbent upon Muslims. They give help unconditionally; and believers are ready to make any sacrifice to encourage others towards what is good. They expect nothing in return, apart from winning the pleasure of God. In Verse 76:9-10, God describes such behavior by believers:

We feed you only out of desire for the Face of God. We do not want any repayment from you nor any thanks. Truly We fear from our Lord a glowering, calamitous Day. Muslims know that God is the Lord of infinite justice, and never forget that their good behavior will be suitably rewarded in the hereafter. Nor do they forget that life in this world is only temporary, and that their true home lies in the sight of God. In the Qur'an, He warns people of their inevitable end, and calls on them all to behave in a manner pleasing to Him:

> *We did not create the heavens and earth and everything between them, except with truth. The Hour is certainly coming, so turn away graciously. (15:85)*
>
> *Worship God and do not associate anything with Him. Be good to your parents and relatives and to orphans and the very poor, and to neighbours who are related to you and neighbours who are not related to you, and to companions and travelers and your slaves. God does not love anyone vain or boastful. (4:36)*

The recompense for those who exhibit pleasing behavior is of great good news for all of mankind, and is revealed in these verses, in these terms:

> *But as for those who believe and do right actions, We will not let the wage of good-doers go to waste. (50:30)*

When those who have done their duty are asked, "What has your Lord sent down?" their reply is, "Good!" There is good in this world for those who do good, and the abode of the hereafter is even better. How wonderful is the abode of those who guard against evil: Gardens of Eden which they enter, with rivers flowing under them, where they have whatever they desire. That is how God repays those who guard against evil. (16:30-31)

Islam Commands Us to Do Good and Avoid Evil

Believers learn the true meaning of good and evil from the Qur'an, a book revealed by God as the Standard by which to discern the true from the false." Concepts such as good and bad, right and wrong, are elucidated in the Qur'an with examples that everyone can understand. The faithful's fear of God gives them light and understanding to help them distinguish between good and bad. (8:29)

Muslims spend their whole lives implementing their awareness of the good and evil, as described in the Qur'an. Yet they take another important responsibility onto their shoulders: inviting others to see the truth, to avoid evil, and live by the morality of the Qur'an. Believers spend their lives telling people about the difference between good and evil, because to the faithful, God has given the following command (3:104):

Let there be a community among you who call to the good, and enjoin the right, and forbid the wrong. They are the ones who have success.

In Verse 3:110, God stresses how those who abide by this commandment are much more auspicious than others:

You are the best nation ever to be produced before mankind. You enjoin the right, forbid the wrong and believe in God. If the People of the Book were to believe, it would be better for them. Some of them are believers, but most of them are deviators.

The faithful perform that Qur'anic duty not only in respect for those ignorant of the difference between right and wrong and with no knowledge of religion, but also in respect for the faithful themselves. People fall into error not only out of ignorance, but sometimes out of forgetfulness, by mistake, or when driven by earthly desires. That being so, the faithful encourage good and prevent evil by reminding one another of the Qur'an's commandments. They warn each other that in this world, those who fail to avoid evil will suffer the torments of hell; that only those who do good and devoutly carry out their religious obligations will be rewarded with Paradise. That delightful responsibility means that they never need feel wearied or discouraged while continuing to warn others compassionately and affectionately, no matter what mistakes they might have made. In many verses, God reveals that He loves those who have patience, and calls on the faithful to be patient when practicing the morality of the Qur'an:

> *You who believe! Seek help in steadfastness and prayer. God is with the steadfast. (2:153)*
>
> *... Those who are steadfast and do right actions. They will receive forgiveness and a large reward. (11:11)*

Islam Commands us to Repay Evil with Good

A good action and a bad action are not the same. Repel the bad with something better and, if there is enmity between you and someone else, he will be like a bosom friend. (41:34)

Ward off evil with what is better. We know very well what they express. (23:96)

In these verses, God promises the faithful that they can secure positive results, so long as they adopt a pleasant attitude in the face of wrongdoing. The Qur'an emphasizes that even when a believer is dealing with an enemy, still he can establish a warm friendship. Responding to evil with good is also an essential part of compassion. When any believer sees others adopting an attitude that will not be pleasing to God, he considers first of all how that will affect them in the hereafter. Then he approaches them with toleration and humility, refusing to let himself become puffed up with pride. Over the course of their lives, believers may come across people of very different characters. Yet they will not change their view of morality according to the people they meet. Others may speak mockingly, use ugly words, become angry, or even behave in a hostile manner. Yet the true believer never ceases to be polite, modest, and compassionate. He will not respond to ugly words with more of the same. He will not laugh at those who mock him, nor answer anger with anger, but remains patient and tolerant. In the face of insulting behavior, he will respond with proper morality, and with such compassion that the other will feel ashamed. That is the morality our Prophet (may God bless him and grant him peace) recommends to us. In one of the hadiths, he says, *"You do not return evil for evil, but excuse and forgive."* — 18 In another hadith, he calls on the faithful in these terms: *"None of you must be the kind of weak person who says, 'He who has no compassion will receive none."*

In the Qur'an (5:13), our Prophet (may God bless him and grant him peace) was told to be forgiving when betrayed by some of the children of Israel:

> *... They have forgotten a good portion of what they were reminded of. You will never cease to come upon some act of treachery on their part, except for a few of them. Yet pardon them, and overlook. God loves good-doers.*

As this verse shows, poor morality displayed by someone else is no justification for displaying the same thing. Each individual is solely responsible to God for his actions. According to the Qur'an, acting with compassion, affection and proper morality in the face of someone else's bad behavior is a sign of superior morality that reveals the extent of a believer's devotion to God. One verse (10:26) reveals the reward that such a pleasing attitude will bring:

> *Those who do good will have the best, and more! Neither dust nor debasement will darken their faces. They are the Companions of the Garden, remaining in it timelessly, forever.*

Islam Forbids the Killing of Innocents

According to the Qur'an (5:32), it is a great sin to kill an innocent person, and anyone who does so will suffer great torment in the hereafter:

> *... If someone kills another person—unless it is in retaliation for someone else or for causing corruption in the earth—it is as if he had murdered all mankind. And if anyone gives life to another person, it is as if he had given life to all mankind. Our Messengers came to them with Clear Signs, but even after that, many of them committed outrages in the earth."*

This verse equals the killing of one innocent to slaughtering all of humanity! Another verse (25:68) expresses the importance that the faithful attach to life:

> *Those who do not appeal to any other deity besides God [alone]; nor kill any soul whom God has forbidden [them to] except with the right to do so; nor fornicate. Anyone who does so will incur a penalty.*

In yet another verse (6:151), God issues the following commandment:

Say: "Come, and I will recite to you what your Lord has forbidden for you": that you do not associate anything with Him; that you are good to your parents; that you do not kill your children because of poverty—We will provide for you and them; that you do not approach indecency – outward or inward; that you do not kill any person God has made inviolate – except with the right to do so. That is what He instructs you to do, so that hopefully, you will use your intellect.

Any Muslim who believes in God with a sincere heart, who scrupulously abides by His holy verses and fears suffering in the hereafter, will avoid harming even one other person. He knows that the Lord of Infinite Justice will suitably reward him for all his deeds. In one of the hadiths, our Prophet (may God bless him and grant him peace) listed the kinds of people who are not pleasing to God:

> *"Those who act cruelly and justly in the sacred lands, those who yearn for the ways of the ignorant, and those who wrongly shed human blood."*

Islam Commands People to Behave Justly

Islamic morality commands believers to behave justly and morally in making a decision, speaking, or working—in short, in every area of their lives. God's commandments in the Qur'an and the sunnah of our Prophet (may God bless him and grant him peace) describe that understanding of justice in great detail. With their warnings, all the Messengers revealed to us in the Qur'an brought peace and justice to all the communities where they were sent. The prophets helped lift cruelty and despotism from the shoulders of the community of the faithful. As God has revealed in one verse (10:47):

> *Every nation has a Messenger, and when their Messenger comes, everything is decided between them justly. They are not wronged.*

A most important feature of Islamic understanding of justice is that it commands justice at all times, even if one is dealing with a person who is near and dear. As God commands in another verse (4:135):

> *You who believe! Be upholders of justice, bearing witness for God alone, even against yourselves or your parents and relatives. Whether they are rich or poor, God is well able to look after them. Do not follow your own desires and deviate from the truth. If you twist or turn away, God is aware of what you do.*

That verse clearly states that to a believer, the wealth or social status of whomever one deals with is of no importance. What is important is fairness—no one should be treated unjustly—and to scrupulously implement the holy verses of God. In another verse (5:8), it is commanded:

You who believe! Show integrity for the sake of God, bearing witness with justice. Do not let hatred for a people incite you into not being just. Be just. That is closer to heedfulness. Heed God. God is aware of what you do.

In that verse, God orders the faithful to act justly always, even with their own enemies. No Muslim can make a spontaneous decision, based on the fact that the person he's dealing with has once harmed him or left him in a difficult situation. Even when he is a personal enemy, if the other side is genuinely in the wrong, any Muslim has the duty to respond with good will and to display the morality God has commanded. To believers, God has issued the following commandment (60:8): "God does not forbid you from being good to those who have not fought you in the religion or driven you from your homes, or from being just towards them. God loves those who are just." Here, He informs Muslims how their relationships with other people should be. These verses are the very foundation of a believer's attitude towards others, formed not by the nature of the people he is dealing with, but by God's revelations in the Qur'an. That is why Muslims with pure hearts always support what is right. Their determination on this matter is revealed in these terms (Qur'an, 7:181): "Among those We have created, there is a community who guide by the Truth and act justly according to it."

Other verses in the Qur'an on the subject of justice read:

God commands you to return to their owners the things you hold on trust and, when you judge between people, to judge with justice. How excellent is what God exhorts you to do! God is All-Hearing, All-Seeing. (4:58)

Say: "My Lord has commanded justice. Stand and face Him in every mosque and call on Him, making your religion sincerely His. As He originated you, so you will return." (7:29)

God commands justice and doing good and giving to relatives. And He forbids indecency and doing wrong and tyranny. He warns you so that hopefully, you will pay heed. (16:90)

All over the world, people are subjected to cruel treatment because of their race, language or skin color. Yet according to the view of justice as set out in the Qur'an, a person's ethnicity, race or gender are of no importance, because Islam maintains that all people are equal. Our Prophet's (may God bless him and grant him peace) words, *"All of you belong to one ancestry of Adam, and Adam was created out of clay,"*14 stress that there is no difference between people. Skin color, social status and wealth confer no superiority on anyone.

According to the Qur'an, one reason why different tribes, peoples, and nations were created is so that they "might come to know one another." All are servants of God and must come to learn one another's different cultures, languages, customs and abilities. One intent behind the existence of different nations and races is cultural wealth, not war and conflict. All true believers know that only godliness —in other words, the fear of God and faith in Him—can impart superiority. As God has revealed in the Qur'an (49:13):

Mankind! We created you from a male and female, and made you into peoples and tribes so that you might come to know each other. The noblest among you in God's sight is that one of you who best performs his duty. God is All-Knowing, All-Aware.

Elsewhere (30:22), He has revealed that:

Among His Signs is the creation of the heavens and earth and the variety of your languages and colours. There are certainly Signs in that for every being.

History offers many examples of the faithful behaving with complete justice towards other peoples, helping Islam grow with unbelievable speed over a wide area, taking in North Africa, the whole Middle East and even the Iberian Peninsula. By means of these conquests, the civility and tolerance of Islamic morality was spread to many races, nations, communities and individuals, bringing together millions in a bond of mutual tolerance, the likes of which had never been seen before. The renowned researcher Joel Augustus Rogers has examined the various races and the relationship between the black race and other countries. In his book *Sex and Race,* he describes Islam's influence on the world in these terms: One reason why Islam was able to survive so brightly for centuries is the almost complete absence in this religion of value-judgements based on race and class, the disregarding of the colour of an individual's skin or his social class and the fact that promotion to the highest levels of a community is based on ability alone... Islam established the greatest and at the same time the freest racial melting-pot in history, and the mixing of these races took place within the body of the most extensive empire the world has ever seen. At the height of its power the Islamic Empire stretched from Spain and central France in the West to India, China and the Pacific Ocean in the East, including Central Asia. The rulers of these extensive territories were of various colours. The colour of peoples' skins was even less important for Muslims than the colours of the flowers in a garden is to the flowers themselves.

Professor Hamilton Alexander Rossken Gibb is one of the world's foremost experts on Islam. In his book *Whither Islam?*, he describes the Islamic view of other races:

No other society has such a record of success uniting in an equality of status, of opportunity, and of endeavors so many and so various races of mankind... Islam has still the power to reconcile apparently irreconcilable elements of race and tradition. If ever the opposition of the great societies of East and West is to be replaced by cooperation, the mediation of Islam is an indispensable condition. Islamic morality aims at a society built on brotherhood and peace, freedom and security.

That is why all communities that come into contact with Islam have given up their oppressive, cruel and aggressive ways and have, instead, built peaceful and civilized societies. In their works, many Western historians have documented Islam's deep and positive affects on communities that came into contact with it. In *The Making of Humanity*, Professor Robert Briffault discusses the relationship between Western society and Islam:

> *The ideas that inspired the French Revolution and the Declaration of Rights, that guided the framing of the American Constitution and inflamed that struggle for independence in the Latin American countries [and elsewhere] were not inventions of the West. They find their ultimate inspiration and source in the Holy Quran.*

These extracts indicate how, down through the centuries, Islamic morality has taught people about peace, tolerance and justice. Nowadays, nearly everyone is seeking just such a model, and there is no reason why such a culture should not come about once again. All that is needed is people's desire to live by the morality of the Qur'an, starting with themselves and later, making efforts to convey it to others. When everyone, from the highest ranks to the very lowest, begins to implement the morality commanded in the Qur'an, they will become just, compassionate, tolerant, full of love, respectful and forgiving. That, in turn, will bring peace to all of society.

Islam Commands The Faithful to be Forgiving, Always

One important sign of compassion is a person's ability to forgive. In Verse 7:199, God calls upon His servants to "make allowances for people, command what is right, and turn away from the ignorant."

Some may find this attitude difficult, but in the sight of God, it will be well rewarded. Those caught up in anger may well refuse to forgive mistakes. But to the faithful, God has revealed that it is better to forgive and, in Verse 26:40, has recommended this morality:

The repayment of a bad action is one equivalent to it. But if someone pardons and puts things right, his reward is with God...

In another verse (26:43), God reveals, "But if someone is steadfast and forgives, that is the most resolute course to follow." Verse 24:22 emphasizes that this is a very superior form of morality:

Those of you possessing affluence and ample wealth should not make oaths that they will not give to their relatives and the very poor and those who have emigrated in the way of God. They should rather pardon and overlook. Would you not love God to forgive you? God is Ever-Forgiving, Most Merciful."

In these words, He encourages the faithful to consider their own positions when it comes to forgiveness. Because everyone wants God to forgive him, to protect and show him mercy, so do we hope that all others will excuse and forgive our mistakes. Therefore, God has commanded the faithful to treat others in the same way they would like to be treated themselves. That important responsibility encourages the faithful to be forgiving towards one another. Our Prophet (may God bless him and grant him peace) encouraged them in these words: *"That person is nearest to God, who pardons, when he has someone in his power, one who would have injured him."*

Believers, knowing that at any moment they may make a mistake, behave tolerantly towards others. Those verses in the Qur'an dealing with repentance make it clear that never making mistakes isn't as important as the determination never to repeat them. One of these verses (4:17) reads:

God accepts only the repentance of those who do evil in ignorance and then quickly repent after doing it. God turns towards such people. God is All-Knowing, All-Wise. Under conditions that reveal an individual's sincerity, the faithful behave forgivingly and compassionately towards one another. If he who has committed error sincerely repents having done so, they cannot judge him for his past deeds. Even when the faithful are totally in the right and the other completely in the wrong, still they have no compunction about forgiveness, because God recommends such behavior as an example of proper morality (3:134):

Those who give in times of both ease and hardship, those who control their rage and pardon other people—God loves the good-doers.

When it comes to forgiving, the faithful don't distinguish between great and small errors, nor do they tailor their view of forgiveness accordingly. Someone may have committed an error inflicting severe harm on others, great financial loss, even loss of life. Yet the faithful know everything happens by the permission of God, as part of His destiny. When it comes to such things, they therefore place themselves in the hands of God and feel no personal anger.

Alternatively, if someone transgresses this Qur'anic rule and exceeds the bounds set by God, only God can judge that person's behavior. It is never up to the faithful to judge—or refuse to forgive—anyone on any matter.

The truly sorry and repentant person will have his reward only in the sight of God. In many verses, God has revealed that apart from "associating partners to Him," He will forgive the errors of the faithful who repent sincerely. Since one man cannot know another's repentance, the faithful simply forgive in the manner God revealed to them. If the Qur'an has anything to say on a particular subject, they treat the person who has committed error in that light.

Islam Commands People To Behave Gently

God has infinite compassion, and is forgiving, protective and gentle toward believers. The Compassionate and Merciful has placed all the blessings in the universe at Man's disposal, supporting him with messengers to reveal the true path. He directs all men to be His sincere servants by means of His revelations, each of which is a guidepost to that path.

Our Lord is the *Halim* (the Clement), *Adl* (Lord of Infinite Justice), *'Afuw* (the Pardoner), *Asim* (the Protector), *Barr* (the Source of All Goodness), *Ghafir* (the Forgiver), *Hafiz* (the Protector), *Karim* (the Generous One), *Latif* (the Subtle One), *Muhsin* (Lord of Infinite Kindness), *Ra'uf* (the Compassionate), *Salam* (the Author of Safety), *Tawwab* (the Accepter of Repentance) and *Wahhab* (the Bestower).

Believers know that they are under our Lord's protection and are aware of His infinite goodness and kindness. For that reason, they are eager to become the kind of servants that are pleasing to Him, who merit His mercy, and Paradise. As we have seen, one characteristic distinguishing believers is they are full of love and compassion. A Muslim behaves very gently, always treating others kindly. God has offered our Prophet's (may God bless him and grant him peace) gentle nature as an example to all believers (3:159):

It is a mercy from God that you were gentle with them. If you had been rough or hard of heart, they would have scattered from around you. So pardon them and ask forgiveness for them, and consult with them about the matter. Then when you have reached a firm decision, put your trust in God. God loves those who put their trust in Him. That verse describes how our Prophet's (may God bless him and grant him peace) gentle, moral nature exerted a positive influence on people, whereby they grew even more devoted to him.

The Qur'an gives the gentle natures of other loving prophets as role models. One verse (11:87) recounts how, when the Prophet Shuayb (peace be upon him) was sent to the people of Midian, they told him, "... You are clearly the forbearing, the rightly-guided!" The superior morality of the Prophet Abraham (peace be upon him) is another example for everyone. The Qur'an tells us that he was sensitive, gentle and full of love. The verses in question read:

Abraham would not have asked forgiveness for his father, but for a promise he made to him, and when it became clear to him that he was an enemy of God, he renounced him. Abraham was tenderhearted and forbearing. (9:114)

Abraham was forbearing, compassionate, penitent. (11:75)

God has commanded his believers always to behave in a pleasant manner, to speak kindly, and to treat others well. His prophets behaved accordingly. For example, when the Prophet Musa (Moses) (peace be upon him) was about to go to Pharaoh, one of the most repressive and cruel rulers of all times, God called on Moses in these terms (20:42-44):

Go, you and your brother, with My Signs, and do not slacken in remembering Me. Go to Pharaoh; he has overstepped the bounds. But speak to him with gentle words so that hopefully, he will be reminded or show some fear.

These verses are an important reminder that everyone has a duty to live by the morality that the Qur'an reveals, and to adopt the morality of the prophets. The Qur'an proposes the following ideals for mankind: Love to all creatures God created; being kind and gentle in the best possible ways; always favoring compromise and tolerance; never speaking harshly, even under the most trying circumstances; making sacrifices happily and willingly; always desiring and seeking the best for others; pushing one's own personal desires to the background; wishing for others exactly what one wishes for oneself; being always quick to offer assistance in cases of need; and rejecting all forms of cruelty. That, no doubt, is exactly the ethical model that mankind is searching for.

Islam Supports Freedom of Belief

In matters of belief, Islam offers people complete freedom, and in the very clearest language. That has been so ever since Islam was first revealed, and forms the basis of today's Islamic morality. The verses on the subject (2:256) are perfectly clear:

There is no compulsion where religion is concerned. Right guidance has become clearly distinct from error. Anyone who rejects false gods and believes in God has grasped the Firmest Handhold, which will never give way. God is All-Hearing, All-Knowing.

According to Islam, people are free to choose whatever beliefs they wish, and nobody can oblige anyone else.

Yes, a Muslim has a duty to communicate Islam and explain the existence of God, to state that the Qur'an is the book of His revelation, that the Prophet Muhammad (may God bless him and grant him peace) was His messenger, to speak of the hereafter and the Day of Judgment and of the beauty of Islamic morality. Yet that duty is restricted to explaining the religion only.

In one verse (16:125), God informs our Prophet (may God bless him and grant him peace) that he is only a messenger:

Call to the way of your Lord with wisdom and fair admonition, and argue with them in the kindest way. Your Lord knows best who is misguided from His way. And He knows best who are guided.

Another verse (18:29) states, "... It is the truth from your Lord; so let whoever wishes believe and whoever wishes disbelieve..." In Verse 26:3, our Lord warns the Prophet (may God bless him and grant him peace), "Perhaps you will destroy yourself with grief because they will not become believers." He also issues His Prophet (may God bless him and grant him peace) this reminder (50:45):

We know best what they say. You are not a dictator over them. So remind, with the Qur'an, whoever fears My Threat.

People are free to choose correctly or wrongly. When Islam—the true path that God has revealed—is explained, they come to believe of their own free will, reaching this decision with no pressure being put on them.

If they make wrong choices, they will face its consequences in the hereafter. On this subject, Verse 10: 99 of the Qur'an contains the clearest command and reminder: "If your Lord had willed, all the people on the earth would have believed. Do you think you can force people to be believers?"

When one of the faithful explains matters, one person might come to believe straightaway, whereas another might adopt a mocking and aggressive attitude. One who follows his conscience might decide to devote his life to pleasing God, even while another, doing as the deniers did, might respond to those same kind words with wickedness. Yet his denial won't lead whoever issued the invitation to suffer or despair. In Verses 12: 103-104, God has stated, "But most people, for all your eagerness, are not believers. You do not ask them for any wage for it. It is only a reminder to all beings."

What's important is that no matter what reaction he meets with, the person who abides by the Qur'an keeps on displaying the kind of morality that is pleasing to God, refuses to make any concessions on it, and leaves matters in God's hands. God has told us that His religion is to be explained in the most pleasing manner. In the words of the Qur'an (29:46):

> *Argue with the People of the Book only in the kindest way—except in the case of those of them who do wrong–saying, "We believe in what has been sent down to us and what was sent down to you. Our God and your God are one and we submit to Him."*

We must not forget that every event, large or small, takes place according to a destiny created by God. He reveals the true path to anyone invited to believe in Him. For that reason, the faithful feel no distress at the behavior of those who reject Him. The Qur'an gives several examples. In Verse 18:6, God tells our Prophet (may God bless him and grant him peace) not to be distressed when those whom he calls on to believe refuse to do so: "Perhaps you may destroy yourself with grief, chasing after them, if they do not believe in these words." Another verse (28:56) reads, "You cannot guide those you would like to, but God guides those He wills. He has best knowledge of the guided."

That means that whatever invitations an individual issues, all his pleasant words, and every detail he goes into can make an effect only by the will of God. A believer's only responsibility is to call people to the Qur'an. He cannot be blamed for atheists' refusal to amend their ways, nor with how they will earn the torments of hell for themselves. In Verse 2:119, our Lord told our Prophet (may God bless him and grant him peace), "We have sent you with the Truth, bringing good news and giving warning. Do not ask about the inhabitants of the Blazing Fire."

God has given mankind both reason and a conscience. His messengers and the divine books revealed to them have shown the true path, and people are responsible for their own choices. Islamic morality can be lived only by a sincere decision to do so—by surrendering oneself to God and listening to one's conscience, which always commands one to do what is right. It is a total violation of Islamic morality to force anyone to believe, because what matters is an individual's surrendering himself to God with all his heart and believing sincerely. If any system obliges people to have faith, then those "converts" will become religious only out of fear. The only acceptable way to live a religion is within an environment that leaves one's conscience completely free. This is what God revealed to our Prophet (may God bless him and grant him peace) (88:21-26):

So remind them! You are only a reminder. You are not in control of them. But as for anyone who turns away and disbelieves, God will punish him with the Greatest Punishment. Certainly it is to Us they will return Then their Reckoning is Our concern.

It's worth emphasizing that Islam leaves people free to make their own choices regarding religion and commands them to respect other religions. Even if someone believes in what the Qur'an describes as superstition, still he can live in peace and security in Muslim lands and freely perform his own religious obligations. In Verses 109:2-6, God commanded our Prophet (may God bless him and grant him peace) to tell those who denied Him:

"I do not worship what you worship, and you do not worship what I worship. Nor will I worship what you worship, nor will you worship what I worship. You have your religion, and I have my religion." Under the morality of Islam, everyone is free to carry out the obligations in accord with his own particular belief. Nobody can prevent any others from performing their particular religious duties, nor can he oblige them to worship in the manner he desires. That violates the morality of Islam, and is unacceptable to God. In the Islamic model of society emerges in which everyone is free to worship and perform the obligations attendant upon his particular chosen beliefs. The Qur'an (22:40) describes monasteries, churches, synagogues, and the places of worship of the Peoples of the Book as all under God's protection:

... If God had not driven some people back by means of others, [then] monasteries, churches, synagogues and mosques, where God's name is mentioned much, would have been pulled down and destroyed. God will certainly help those who help Him— God is All-Strong, Almighty.

Our Prophet's (may God bless him and grant him peace) life is full of such examples. When Christians came to see him pray in his own mosque, he left it for them to use. That kind of tolerance was maintained during the times of the caliphs who succeeded the Prophet (may God bless him and grant him peace). After Damascus was captured, a church that had been turned into a mosque was divided into two, so that Christians might worship in one half and Muslims in the other.

"ORNAMENT AND CRIME" AND RELIGION

In 1908 the Austrian Architect and thinker Adolf Loos delivered an influential paper laying out the principles for what became the modernist ethic. Who, asked Loos, in this day and age wilfully decorates themselves and their environments with unnecessary decoration and ornamentation in the manner of the undeveloped child or the uncivilized Papuan? Only two groups: those with criminal tendencies and the degenerate aristocrat. To be modern, to be progressive, to be cultured, to be civilized was and is to live your life with control, order and discipline. It is to live your life without the support and excess and distraction of unnecessary ornamentation; and that ornamentation, post-Nietzsche, included God. Loos' claim was that unnecessary ornamentation was a sign of arrested cultural development, the expression of a primitive outlook, the signal of a criminal tendency or the mark of a degenerate aristocrat. This resulted in unnecessary ornamentation being labelled a sign of deviancy. For Loos, the child or "the Papuan" may be free to scrawl and decorate because they had not yet "come of age" in either a physical or cultural sense. Those who lived in a mature, civilized culture having achieved adulthood (culturally and developmentally) would only unnecessarily disorder their world through deviance. While Nietzsche had proclaimed the death of God some twenty years earlier and Marx had made him an opiate, Loos now made him an unnecessary ornament. God was no longer the great architect, the one who ordered the world. Rather, in an act of Gnostic reversal, God was seen at that who disordered humanity. What Loosian modernism does is introduce the possibility of a modernist secular fundamentalism that reads "the world" as it "literally is".

Modernism is an act of utopian "progressive" secularism, an attempt to order that which God was seen to disorder: an act of humanism over and against religion. It is the secular apocalypse, the attempt of living in an immanent kingdom of the absent God – as Thomas Altizer, prominent 1960s proponent of the death of God would claim:

If there is one clear portal to the twentieth century, it is a passage through the death of God, the collapse of any meaning or reality lying beyond the newly discovered radical immanence of modern man, an immanence dissolving even the memory of the shadow of transcendence.

Altizer states that out of this has "come a new chaos" of Nietzschean-forecast nihilism. Loos' title was wilfully mistranslated by those of Purist sympathy in the France of *Le E'spirt Nouveau* as "Ornament *is* Crime". This act changed the nature of modernism as those who followed the Purist manifesto came to assert a form of sub-Nietzschean nihilism. If the Loosian aesthetic is one of less, the Purist aesthetic is one of imposed loss. Loos looked to banish what was perceived as the unnecessary; his is a reduction in the name of culture and civilization, an assertion of a humanist, modern, progressive ethic. The Purist, in contrast, came to reduce for reduction's sake; theirs is a machine aesthetic in that technology is the*raison d'etre*. While the Purist ethos is that of white purity (and control), the Loosian desire to control is not far removed from that of Marinetti and the Furturists who worship at the altar of secular modernism.

THE CHALLENGE OF FUTURISM

The banishing of ornament, the signal of God as deviance, the flat roof of an immanent transcendence, the Purist white wall, each sought not only to banish the chaos of *fin de siecle* ostentation and the horrors of World War One, but were also an attempt to embrace the new hope of technology and a Futurist inspired machine age. In Marinetti's Futurist Manifesto: "The New Religion – Morality of Speed", speed is the new location and expression of divinity. Marinetti, viewing the Great War as "liberating", expresses a Futurist morality that: "...will defend man from the decay caused by slowness, by memory, by analysis, by repose and habit. Human energy centupled by speed will master time and space". This creates a new secular religious response: "If prayer means communication with the divinity, running at high speed is a prayer. Holiness of wheels and rails. One must kneel on the tracks to pray to the divine velocity". This also means that "one must persecute, lash, torture all those who sin against speed". Futurism deepens and extends Loosian modernist fundamentalism raising it to a kind of secular religion. Out of this Marinetti expresses a new Futurist-Purist doctrine of modernity:

Speed, having as its essence the intuitive synthesis of every force in movement, is naturally *pure*. Slowness, having, having as its essence the rational analysis of every exhaustion in repose, is naturally*unclean*. After the destruction of the antique good and the antique evil, we create a new good, speed, and a new evil, slowness. Speed = synthesis of every courage in action. Aggression and warlike. Slowness = analysis of every stagnant prudence. Passive and pacifistic. Speed = scorn of obstacles, desire for the new and unexplored. Modernity and hygiene. Slowness = arrest, ecstasy, immobile adoration of obstacles, nostalgia for the already seen, idealization of exhaustion and rest, pessimism about the unexplored. Rancid romanticism of the world, wandering poet and long-haired, bespectacled dirty philosopher.

Marinetti's linking of speed, destruction, modernity and war as the hygiene against the unclean slowness of that seen to be in decay sits at the heart of religious terror. This is an interesting overlap between the secular modernist fundamentalist of a century ago and the modern religious terrorist. Baudrillard, comments on this in way that makes the link explicit noting:

...that generation you see everywhere, in all latitudes, running, jogging or walking, and high on phobic concern for their bodies. This is the New International Hygienic Order...This is the hygiene of the Assassins. (The self-terrorism of the West is therefore just another version of the terror that seeks to eliminate the West in the name of a religious hygiene).

Marinetti's Futurism can be read in tandem with Loos prophetical statement: "I have discovered the following truth and present it here to the world: *cultural evolution is equivalent to the removal of ornament from articles in daily use*". This Loosian truth signals the modernist desire to control and order all that is disordered: religion, sex and ornament. All are to be removed from daily use – all (as ornament) are no longer "organically linked" nor "an expression" of our (modern) culture. Loos links the absence of ornament to a religious view by articulating what is clearly the salvific status of non-ornamentation. The absence of ornament is that which will enable humanity to create the city of fulfilment where, having won through to lack of ornament: "...the streets of the town will glisten like white walls. Like Zion, the holy city, the metropolis of heaven. Then we shall have fulfilment". As Baudrillard notes of the "immanence" of modernity:

The whole movement of modernity, its negative destiny, lies in the fact of transcribing all that was of the order of the imaginary, the dream, the ideal and utopia into technical and operational reality.

Those who live in this new Zion of secular modernity are aristocrats – not the ornamented degenerate aristocrats Loos is opposed to, but a form of Gnostic-elite; aristocrats who are evolved beyond those who have need for ornamentation. Loos tellingly uses the example of an old woman with a roadside shrine. He claims that the revolutionary confronted with this would challenge her with the words "there is no God"; but the Loosian atheist aristocrat "raises his hat on passing a church". This means religion is seen as a form of cultural evolution – in a sense it is "the opiate of the masses". Not being a revolutionary, the Loosian aristocratic modern has no desire to tear down the ornament and attempt to make "aristocrats" of those who are as yet unable and unprepared to adopt such a position. Those who have moved on from the peasant world – that is, those who have left the village mentality and existence behind and become urban (the Loosian location of modernity) – will only wilfully turn to unnecessary ornamentation if they are degenerate aristocrats or have criminal tendencies. The church deserves true aristocratic modern respect and good manners for what it symbolizes – but the true aristocratic modern is beyond needing it. For only the revolutionary will wish to erase the past, the aristocrat is aware that it can be and always is being supplanted.

TOWARD A LOOSIAN THEORY OF RELIGION IN MODERNITY

If we look back over the century of modernity, we can re-read it as a Loosian battle where religion comes to be viewed as a form of ornament. Contemporary religious fundamentalism is another form of Loosian-like move against ornament, but it is an inverted move, whereby the modern unornamented world is seen as a form of unnecessary ornamentation. In response, modern religious fundamentalism often retreats to what Loos or a secular modern would see as a world of ornamentation, a costume of literalism which draws on pre-modern belief – but for very modern purposes:

O ye who believe! When ye meet a force, be firm, and call Allah in remembrance much (and often); That ye may prosper. God, who sent the book unto the prophet, who drives the clouds, and who defeated the enemy parties, defeat them and make us victorious over them. Our Lord! Give us good in this world and good in the Hereafter and save us from the torment of the Fire! [Koranic verse]. May God's peace and blessings be upon Prophet Muhammad and his household.

The New Age, seen from a secular modern Loosian viewpoint, can be understood as the return of unnecessary ornamentation. In a physical manner, buildings, lives and bodies became newly unnecessarily ornamented – all are costumed, tattooed, decorated. In a manner similar to modern religious fundamentalism, the interior *Raumplan* of spirituality became inverted over and against the white walls of modernity. Religion and secularity are now both seen as forms that the necessary ornamentation of postmodern spirituality and the New Age reacted against. Conversely, the return of conservative religious movements signals a reaction against such decoration. Viewing both the inverted interior spirituality of the New Age and the lingering late modern secularity as forms of unnecessary ornamentation, modern (and postmodern) religious conservatism attempts to both banish what is seen as unnecessary and, paradoxically, enforce a modernist-derived order of necessary ornamentation. This "soft modernism" can hold together both Peter Berger's desecularization and Steve Bruce's continued secularization theses. Both can view the other as forms of costume that limit the Loosian pursuit of the expression of "our time" – they are types of "bad form". Therefore, what sits at the heart of the modern condition (whether modern, postmodern, anti-modern or soft modern) is the question of the necessity or otherwise of ornament; and the continuing, debatable, contestable question of what exactly constitutes ornament when, as Loos demanded, we "think and feel in the spirit of our time".

RETHINKING TERROR, RELIGION AND MODERNITY

To respond to the *religare* of terror in modernity, we could turn to the Loosian response to the roadside shrine: the confrontation with that which posits an alternative to secular modernity. Unfortunately, we tend to respond like the revolutionary and see it (the *religare* of terror) as an affront. Rather, we could view it for what is actually is, the survival of religion *as a provocation* to the modern world, seeking affirmation in and from the attempt to destroy it. An alternative for secular modernism is to remember what Nietzsche claimed caused the death of God: not the frontal attacks and dismissals, but rather, in the end, the turn of indifference. Thus, instead of the current ongoing exchange of affirmation in which both the fundamentalist terrorist and those who respond symbolically affirm each other, we could seek to adopt a position of indifference. This of course does not mean fundamentalist terror will fade away completely, but it could lead to its marginalization from the everyday, whereby terror is located as sectarian. Every response to terror actually affirms the destruction that takes place as being necessary for it and its claimants to be noticed.

Here we can look to what Brian Tamaki has done with a small (7000 strong) sectarian religious movement, Destiny Church, in New Zealand. Understanding the importance of the mass media to articulate (a media-derived) legitimacy – to be seen is to exist – he moved into the public media, creating a deliberately provocative presence on both television and the internet , by opposing the proposed extension of civil unions to homosexuals and the reform of prostitution laws. His central message decries moral and spiritual decay, calling the nation back to a proposed theocracy of the kingdom, allied with a strongly protestant gospel of prosperity. What makes Tamaki important is his recognition that public appearance is, in a postmodern-inflected world of image and spectacle, *itself* an act of self-legitimacy. To appear on television, in a localized version of American televangelism, even if within the early-morning dead-zone of church-funded "infomercial" preaching, is to recognize that it is the *appearance* on television that creates the real for those uninitiated in post-structuralist semiotics. For those able to decode such action, his infomercial televangelism is a simulacra; but for those who do not decode, this becomes a form of "real presence". He "made real" his presence, in what was a carefully stage-managed "return to the real" – but as simulacra that was based – albeit vigorously denied – in good modernist, futurist fashion, on the hyper-real mythic history of Mussolini's act of legitimacy: his fascist march on Rome of 28 October 1922.

Tamaki's simulacrum of this occurred on 23 August 2004 with a rally of his Destiny Church followers down the main street of the capital, Wellington, culminating in a march on Parliament, accompanied by body-guards and lead by a crowd of predominantly Maori and Pacific-island men, in black t-shirts, waving their fists and chanting "enough is enough". This courting of public notice by partaking in what was a pseudo-event, a spectacle, was an act of public terror with its fascistic overtone and black-shirted associations of masculinity, power and the war-dance confrontation of a mass haka. It worked – the indifference of the general public and the media to Brian Tamaki lasted only as long as he and his cult were *not* a pseudo-event, were *not* a public spectacle, as long as they did *not* evoke a response of fear that was out of all proportion to the size of his organization.

In the months since his pseudo-spectacle he has become a form of alternative legitimate voice of religion in New Zealand – the one that the media turn to because of the "terror" of his provocative stance. To counter the hyper-real terror of Bin-laden or Tamaki is actually to seek to control the reproduction of the hyper-real – the circulation and mass-media production of the image. Mass-media provides a hyper-real "*religare*" – a binding together, a communal presentation and affirmation as to the efficacy and indeed legitimacy not only of the circulation and presentation of the event, but of the event itself. Yet conversely, to seek to limit the spectacle is to enforce the control of image and truth that is sought by the terrorist.

In effect, terrorism occurs and is "justified" when the spectacle is reported and repeated. This is because it is in the *religare* of the mass media that terrorism really occurs. It frees the act of terror and intimidation from its physical location in the event and makes it national – and increasingly transnational. This means we now "believe" in terror because we respond to its representation: that is, to its image. It has actually become a form of *religare* that binds us all together – "we believe in terror" – and in our belief we give it a form of efficacy and legitimacy. Yet is important that we remember that a *religare* binds different groups together in different ways. Therefore, if religion arises in a multiplicity of ways from *religare* (that which binds us together) then terrorism itself has become a cause of – and expression of – a new global religion that is basing itself on a theory of exchange and sacrifice to institute an alternative modernity. Or rather, to institute alternative forms of modernity that challenge what is seen as the chaos occasioned not only by secular modernity but also the conversant multiplicity of chaos that arose out of postmodernism and its turn to the multiplicities of others and the pluralism of truth and identity. Terrorism is a hyper-real apocalyptic event that provides an alternative teleology. In fact, *after* the event we now live in terror of the "pseudo-event": not that which *has* occurred, but rather something that we believe *may* or *will* "occur". In many ways we are living in our own version of millennial apocalyptic cults, seeking an *eschaton* that will affirm that our hopes and fears are correct.

THE CHANGING NATURE OF MODERN TERRORISM

Australians are confronted as never before by terrorism. Our sense of vulnerability to attack is new. So are the force, global reach and ambition of the distinctive threat from transnational terrorism now perpetrated in the name of a Muslim extremist cause. Understanding these changes is the first challenge. That is not easy for a nation neither expecting nor used to being targeted like this. But it is essential to maintaining an effective national response.

Open and pluralist societies like ours are now confronted in fundamental ways. These terrorists seek to undermine our security and prosperity. They feel threatened by the values and aspirations that make us an open, tolerant and creative country with a confident future. Australians know that preserving these qualities is vital to our health as a community in all its diversity. It is central to our resilience in the face of this threat. It is the key to our appreciation of the many Muslims who are part of us and to the continuing strength of our links with Muslim-populated countries overseas.

But, naturally enough, we struggle to come to grips with the dimensions of contemporary terrorism. It is not easily understood as a nationalist or political campaign such as Irish, Basque or Tamil separatist terrorism. It bears little resemblance to familiar examples in the public memory when Australians were occasionally incidental victims. While these previously known forms of terror continue, they are peripheral to the nature and scale of the security challenge Australia now confronts. We find it hard to comprehend the rhetoric of these terrorists, who condemn anyone who does not agree with their approach to Islam. For us, the terrorists' assertions of an international conspiracy to repress and defeat Islam makes no sense. It has no connection to everyday reality, however much we understand and sympathise with the plight of Muslim and other communities in distress. We cannot easily relate their assertions to a territorial dispute, political ideology or historical injustice. For Australia, these are no longer issues of global distance - or ones that can be left for others to contemplate. The terrorists' challenge is now direct and immediate. Their goals confront us. They want to drive the West's presence and influence from Muslim lands. They want to replace governments there with regimes that reflect their extremist interpretation of Islam. Ultimately, they want to reshape the international order to accommodate a pan-Islamic super-state. Their objectives are inherently political regardless of their religious trappings. To achieve this they are set on intimidating those who do not support them - Muslim and non-Muslim alike.

For the first time, Australians are having to come to terms with a security threat neither constrained nor defined by national borders, traditional power structures or formed armies - one that is neither dependent on sponsoring nation states, nor responsive to traditional deterrence. Rather, it is driven by an ideology that is inaccessible to reason, and with objectives that cannot be negotiated.

DEFINITION OF AN ACT OF TERRORISM

There is no internationally accepted definition of terrorism. Not even the United Nations has been able to achieve consensus on this contentious issue. The old adage that 'one man's freedom fighter is another man's terrorist' goes to the root of the ongoing debate. Individual states, therefore, have been compelled to develop their own definitions for the purposes of enacting legislation to counter the threat.

In Australia, what constitutes an act of terrorism is defined in Commonwealth legislation. The Criminal Code Act 1995 states that a terrorist act means an action or threat of action where the action causes certain defined forms of harm or interference and the action is done or the threat is made with the intention of advancing a political, religious or ideological cause. Further, the Act states that 'the action is done or the threat is made with the intention of:

i. coercing, or influencing by intimidation, the government of the Commonwealth or a State, Territory or foreign country, or part of a State, Territory or foreign country; or
ii. intimidating the public or a section of the public; and where the action
    (a) causes serious harm that is physical harm to a person; or
    (b) causes serious damage to property; or
    (c) causes a person's death; or
    (d) endangers a person's life, other than the life of the person taking the action; or
    (e) creates a serious risk to the health or safety of the public or a section of the public; or
    (f) seriously interferes with, seriously disrupts, or destroys, an electronic system including, but not limited to: (i) an information system; or (ii) a telecommunications system; or (iii) a financial system; or (iv) a

> system used for the delivery of essential government services; or (v) a system used for, or by, an essential public utility; or (vi) a system used for, or by, a transport system.

The Criminal Code makes it an offence if a person commits a terrorist act, provides or receives training connected with terrorist acts, possesses a thing connected with terrorist acts, collects or makes documents likely to facilitate terrorist acts, or does any act in preparation for or planning of terrorist acts. The penalty for engaging in a terrorist act is life imprisonment.

The penalty for other terrorism-related offences outlined above ranges from ten years to life imprisonment.

We have to adjust to a threat that is not only alien, but unconventional and unpredictable. Its presence is largely unseen and unknown. But it commands frequent headlines and commitment of our resources on a national scale. We seek to protect and defend ourselves in the knowledge that there can be no guarantees from successful attack in open societies like ours. This is an 'asymmetric' threat with disproportionate advantage to the smaller but determined aggressor operating beyond any accepted rules of behaviour.

Our exposure is magnified by globalisation. An interdependent world allows terror to be transmitted to remote victims. Borders and distance offer little protection to a terrorist enterprise proficient at using technology to recruit, communicate and operate transnationally. With more extensive international interests than ever before, we must increasingly work with international partners to protect ourselves. Our economy is linked to global systems that are exposed to terrorist sabotage. The networks we rely on for transportation, energy, finance and communication can be protected, but not made immune. More so than in the past, Australia's people, its economic links and its contributions to international security and prosperity have spread to parts of the world where the terrorist danger is even more direct - and where we have less control over how we are protected.

We must adapt to living in a more dangerous world. These new terrorists have used aircraft as weapons. They have used public transport to kill indiscriminately. They have made bombs from materials used in farming and mining. They have experimented with chemical and biological weapons. They are limited only by imagination and opportunity.

And we must adapt to these harsh new realities in a changed strategic environment. These changes began with the end of the Cold War and the new strategic uncertainties that followed. The emergence of the United States as the pre-eminent military and economic power remains the overwhelmingly dominant factor in the global strategic balance today. The balance it struck with other big powers brought advantages and opportunities for countries like Australia, open and capable, and committed to the benefits of international cooperation in an increasingly globalised world.

The deadly and unprovoked terrorism of 11 September 2001 has further recast these international settings - for the United States, Australia and the broader international community. Not only did a potent new enemy demonstrate strategic reach, but it wrought unprecedented damage on the homeland of the world's biggest power, exposing unimagined vulnerabilities. In doing so, it instantly created an adversary determined not only to remove terrorist enemies but to confront existing and potential security threats with great vigour and resolve.

The menace to Australia of weapons proliferation has also been compounded by this new form of terror. We must address the possibility that these transnational terrorists may acquire and use chemical, biological, radiological or even nuclear capability. This prospect presents us with dangers of grave proportions. These twin dangers remain key drivers of United States strategic policy, as they do for Australia and other key partners.

The asymmetric nature of the threat posed to Australia demands a disproportionate scale of response. National security is higher on the Australian Government's policy agenda than it has been for decades. The national resources deployed to counter the threat are major - and still growing.

The transnational terrorist capacity to inflict harm disproportionately, without restraint or warning, means Australia's response must be broad-spectrum. It has demanded adjustment to the conventional defence posture we maintain to fight conventional wars. And it has put a new cast on our broader security policies, including our approaches to other transnational issues, such as people smuggling, money laundering and organised crime. Good intelligence has become an even more vital element to our protection. So too has better law enforcement and improved counter-terrorist legislation.

Our counter-terrorism response has meant changes to the environment in which Australians lead their everyday lives. Protection against terrorism is essential to preserving the right of each Australian to security.

This allows us to participate freely in a society based on shared values of freedom and respect for the dignity of human life. We need to recognise this - and to make sure the inevitable cost of our preparedness does not also tax our values, our tolerance and our fundamental way of life.

AUSTRALIA'S PAST EXPERIENCE OF TERRORISM

The extent to which Australia has been affected by terrorism significantly changed with the 11 September 2001 attacks in the United States and the Bali bombings of 12 October 2002, in which a combined total of 98 Australians were killed.

In the past, few Australians had been killed as a result of terrorism. Most of those few were killed overseas and not deliberately targeted as Australians. Two Australians killed by the Irish Republican Army (IRA) in the Netherlands in 1990 were the victims of mistaken identity, the terrorists believing them to be British.

In Australia, past acts of terrorism have generally involved attacks against foreign interests - including those of Turkey, Iran, India and Israel. Although Australians were killed in these attacks, Australia was not itself the target. Rather, Australia was the venue for the expression of extremist violence directed at other nations' governments in reaction to events overseas. The bombing of the Hilton Hotel in Sydney on 13 February 1978, in which three Australians died, was targeted at Indian officials attending a Commonwealth Heads of Government Meeting (CHOGM).

Australia is now a target of transnational extremist-Muslim terrorism and Australians are being targeted overseas. The threat Australia faces is enduring. It requires a sustained national response. While we have already made many changes in order to better protect ourselves, we may need to make more. We can expect our national resilience to be put to future tests. The dynamic nature of the threat will continue to demand heightened awareness and vigilance of all Australians.

A New Kind Of Foe

Transnational terrorism confronts us with a new kind of foe. It is diverse, complex, adaptable and continually evolving. It is uncompromising, global in reach, and its operations are highly networked. Its approach is asymmetric, using unconventional and unexpected means to wreak maximum damage. It is of a previously unknown scale. It is being perpetrated in the name of an extremist Muslim cause but it is a type which, in a future world order, could be applied by others. It signals a new era of conflict.

ASYMMETRIC WARFARE

Terrorism is a form of asymmetric warfare: an approach that uses non-traditional methods to counter an opponent's conventional military superiority. It uses unconventional means to attack unexpected targets. It turns perceived strengths into weaknesses and exploits vulnerabilities to deadly effect. It may also involve the capability to attack an adversary with means for which they are unprepared or incapable of responding in kind.

The new transnational terrorists have adopted a strategy that responds to the unprecedented dominance of the United States and other highly developed Western countries in all aspects of conventional military power. The terrorists therefore seek means other than conventional warfare with which to confront the West.

Terrorism pits clandestine methods against open societies. It uses small teams whose operations are cheap, but demands a response that is enormous in scale and expensive in resources. It exploits the foundations of civil society, such as principles of human rights, efforts to avoid civilian casualties, and adherence to the rule of law - including the laws of armed conflict.

The terrorists' asymmetric approach demands a sustained, comprehensive and coordinated response at national and international levels, incorporating a wide range of Australia's assets.

An Extreme Ideology

As with most previously known forms of terrorism, extremist ideology is the driver. The threat we face today is driven by an extremist interpretation of Islam. This form of extremism is absolutist. It leaves no room for compromise and it seeks no place at the negotiating table. It uses violence to signal its committed path to a final end. It is not bound by social norms, laws or values.

These terrorists justify and feed their ideology through skilful exploitation of dynamics within mainstream societies. They use adverse political, social and economic conditions as a rallying cry to recruit and motivate their members. They exploit distrust of the West and feelings of humiliation and anger. They invoke events that resonate with most Muslims, such as the Israeli-Palestinian conflict and the war in Iraq, as justifications for their ideological cause. They are also driven by a need for continued action. Militant jihad - as interpreted by transnational extremist-Muslim terrorists - is a process of constant struggle against their enemies. They therefore seek to constantly strike their enemies to maintain the momentum of their cause.

Global Goals and Scope of Operations

Although they act in the name of a religious cause, these terrorists have political goals. They want ultimately to establish a caliphate - a pan-Muslim super-state that unites all Muslims and all lands now or ever part of the Islamic world. This includes the Middle East and North Africa from the Red Sea to the Atlantic coast. It includes Andalusia in Spain, parts of the Balkans, Central and South Asia through to the Indonesian archipelago, and parts of the Philippines in South-East Asia.

They seek to drive the West's presence and influence from these lands. They oppose governments in Muslim countries - criticising them for being 'un-Islamic' and therefore illegitimate - and seek to replace them with ones that accord with their extremist views. Their operations are global in scope. They do not limit their attacks to previous theatres of 'militant jihad'. Al Qaida's so-called fatwa (religious decree) of February 1998 called on supporters everywhere to attack the United States and its allies - including civilian targets - anywhere in the world. Terrorism previously directed against Western interests in other countries has since spread to Western countries themselves.

This illustrates the global reach of the new terrorism since 1992. The network of these terrorists is also global. There are extremist-Muslim terrorist elements and supporters - with varying degrees of connection - in the Middle East, South, Central and South-East Asia, North Africa, Europe and North America.

This network extends to Australia. Some terrorist groups have small numbers of supporters in Australia and some Australians have trained in extremist camps in Afghanistan, Pakistan and Kashmir. We know the terrorists have considered planning attacks in Australia. The new enemy also recruits globally. That means Western countries are a source. There is no simple 'terrorist profile' based on nationality or ethnicity.

TERRORIST OPERATIONS - SOME FEATURES

A Network of Networks

Transnational terrorist operations are highly networked. Small, dispersed teams and individuals work semi-autonomously to achieve a general goal. Leaders communicate their intentions periodically and non-specifically, including through public pronouncements.

Groups are affiliated through both formal and informal links. Decision-making and operations are often highly decentralised.

Al Qaida is the most visible manifestation of the terrorist threat, but the new transnational terrorists are not organised as a hierarchy with Al Qaida at their head. The threat comes from a 'network of networks', made up of dispersed groups and movements. Some of these groups are themselves a network, with limited central command and control. The autonomy of small teams within this loose structure helps the terrorists survive. Even if the heart of a network is destroyed, the small teams can survive, operate independently, and tap into another part of the network. When a terrorist group is destroyed or its capability degraded, other groups or teams can take over their functions relatively easily.

Networked operations make it more difficult to identify indicators and forewarnings of terrorist attacks. They also make it harder to target the threat. But understanding how the networks operate is critical to devising a strategy to deal with them.

A Skilled Enemy

Many of the methods applied by these transnational terrorists are sophisticated. The New York and Washington attacks of 11 September 2001 showed an ability to plan, coordinate and execute multiple, simultaneous attacks. We have seen further examples in East Africa, Riyadh, Casablanca and Madrid.

Many are technically skilled, intelligent and educated people. Some have received professional military training, including in Western forces. Many more have had professional instruction in advanced terrorist methods in training facilities in Central, South and South-East Asia and the Middle East. They are good at planning and logistics. They use modern technology to their advantage. Their security practices are also well developed. Their cell tructure, combined with good counter-intelligence tradecraft, keep their identities, operations and methods secret. Not everyone in a team knows the plan or the mission (e.g. the target and the exact method or timings). This is sometimes only revealed at the last moment - lessening the risk that the exposure of part of a plan, or the capture of one terrorist, will undermine an operation.

They are often knowledgeable about Western countries, customs and culture. Some were born or live in the countries they target. Their knowledge and familiarity helps them maximise physical harm and psychological impact. It also allows them to live in target countries without arousing suspicion and plan for terrorist attacks undetected.

They use converts to Islam for terrorist operations - including those from European backgrounds. People from such backgrounds can attract less security scrutiny than those who meet certain nationality and ethnic profiles used in some countries.

Above all, the new transnational terrorists are patient. They strike at times and by means of their own choosing. They conduct meticulous long-term planning. There may be years between conceiving and conducting a major attack. Plans that in the past proved impractical are often revisited. Targets are pursued with great persistence, and planning is developed and refined - we know this from examples like the World Trade Centre in New York, which was first targeted in 1993.

Resources are sometimes moved to target locations well before an attack - in some cases years ahead. These terrorists may infiltrate and obtain the necessary documents, vehicles, weapons and explosives well in advance.

The Targets of Terrorism

These new terrorists deliberately attack civilian targets to cause, where they can, mass casualties. The September 11 attacks in the United States caused human casualties on an unprecedented scale for a terrorist attack. The 2002 Bali attacks presented terrorism of a scale previously unknown in our region. The more recent Madrid attacks deliberately targeted a crowded urban public transport system. Based on recent experience and terrorist statements, we can expect more attempted mass casualty attacks in the future.

As defences improve, the terrorists have demonstrated a willingness to widen their focus from well-protected, or 'hard', targets to also include less well-protected, or 'soft', targets. 'Soft' targets such as restaurants, bars and clubs also afford the potential for causing mass casualties.

'Hard' targets, however, remain attractive to terrorists. Destroying well-protected high-value targets - such as diplomatic missions and military facilities - has great symbolic value. Table 1 illustrates the scale of impact of global terrorism since 1992 in terms of loss of human life. We know that terrorists have also sought to target critical infrastructure in a deliberate attempt to cause maximum damage and disruption to facilities and services vital to a nation's government and economy. Recent attacks in

Saudi Arabia are examples of how the terrorists have targeted the oil industry sector. These attacks have served the multiple purposes of singling-out and killing Westerners, undermining confidence in the Saudi economy, and having a global economic impact on oil prices.

CRITICAL INFRASTRUCTURE

The Australian Government defines 'critical infrastructure' as physical facilities, supply chains, information technologies and communications networks which, if destroyed, degraded or rendered unavailable for an extended period, would significantly impact on the social or economic well-being of the nation, or affect Australia's ability to conduct national defence and ensure national security.

Critical infrastructure includes:

- communications (telecommunications, electronic media, postal services)
- finance (banking, insurance, trading exchanges
- transport (air, sea, road, rail
- utilities (water, waste water)
- energy (oil, gas, electricity)
- health (hospitals, public health, laboratories)
- food supply (bulk production, bulk storage)
- manufacturing (defence industry, heavy industry, chemicals)
- government services (parliament, defence, intelligence, law enforcement, fire services, also including foreign missions in Australia
- community assets (national icons, buildings, sports facilities).

Terrorist Methods

Transnational terrorism is highly lethal, using old and new weapons to devastating effect. Advances in weapons technology are making them more lethal than ever before. The range of weapons at the terrorists' disposal is wide and increasing.

TERRORISTS HAVE GREATER LETHALITY

Transnational terrorists have access to weapons of unprecedented lethality. Access to a vast array of new, highly lethal weapons is spreading, aided by the transfer of knowledge, funds and weapons systems internationally. These include anti-aircraft and anti-armour missiles, and enhanced-blast explosive devices. Many of these weapons are cheap, readily available and can be carried, concealed and operated by a single individual. The terrorists have already used some of these weapons.

The use of hand-held missiles to attack aircraft is an example of the greater lethality able to be posed by a single individual with sufficient training in their use. The transnational terrorists' preferred method of attack is bombings. They have hijacked aircraft and used them as weapons. Assassinations, kidnappings and hostage-taking are also used, although to a far lesser extent. Terrorists will use whatever methods suit their purpose at any given time.

Training in techniques and tactics covers the use of a range of weapons and explosives, vehicles and other craft. One preferred method is the truck or car bomb. These enable terrorists to deliver substantial quantities of explosives to the target. They are often, but not always, conducted by suicide bombers. Terrorists also use remote control to detonate their bombs, demonstrating a degree of sophistication in their operations. The transnational terrorists have demonstrated maritime attack capability. On several occasions they have used small boats packed with explosives. Since January 2000, there have been maritime attacks against the USS Cole in Aden in October 2000 and against the French-owned oil tanker MV Limburg off the coast of Yemen in October 2002. Further attacks have been planned but disrupted. Most attacks occur (or are planned) in coastal waters.

Use of 'stand-off' weapons such as rockets, missiles and mortars are also part of their methodology. They enable the attackers to keep a safe distance from any defensive countermeasures. These weapons are readily available in some parts of the world and have been acquired and used by these terrorists, including surface-to-air missiles against passenger aircraft.

Suicide Tactics

Suicide tactics further boost the lethal reach of these terrorists. The willingness of extremists to die in the act of terrorism makes planning easier, because the attacker has only to reach the target. There is no need to plan for escape, one of the most difficult stages of an attack. Suicide tactics are not new, but they are a major feature of the new transnational extremist-Muslim terror.

Innovative forms of Attack

Transnational terrorists are innovative in developing new forms of attack. They adapt their methods to specific targets. If a hard target is of high symbolic importance, the terrorists will build on experience and develop new methods of attack.

They showed this by using several teams to breach the multi-layered defences of hardened targets in the Middle East.

Innovative approaches turn everyday items into lethal weapons. For example, in the September 11 attacks individual terrorists used box cutters to seize control of passenger aircraft with full tanks of fuel, turning them into large flying bombs. They have also manufactured explosives from everyday chemicals and garden fertilisers.

Non-conventional Weapons

Terrorists have shown a growing interest in chemical, biological, radiological and even nuclear (CBRN) terrorism - adding a significant new dimension to the threat. If the terrorists obtained chemical, biological or nuclear weapons or materials, there is little doubt they would use them.

Transnational terrorists have sought chemical, biological and radiological materials capable of causing human casualties and economic harm.

So far, all known large-scale chemical, biological or radiological attack plans initiated by the terrorists have failed or have been disrupted. We expect more such plans will surface. Any successful chemical, biological or radiological attack by these terrorists would be a grave development and would likely encourage others.

WEAPONS OF MASS DESTRUCTION

The terms weapons of mass destruction (WMD) and chemical, biological, radiological and nuclear (CBRN) weapons are often used interchangeably. WMD refers literally to any device that causes large-scale destruction, but is commonly taken to mean weapons capability employing chemical, biological, radiological or nuclear materials.

Chemical and biological agents may cause mass casualties but this need not always be the case. Terrorists might equally use them to assassinate one, perhaps high-profile, individual. Radiological weapons cause no physical destruction as such. But radiological materials, in combination with conventional explosives, can contaminate an area (the so-called 'dirty bomb') and may have lasting effects which result in casualties. Radiological weapons are not a serious part of any country's weapons program.

Transnational terrorist groups have ready access to information on chemical, biological or radiological materials and, to some extent, nuclear weapons, via publicly available information, including on the Internet. The spread of information from state programs producing CBRN materials has further increased the potential for terrorists to develop or acquire offensive CBRN capabilities.

A range of terrorist plans involving chemical and biological capability have been disrupted in recent years. It appears that years of research and training were to be translated into practice in late 2001 when extremists in Italy discussed plans to transport 'a liquid that suffocates people'. This was reportedly with intent to attack a cathedral in Paris with 10 litres of an unknown chemical agent. In December 2002, French authorities disrupted a network and found materials suggesting it was planning a cyanide gas attack. And in January 2003 UK authorities arrested a group of extremists apparently planning a ricin attack in London.

Users of the Tools of a Globalised World

The tools available to a globalised world are used to great effect by transnational terrorists. The Internet, mobile telephones and satellite telecommunications give them a truly global reach. They can run their networked operations more smoothly and coordinate action between geographically dispersed groups. They use the Internet to collect information and for operational planning. They conduct research and reconnaissance, identifying targets and vulnerabilities. They have access to a wealth of public information they can exploit.

So one-time reassurances - such as distance and geographic isolation in the case of Australia - provide little or no protection against the new transnational threat. Attacks can be coordinated and launched 'virtually'. Theatres of operation are no longer limited by geography.

Propaganda is an important weapon in the terrorists' arsenal. It helps them issue threats, spread disinformation and create terror. The threat of violence, to coerce or intimidate opponents, is a form of terrorism in itself. Terrorists have always used fear as a tactic, but modern technology has made it much more powerful. We see increasingly adept use by transnational terrorists of the mass media to get their fear-inducing headlines. Both the media and the Internet have proven similarly effective in conveying the terrorists' message to their supporters worldwide - and boosting their global recruitment efforts. Globalisation has made financing transnational terrorism easier. Financiers can transfer funds electronically and rapidly to operational elements across international boundaries. International money-laundering to support terrorist operations is also easier.

All these aspects of globalisation have helped reduce the terrorists' dependence on state sponsors. Past terrorists often relied on state sponsors for capability beyond geographic borders. Today's transnational terrorists do not. Before the fall of the Taliban, Afghanistan provided a useful base of operations and training. But it was not essential for the terrorist network's survival or its ability to plan for and conduct complex operations.

Areas outside effective government control, such as tribally administered territories in parts of South Asia, or areas where civil government is weak, remain important to terrorists as a base for training and operations and a source of recruits. This is why failed and failing states pose such a risk - they may easily develop into safe-havens for terrorists. While transnational terrorists are adept in using the tools of globalisation they also use 'low-tech' means that make them harder to detect. For example, in transferring money they use personal couriers and traditional banking networks that operate outside international financial controls. Using these methods, funds can be transferred rapidly and reliably with a limited or no audit trail. That makes it harder for government agencies to identify terrorist funding channels.

Cyber-terrorism

Muslim extremists call it 'cyber-jihad' - an actual or threatened attack on a computer network to coerce or intimidate governments or the public. While there have been no instances of cyber-attack by terrorists to date, this remains a potential threat against which we must protect ourselves. We know some extremists view computer network attack as a means of waging asymmetric warfare. Direct physical attack - which often results in human casualties and physical damage - will remain the terrorists' preferred method in the medium term.

But computer network attack on critical infrastructure offers the potential for significant damage of its own kind. Cyber attacks can be launched from anywhere in the world and from multiple locations at the same time.

They could cause serious damage or disruption to critical infrastructure. Since our critical infrastructure is more and more interlocked with its underlying information infrastructure, that information infrastructure may be one avenue through which to attack a high-value target. The possible consequences include disruption to e-commerce resulting in financial and economic loss, and an undermined public confidence in information technology systems. Terrorists may seek to mount cyber-attacks in combination with a physical attack to intensify its effects. They could also use cyber-attack to provide a decoy or cover for a physical attack. Individuals and groups sympathetic to terrorist causes have engaged in cyber activities, including website defacement and multiple messaging intended to deny service for a period.

An Adaptable Enemy

These terrorists are highly adaptable to changes in the strategic environment. They shift regional hubs of operations in response to changes in political and security circumstances. Their networked mode of operations makes this easier for them. They understand their environment and readjust their strategy accordingly.

They are particularly adept at responding to change in tactical circumstances. Their planning is flexible and unforeseen considerations are incorporated in the planning process. They have shown they can learn from experience and mistakes. They have demonstrated a capacity to identify and exploit weaknesses in security arrangements and they continually seek new methods to defeat countermeasures.

The adaptable nature of these terrorists means that their past actions will not always be a useful indicator of their future plans.

5

The Symbolic Nature of Terror

Baudrillard, writing in *The Spirit of Terrorism*, mentions the importance of not so much providing explanations but rather the importance of "an analysis which might possibly be as unacceptable as the event, but strikes the ...let us say, symbolic imagination in more or less the same way".

What Baudrillard wants to emphasize is the symbolic nature of acts of terror – and the importance of what is destroyed or attacked. In discussing the attacks on the World Trade Centre and the Pentagon, he stresses that we should not forget that the focus was actually the symbolic object, rather than the architectural object. This leads him note that "most things are not even worth destroying or sacrificing. Only works of prestige deserve that fate, for it is an honour".

While we must discuss the central issue of the sacrificial act, I also think that this insight is an important element for considering actions undertaken by Maori activists in New Zealand over the past decade. In every case – the theft and threatened destruction of the painter Colin McCahon's iconic *Urewera* mural in 1997, the chainsaw attacks on the iconic tree on One Tree Hill in Auckland in 1994 and 1997, the decapitation of the statue of the colonial Premier John Ballance during the 1995 Moutoa gardens protest, the attack on the America's Cup in 1997 and the activist Tama Iti's shot-gunning of the New Zealand flag, in front of a governmental delegation and captured on television news in January 2005 – all point to the possibilities of acts of symbolic terror associated with Maori radical movements. Each was a symbolic attack upon something representing prestige – but a prestige that is perceived as an affront.

As Baudrillard notes: "Terrorism invents nothing, inaugurates nothing. It simply carries things to the extreme, to the point of paroxysm. It exacerbates a certain state of things, a certain logic of violence and uncertainty". That is, the effect of terrorism *is in its effect* – in other words, it is our response that makes what is terror "terror". We "believe" in its stated aims by responding as if it is terror – in effect legitimizing it by making it an authentic act of symbolic affront and a sacrifice. To accept the offer of the gift of terror and death, to accept the gift of symbolic affront is to participate in the logic of exchange which affirms the action of the terrorist as both legitimate and of worth. This results in a situation whereby both "terrorism" and "the war on terror" actually affirm and legitimize each other because global disorder is both believed in and perceived as "the norm". It is also a situation whereby both sides – "terror" and "war on terror" – are each seeking to impose alternative forms of "order" which are viewed as the solution to the disorder which is perceived as forcing the act of terror in the first place. In other words, attempts to impose "order" merely serve to perpetuate the disorder that each form of order seeks to overcome. We end up with a terrorist war on terror, all the more terrorist for the fact that it now seems endless. To impose a Hegelian-derived dialectic, where "terror" is the thesis and "war on terror" is the antithesis, the synthesis is this hyper-real "terrorist war" – a synthetic event that is increasingly taken as an end-state.

For Nietzsche the "death of God" was caused by human indifference – and indifference to religion (specifically Christianity) as the expression of that God. Today in a world where we seem to believe in the *religare*of terrorism, that "terror" has become the new global god we seek to oppose or affirm. In a sense terror is actually the religion of globalization. That is, terrorism occurs and exists as the *religare* of globalization, that which occurs out of it and authenticates it, that which provides an ontology of violence and uncertainty, that which justifies the expansion of globalization by its occurrence. As Baudrillard notes: "And it is the real victory of terrorism that it has plunged the whole of the West into an obsession with security – that is to say, into a veiled form of perpetual terror …The spectre of terrorism is forcing the west to terrorize itself". This *religare* of fear, this self-affirmation by terror is actually a response that arises out of the meaninglessness of modernity – and the rejection of the cosmopolitan pluralities offered by postmodernism. In effect the recourse to terror is the rejection of both the plurality of contemporary society and the challenge of "the other" that pluralism offers. It is the return to the central question presented by modernity: that of meaning in the face of indifference. As G. Clarke Chapman put it, the issue with the rise of terrorism – and its response – is that of what to do "that enables us to cope with the acute sense of vulnerability imposed by engulfing modernity"?

In response to this question, I believe we need to note that the erosion of old norms and stabilities, the rejection of the cosmopolitan uncertainties and provisionality of postmodernism, allied with the "indifference" that leads to the death of God, have all resulted in a sense of communal identity and meaning being provided by the new religion of fear. Over the past fifteen years since the decline of the threat of the cold war, there has been the media-driven explosion of a succession of new eschatological fears, of disease, pandemics, global warming or cooling, biogenetics, Y2K, immigration etc, which are but forms of global terror which seek to overcome the indifference of the western world.

Terrorism is the embodiment, the clarification, of this indifferent religion of fear, this *religare* of terror. In other worlds, fundamentalist terror is manufactured, presented and believed in *as* the religion of the modern indifferent world. Its worship of both the speed of destruction and of the speed of spreading its event-message using global media, allied with its focus on a destructive purity, make it the latest embodiment of Futurism.

RELIGION, TERROR AND SACRIFICE

To disenchant terrorist discourse also means, in a multi-religious and multicultural society, the necessity of disenchanting the state and public rhetoric. The turn to talk of religion and spirituality, that talk of re-enchantment and desecularization, not only serves to act as public space for religious diversity to state their claims of communal legitimacy, it also provides a public space for the religion of terror and terror discourse. To disenchant is not to dismiss the various religious claims or affiliations, but to effectively seek to secularize them into the realm of privatism. Yet in order to do this we need to be also aware of the claims of the sacred, especially in claims of sacrifice and transgression that *exist still* within our society – and which are repositioned into the public sphere by acts of terror.

Georges Bataille offers a provocative take on the challenges of sacrifice and transgression, in which the sacred unleashes itself in acts of passion which are contrary to reason. He notes the links of horror, terror and the sacred and how, in the contemporary world, with the reduction to symbolic passion in our religion we have attempted to domesticate our fascination with death and destruction that sits at the heart of religion. This is the basis of the *religare* of terror – our fascination with death as *sign and symbol* of the sacred. Therefore the challenge of terror is the return of the sacred as transgressive in a world seeking to limit and contain it, to reduce it. The problem is that we fail to see acts of terror as acts of exaltation and intoxication in the sacred, failing to acknowledge Bataille's claim for the transgressive eroticism of terror:

> The inner experience of eroticism demands from the subject a sensitiveness to the anguish at the heart of the taboos no less great than the desire which leads him to infringe it. This is religious sensibility, and it always links desire closely with terror, intense pleasure and anguish.

This is why terror has become the new global religion. It reflects and provides the religious sensibility in the contemporary world – it transgresses the space given to religion in the postmodern turn and rejects both the restraints of controlled plurality and the turn away from plurality in the turn back to a new modernity. Today, terror is a religion that acts as transgression and taboo to *both* modernity and postmodernity. In a sense, following the Nietzschean nihilism of *Beyond Good and Evil* we now exist in a world of taboo and transgression, a world of sacred violence. As Bataille notes: "the transgression does not deny the taboo but transcends and completes it". In this we need to now view the transgression of terror as that *which transcends and completes* both taboos – those of death and of religion/sacred in public space – in the modern world. As "the taboo is there to be violated" and is "at the very least...the threshold beyond which murder is possible", our taboos on public death and public religion are in fact those which paradoxically issue a form of demand *for* the transgression of terror – and the terror of transgression. In effect, notes Bataille, for our profane world to exist we require the complementary acts of transgression that exceed its limits but do not destroy it: "the profane world is the world of taboos. The sacred world depends on limited acts of transgression".

This means that acts of terror are acts of transgression for the expression of the reality of the sacred world. In other worlds, acts of terror are a form of sacrifice. What the act of sacrifice does is not a killing but rather a relinquishing and a giving. What is sacrificed is what is useful – it "restores a lost value by relinquishment of that value". As bin Laden would have it:

When you talk about the invasion of New York and Washington, you talk about the men who changed the face of history and went against the traitors....These great men have consolidated faith in the hearts of believers and undermined the plans of the crusaders and their agents in the region. Terrorism against America deserves to be praised because it was a response to injustice, aimed at forcing America to stop its support for Israel, which kills our people.

The acts of terror are, from a religious viewpoint, acts of sacrifice: they give up what is useful – the life of the terrorist, the life of the believer, the sacrifice of people in the profane world – in a manner of transgressive action that seeks to transcend the taboo on violence, death and the sacred. As Bataille notes: "The sacrificer declares ...I call you back to the *intimacy* of the divine world, of the profound immanence of all that is...".

The spectacle of terror is therefore on one level the intimacy of sacrifice in the intimacy of our daily lives, in the intimacy of our living rooms, in the intimacy of our public and private spaces. It is on one level, as Bataille states of sacrifice, "the communication of anguish". So what is this anguish? Perhaps it is as Slavoj Zizek notes, the cry of anguish of sacrifice, of terror, of violence. Furthermore, that our transgressive avidity for these is our passion for the "Real" – that which he notes Alain Badiou as claiming is "the key feature of the twentieth century". This passion for the Real is what sits at the heart of Loos' call for the overthrow of unnecessary ornamentation; this passion for the Real sits at the heart of the Futurist worship of the cleansing effect of technology, war and death; this passion for the Real is what lies in modernity's rejection of transcendence – and in Postmodernity's rejection of modernity's secularity. In effect, the dualistic battle in modernity between what is seen as order and what is seen as chaotic *is* this battle over what is Real and where the Real is located. Violence, taboo, transgression and sacrifice are those acts that serve as both statements of the Real – and the rejection of what is perceived to be non-Real. Acts of terror, made possible by the space given in postmodernity for the articulation of varieties of transcendent "Real", are an act of the rejection of these possibilities in a challenge of what is seen as the Real. Yet in their symbolic intention, they participate in the postmodern spectacle as an attempt to evangelize by effect. The passion for the Real and the attempt to represent it are actually transgressive to modern world where we attempt to keep the Real controllable by not confronting it. The response to the rise of transcendence as the location of the Real was not to confront it but rather to seek to splinter it by postmodern tolerance. Yet all this did was to give consent to those who sought to destroy even the possibilities of competing Reals.

In effect, contemporary terrorism is the Real of modernity (a battle beyond good and evil, of order and chaos) confronting itself with the non-reality of terror and spectacle that act as transgressive to that which we seek to hold as Real. The effect is not concerned with the reality of the chaotic act, but rather with the chaos that is the response to the reality of the act. In effect we say "we cannot believe this act has occurred" and this stating of our inability to believe in the Real is the chaos that the act of terror seeks. We then search to ascribe a meaning to the event that may mean *we claim to see the reason behind the act*, the "cry of anguish" that caused this act. To ascribe meaning to the act is to order it, in effect to attempt to "make it real" – and in making it Real paradoxically giving a form of inverted value and meaning to the actions and beliefs of those who undertook it.

Yet often what happens in response is the turn away from the liberal tolerance of dissenting beliefs that (perhaps) marks off a Western sense of the Real: a form of order that exists by ordering chaotic elements within pluralism. Yet the act of terror is a rejection of Western liberal pluralism, a rejection of the type of Western order that secularizes its taboos and transgressions.

HOW TO DEAL WITH TERRORISM

After the attacks of 9/11, the American president declared a "Crusade" against terrorists.

This "Crusade" was, after some think-ing, changed into a "War Against Terrorism." This war on terrorism is totally based on deterrence and preemptive strikes. Ac-tual and prospective terrorists must be wiped out by killing or at least capturing them, hold-ing them prisoner, or (perhaps) putting them on trial and sentencing them to imprisonment for long periods or indefinitely. Such treatment is expected to make the penalty for the crime so harsh that no individual will engage in ter-rorist activities in the future.

INEFFECTIVENESS OF DETERRENCE

History and recent experience suggest, however, that deterrence is ineffective and may even be counterproductive in dealing with terrorism. Moreover, the extent of terrorist acts may well increase rather than decrease. A poli-cy based on deterrence has a second disadvan-tage—It threatens civil and human rights in the countries engaged in fighting terrorism. Deter-rence thus tends to undermine exactly those values it claims to protect.

Many people share this concern but see no alternative to deterrence. I want to show that such alternatives do exist and are viable. Three strategies are proposed:

(1) Reduce vulnerability by decentralizing society;

(2) Strengthen positive incentives to leave the terrorist camp;

(3) Divert media attention from terrorist groups.

DECENTRALIZATION REDUCES VULNERABILITY TO TERRORIST ATTACKS

Any system with many different centers is more stable due to the ability of the vari-ous centers to substitute for each other. When one part of the system is negatively affected, another part or parts can take over. This ba-sic insight also applies to terrorism. A target's vulnerability is lower in a decentralized society more so than in a centralized society. The more centers of power there are in a country, the less Economists' Voice www.bepress.com/ev August, 2006

Terrorists are able to hurt it. In a decentralized system, terrorists do not know where to strike because they are aware that each part can sub-stitute for the other so that a strike will not achieve much. In contrast, in a centralized sys-tem most decision-making takes place in one location. This power center is an ideal target for terrorists and therefore is in great danger of being attacked.

As a means of reducing vulnerability, decentralization can be achieved in various ways:

- Decentralize the *economy* by relying on the market as the major form of resource allocation.
- Decentralize the *polity* by resorting to the classical division of power between the government, the parliament and the courts. Decentralization over space is achieved by a federalist structure with decision-making power attributed to lower levels of the polity (states, provinces, regions and communes).
- Decentralize the *society* by allowing for many different actors such as churches, nongovernmental organizations, clubs and the family.

POSITIVE INCENTIVES TO ACTUAL AND PROSPECTIVE TERRORISTS NOT TO ENGAGE IN VIOLENT ACTS

Positive sanctions consist in providing people with previously nonexistent or unattainable opportunities increasing their utility.

The *oppor-tunity costs of remaining or becoming a terrorist* are raised because other valued possibilities are now available. Various approaches are possible.

Terrorists can be reintegrated. One of the most fundamental human motivations is the need to belong, and this also applies to terrorists. The isolation from other social entities gives strength to the terrorist group because it has become the only place where a sense of belonging is nurtured. An effective way to overcome terrorism is to break up this isolation. The (potential) terrorists must experience that there are other social bodies able to care for their need to belong. Interaction between groups tends to reduce extremist views, which are more likely to flourish in isolated groups of like-minded people. Segregation reinforces extremism and vice versa. Therefore, breaking up this vicious circle of segregation and extremism should lower terrorists' inclination to participate in violent activities.

There are various methods of motivating terrorists to interact more closely with other members of society, thus overcoming their isolation. The terrorists can be involved in a *discussion process,* which takes their goals and grievances seriously. Moreover, terrorists can be granted *access* to the normal *political process.* This lowers the costs of pursuing the political goal by legal means and hence raises the opportunity costs of terrorism.

The same principle of anti-terrorist policy can be applied to nations supporting or harboring terrorists. If such countries are internationally isolated and identified as "rogue states," they tend to become more extreme and ideological. A more fruitful strategy is to help them to re-enter the international community and to adopt its rules.

Repentants can be welcomed. Persons engaged in terrorist movements can be offered incentives, most importantly reduced punishment and a secure future life if they are prepared to leave the organization they are involved with and are prepared to talk about it and its projects. Terrorists who credibly show that they wish to renounce terrorist activities should be supported and not penalized (Principal Witness Programs).

A member's opportunity costs of remaining a terrorist are therewith increased.

Valued opportunities can be offered. Persons inclined to follow terrorist ideas and undertake terrorist actions can be invited to visit foreign countries. Universities and research institutes, for example, can offer such persons the opportunity of discussing their ideology with academics and other intellectuals. Liberalism is based on the conviction that the atmosphere of discourse existing in such places of learning tends to mellow terrorist inclinations. If prospective terrorists do not change their views, the situation is not worse than before. The very least to be achieved is that the (potential) terrorists have access to new and radically different ideas, compared to the situation in which they live within a closed circle of other extremists.

Providing terrorists positive incentives to no longer engage in violent actions represents a completely different approach from the conventional anti-terrorist policy of deterrence based on coercion. An effort is made to break the organizational and mental dependence of persons on the terrorist organizations by offering them more favorable alternatives.

ATTENTION TO BE DIVERTED FROM THE TERRORIST GROUPS

The relationship between terrorists and the media can be described as "symbiotic." The interests of the terrorists are similar or even identical to those of the media: Both want to make news, and both want the terrorist act to remain in the news as long and as prominently as possible.

Terrorists have become very skilled in using the media to achieve a maximum effect. They have learned to exploit the media to propagate their political demands to millions and even billions of people. Terrorists have fully adjusted their tactics in order to accommodate media needs.

Terrorists can be prevented from committing violent acts by reducing the utility gained from such behavior. A specific way for terrorists to derive lower benefits from terrorism consists in the government ascertaining that a particular terrorist act is *not attributed to a particular terrorist group*. This prevents terrorists from receiving credit for the act and from gaining the public's attention associated with committing the act. The government must see to it that a particular terrorist group does not monopolize media attention.

This does *not* mean that the government should suppress information. This is not possible in an open society. The government can divert attention from terrorist organizations and their goals by supplying *more* information to the public than desired by the terrorist group responsible for a particular violent act.

It must be made known that *several* terrorist groups *could* be responsible for a particular terrorist act. Experience shows indeed that in the case of most terrorist attacks *several* groups of terrorists have claimed to be responsible. The authorities have to reveal that they never know with certainty which terrorist group may have committed a violent act. Rather the government must publicly discuss various reasonable hypotheses.

The strategy of refusing to attribute a terrorist attack to one particular group systematically affects the behavior of terrorists. The benefits derived from having committed a terrorist act decreases for the group having undertaken it because the group does not reap the public attention hoped for.

The political goals it wants to publicize are not propagated as much as desired. This reduction in publicity makes the terrorist act (to a certain degree) senseless, as modern terrorism essentially depends on publicity. Terrorists who are ready to take a high risk, even the risk of death, in order to put forth their political beliefs, feel deeply dissatisfied. Their frustration is intensified by the feeling that other, not equally as "brave" political groups, are given a free publicity ride. This frustration is often intense because terrorist groups tend to be in a state of strong competition even when they have similar political beliefs.

CONCLUSIONS

The proposed anti-terrorist policy based on a *positive approach* has two important ad-vantages over a coercive policy:

- The whole interaction between terrorists and the government takes the character of a *positive sum game*: All sides benefit. The effort of the government is no longer directed solely towards destruction. Rather, the government makes an effort to raise the utility of those terrorists who choose to enter the programs offered. It provides alternatives to persons considering becoming terrorists. In contrast, deterrence policy by necessity produces a worse position for both sides. The terrorists are punished (incarcerated, killed, or mutilated), while the deterrence strategy is very costly in terms of resources and civil rights.
- The strategy *undermines the cohesiveness of the terrorist organization*. The incentive to leave is a strong threat to the organization. The terrorist leaders no longer know whom to trust because, after all, most persons can succumb to temptation. An effort to counteract these temptations by prohibiting members from taking up the attractive offers leads to conflicts between the leaders and the rank and file. With good outside offers available to the members of a terrorist group, its leaders tend to lose control. The terrorist organization's effectiveness is thereby reduced.

The application of the economic approach to terrorism offers a range of superior anti-terrorism policies to deterrence. They are effective in dissuading potential terrorists from attacking. All of these policies are based on the notion that a positive approach is preferable to one based on the use of force.

The policies are "positive" as they do not seek to harm or kill potential and actual terrorists, but to reduce terrorist activities. The policies are not retributive but anti-terrorist. The positive approach here championed is not the only effective strategy and it does not work in every case; but, compared to the now dominant deterrence and preemption policy, the favorable features by far prevail. There is no need to restrict policies to deterrence; the positive approaches presented are in many respects superior alternatives.

A crucial question is why deterrence policy is so often undertaken though it is far from successful, and why the positive policies are disregarded. The reason is that government politicians derive additional private benefits from using force. The same holds for the military, the police and the secret service. In contrast, the proponents of positive anti-terrorist policies are weak, at least in the short run. However, the outcome of the political struggle can be influenced by political persuasion, giving the positive approach a better chance.

THE RESPONSE TO TERROR

The type of modernity in which we currently find ourselves is, in a Zizekian sense, one where we have a series of competing claims as to both the validity and location of the Real – and a series of competing claims as to what are acceptable actions to institute its recognition by the wider population. Fundamentalist terror sees what it seeks to destroy as chaotic, as unnecessary, as an affront to what is Real, what is ordered, what is necessary. Fundamentalist terror is the violence of the Real in the service of what is seen as the *necessary alternative*. The type of symbolic violence undertaken is a reflection of the type of claims of reality being made. Symbolic action as has been undertaken so far in New Zealand reflects a society that is secular by inclination. The Real is contained in symbolic action that can be reported and represented as secular in effect and motivation. Other acts of symbolic action in New Zealand such as desecration of Jewish graves, and graffiti attacks and vandalism of mosques and synagogues can, in a secular society, be contained as criminal acts of a non-legitimate extreme minority. The challenge presented by Destiny Church is not its symbolic nature, but rather the media response that gives credibility to religiously motivated symbolic events as being effective – and as being a means of effecting a form of legitimacy. Yet paradoxically, what will keep Destiny under control is its obsession with a gospel of prosperity – they will not seek to destroy the type of society that they believe will reward them. The danger to a country like New Zealand is the recourse to symbolic violence by those marginalized by both belief and culture – and yet given postmodern tolerance for their intolerant beliefs. The Real of the modern secular pluralist state is ever open to the challenge of the competing modernity of the religious Real that understands the nature and efficacy of symbolic violence. As Paul Piccone and Gary Ulmen noted in response to September 11: The first thing that will have to go is the criticism of the concept of tolerance for the intolerant – and therefore of its pseudo-universalism. Tolerance is a particular western value, which applies only to those who practice it. It excludes not only those who reject it, but also those who tolerate its rejection.

The religion of terror is linked to the religion of modernity, the belief in the pluralist secular nation state, the belief in a future that unfolds through rationality and progress – and in particular to a distinct form of western modernity. The failure of the postmodern can now be seen as the failure of the extension of tolerance to the intolerant, to those who seek to reject that which enables them to dissent. The recourse to symbolic violence is the challenge of the transgression of the taboo of intolerance; that which seeks a response that will assert the validity of the claims of the Real being made by the terrorist. As Baudrillard notes: "The tactic of the terrorist model is to provoke a surplus of reality and to make the whole system collapse under it".

To oppose the surplus of the reality of taboo and transgression that is to be found in the act of terror, the system under attack needs an alternative Real that can neutralise any attempts to impose any religious Real upon the general public and the nation. This occurs either by the symbolic actions that terrorise the liberal State's fear of being viewed as intolerant, or in specific actions that by act of violence seek to spread the terror of the Real through the *religare* of the mass media and so constitute the grounds for a new *religare* of terror. The challenge is that it is the freedom of the mass media that allows the circulation of the spectacle of terror – yet to limit the spectacle is to enforce the control of image and truth of the kind sought by the fundamentalist terrorist.

Contemporary terrorism is not a challenge against modernity, but rather a challenge that rejects the offer of postmodernity, an offer made by the post-Christian West and yet rejected by those who that West sought to include. What is offered in the act of fundamentalist terror is the challenge of an alternative modernity, an alternative way of ordering the chaos of life, an alternative belief system that uses the synthesis of mass media and terror to provide a new *religare* of terror that, in our response, serves to validate, from the point of view of the terrorist, the sacred necessity and justification for the act of terror: "We realized from our defence and fighting against the American enemy that, in combat, they mainly depend on psychological warfare. This is in light of the huge media machine they have".

To oppose the *religare* of terror the state may opt to secularize symbolic recourse as criminal behaviour, as has been the case in New Zealand, in effect trying to neutralize terrorism claims to efficacy as religious act and as *religare,* through a response of indifference. Secondly, it may be recognized that the privatization of belief and culture that occurs in modernity can also serve to allow the legitimization of intolerance within those groups. A cosmopolitan society is therefore confronted with the reality that calls for religious and cultural difference which can locate and express themselves in statements and actions of intolerance. Thirdly, this means that the secular *religare* of a cosmopolitan society *will* result in symbolic acts by those who seek to reject it. With the increasing recourse to religion as a form of identity politics (beliefs and communities as tangible *religare*), the state's dismissal of these to the privatist sphere may force the recourse to further symbolic action and this will be seen by some as a necessary risk. The alternative will be understood as responding *as if* the global*religare* of terror paradoxically legitimizes the unnecessary ornamentation of communal religious expression *within* the public sphere.

As Baudrillard notes, already the West is responding to "the spectre of terrorism" by terrorizing itself. In effect we are unsure how to respond to what he notes is the inversion of the master and slave relationship because the non-terrorist is "deprived of death and destiny" while the terrorists, the ones who control death, are the symbolic master. The western terrorising of "itself" occurs when, seeking to remain "tolerant" it provides the symbolic space for the terrorist "master" impose a hyper-real condition of REAL EVENT-DEATH as a permanent condition of the *religare* of fear and "*eschaton* expectation" – the "crystallization" of "all the ingredients in suspension".

The dilemma for the secular, cosmopolitan society is therefore when the private belief attempts to act within the public domain in a manner that seeks to impose its particular values and identity *upon all* within the society, this is particularly true of any recourse to religious fundamentalism. To avoid the self-terrorism that is the common response, perhaps in the end all private beliefs are to be equally unequal – and so exist in a form of oppositional equality. This is because in a Loosian-derived modernity, unnecessary ornamentation is itself the location of definition in a pluralist society. To proceed from locating *all* religious identity as unnecessary ornamentation is perhaps the only way to achieve equality, but also the groundwork toward the articulation of a pragmatic common narrative of modern identity. To privatize religion may protect an individual's identity, but it may also impede it. So, on the one hand the state may attempt to reply to fundamentalist terrorism with indifference. But what about the terrorism of the state and the uncertainty that the state – terror relationship bring to any discussion of either?

Jean-Luc Nancy, who raises the question of "what is to be done?" also offers a possibility which in its articulation of the necessity of the provisional possibility is a possible (non)solution:

> Perhaps though, we know one thing at least: 'What is to be done?' means for us, how to make a world for which all is not already done (played out, finished, enshrined in a destiny), nor still entirely to do (in the future for always future tomorrows).

This challenge sits against the claims of necessity and certainty, the dualist battle that "terror" and "the war on terror" encompass. That this is a war of rhetoric – a rhetorical war – is also beyond a doubt. This is a point acknowledged by Kevin Roberts, CEO Worldwide of SAATCHI & SAATCHI Ideas Company in his recent "presentation to various U.S. Defense Intelligence Agencies". Robert's claim was the need for the rebranding of the rhetoric of "the War on terror", with the aim to create a new "loyalty beyond Reason", what Roberts calls a Lovemark: "these are brands that make deep emotional connections with consumers. Passionate connections that go inside people's lives and make a difference". These are brands that have "High Love, High Respect" such as

Harley Davidson, Apple and JFK. For Roberts "brand America" currently has "High Respect, Low Love". His rebranding of "brand America" and of the "War on terror" is based on his "Lovemark" credo: "Mystery, Sensuality and Intimacy". This could be termed the seduction, the eroticism of the brand, the pornography of global capital.

Roberts' rebranding is to what he terms the "fight for a better world", a fight launched alongside the war on terror that seeks to tackle geopolitical issues such as "global AIDS, malnutrition and malaria". But Roberts' call "to create America as a lovemark" is a response that needs to be added to the already empty rhetoric that "terror" inspires. This is capitalism as hyper-real benevolence, a simulacrum of compassion that is pushing a global product. It merely swerves to emphasise Zillah Eisenstein's critique that: "Anti-terrorism rhetoric fits well with global capitalism ...there is no single country that houses terrorism...or capitalism. Both are networked transnationally.

What this demonstrates is that the *religare*, the religion of terror has already become just another product, something to be consumed in a form of globalization. Baudrillard encourages us to think about the problem of fundamentalist terrorism by reversing several of our standard assumptions. What if it were Islam, he asks, that were spreading through the West and rising to dominate the globe? Baudrillard tells us that if this were the case then "...terrorism would rise against Islam, for it is the world, the globe itself, which resists globalization".

What we need to consider, perhaps even confront, is the challenge that the *religare* of globalization is the *religare* of terror which is both product and consumption of capitalism and its other – terror. For terror is the inside of capitalism; that which acts as perhaps the "lovemark" of the inverted fight against the global. This link of religion, modernity and capitalism was noted by Marx in his call that "the criticism of religion is the prerequisite of all criticism". One could perhaps invert and expand it and say also that "the religion of criticism is the prerequisite of all terror". This dualism is what perhaps sits under all questions involving the modern, capitalist state and terrorism. Both the state and terror are built on certainties – yet both are certainties under attack from their other within the *religare* of the global. As Nancy has also noted: "Where certainties come apart, there too gathers the strength that no certainty can match.

The collapse of certainty is perhaps the collapse of the real, or rather the collapse of the belief in the real, a collapse that forces a struggle to assert the claim of the real (terror/war on terror) over and against the uncertainty and the indifference that the collapse of the real engenders. As Baudrillard notes: "There is no corpse of the real, and with good reason: the real is not dead, it has disappeared.

The unacceptability of terror is only as unacceptable as the *religare* of modernity, of the global, of global capital, as the drive to non-ornamentation. All are drives for the real arising out of claims of certainty as to the location and representation of the real. The *religare* of the real is the religion of terror – and of the war waged against it – a war of mutual rhetoric that by transgressive public religion/*religare* and public death affirm the Manichean centrality of modernity itself. Baudrillard's aphorism that "He does not have room for both the world and for its double – but no one knows which will have the last word" sits under any consideration of a response. Perhaps the only response is not to fall into the impatience of desiring a response, for out of impatience could possibility eventuate that which we do – but deny – desire:

Impatience is a millenarian passion which desires the immediacy of the end. Now today, wherever time has been abolished by the operation of 'real time', events no longer come to maturity, either immediately or with a delay. But impatience is not consoled by that: having nothing left to devour, it devours the remains of the real.

The immediacy of the end, the desire to immediately end "terror/the war on terror" or that which terror strikes at, are reminiscent of the drive to hygiene of futurism, the banishing of ornament, the self-implosion of Modernity at Pruitt-Igoe. The state that desires the immediate end to terror by self-terrorising itself is itself devouring what it believes is the remains of the real (itself as bureaucratic state) out of a millennial passion for the end.

This self-terror of the self-devouring response has, as Baudrillard notes, its immediate prior expression in the West's hyper-real Iranian *Fatwa* it carried out for the Iranian state on Salman Rushdie: "The Iranian strategy consists in inflecting Western culture with fear, duplicity and self-pity".

Perhaps the issue is the centrality of the Loosian modernist rejection of disorder – a pursuit of order as *religare* that terror seeks to deny and discredit. Writing of the 1988 Libyan terror bombing of the plane over Lockerbie, Baudrillard notes: "What fascinates thought is this terrorist enchanting of things, the symbolic disorder of which terrorism is merely the visible epicentre".

The choice is therefore a degree of no-choice, the enchanting of terror by the state, the enchantment of terror by the terrorist, both symbolize a disorder against the Loosian claims of the realised real in ordered modernity, in the systems of order that the bureaucratic state now activates to self-terrorise itself, in effect to institute its internal *Fatwas* on its own citizens in the recognition that: "Every society must choose itself an enemy, but it must not try to exterminate it".

The state and the self-instituting terrorist act both have each other as enemy, but cannot act for a final extermination, a fulfilled millennial, apocalyptic passion for then their claims of and for the real are finished. The act of extermination is the internal destructive act of Pruitt-Igoe, the real terror is that turned by the state upon itself, to clear the space for the self-transcendence of its prior claim for the real.

As the French novelist Frederic Beigbeder notes in his mediation on the final hours of the twin towers: "Since September 11, 2001, reality has not only outstripped fiction, it's destroying it. It's impossible to write about this subject, and yet impossible to write about anything else. Nothing else touches us". The Western *Fatwa* has been extended – we all now live as Rushdie: self-imprisoned not by the original action but by our (Western) reaction to the original event-death. The Irony is that the modern Western dismissal of the ornamentation of religion has been supplanted by a *religare* of terror that ornaments us continually in the hyper-real self-*Fatwa*. Maybe our best case scenario is to hope that Baudrillard is right when he says: "terror is dissipated by irony" Neither are in short supply today.

DEVELOPMENT CHALLENGES FOR AND OTHER BIOLOGICS TO ADDRESS TERRORISM

The FDA plays an important role in multiple stages of the product development process, from initial clinical studies through licensure, manufacturing and post-marketing studies which may be used to further evaluate safety and effectiveness.

For these reasons, FDA is committed to working together with the scientific and clinical communities and with industry and the public to fulfill its regulatory and public health role in facilitating the development of biodefense biologics and therapeutics. Recent and ongoing FDA biodefense-related activities include, for example, meeting with sponsors and sister agencies and departments to encourage interest in developing safe and effective new products needed for public health biodefense, performing research that ultimately facilitates the development of these products; and providing intensive and early interactions with product sponsors to speed their availability.

As with any medical product, bioterrorism products need to be regulated to ensure consistent and objective protection of the public safety. While there is currently a sense of emergency and a set of urgent needs to address, the desire for rapid and innovative responses must not be allowed to compromise the objective assessment of safety and effectiveness.

Thus we need a regulatory agency that can step back and provide a more objective perspective. If and when things go wrong in the wake of decision(s) made in a time of crisis, few people will remember the crisis and that the decision was in fact made with the best intentions.

The public expects safe and effective products, and safety expectations are especially high for vaccines administered to healthy individuals. Maintaining public confidence in vaccines and medical products, in general, is critical to maintaining overall confidence in our nation's public health programs and leadership in matters extending far beyond bioterrorism. For these reasons, even in difficult times, we must continue to make and communicate clearly the best possible scientific and public health decisions about product development, licensure, availability and use.

Furthermore, bioterrorism is a moving target, not a single disease of predictable epidemiology, and all potential product uses may not be anticipated. This complicates many decisions about product use. For example, a vaccine, such as the licensed anthrax vaccine, which may have been originally studied and used in a limited population effectively and without major safety concerns may raise more significant public concerns about uncommon adverse events, whether coincidental or due to the vaccine, if and when it is administered for similar reasons to hundreds of thousands of people or when unanticipatedly used for post-exposure prophylaxis. There are several factors that account for why we do not have an adequate supply of vaccines for bioterrorism defense:

Financial Disincentives

- Uncertain markets, especially for potentially more limited use products such as a tularemia or plague vaccine.
- Uncertain longevity of the needs, markets and of resources; short attention spans in government budgeting.
- The fact that vaccines are complex biological products that carry a high risk of uncertainty, unpredictability of success, and financial loss.
- The rigorous safety requirements and low public tolerance of risk—in part because they are often administered to healthy people as a preventative measure—and associated costs of developing biologics.
- The fact that preventive measures are generally undervalued, both perceptually and financially. Vaccines are often expected to be sold for very low prices, and the expected profit for the producer is therefore lower than for other products (e.g., drugs for treatment) competing for the same resources. However, while difficult to model when risks are unclear, it would be interesting to conduct more comprehensive and long-term cost-benefit analyses

concerning the personal health impacts and the social and economic costs versus potential benefits of vaccine compared to treatment strategies for specific agents of interest.

- The added cost of the large clinical trials needed to address potential wide use including in diverse populations.
- The presence of advocacy groups with various points of view.
- A fair amount of concern about possible adverse effects of vaccines, ranging from specific disease issues to more general anti-vaccine sentiment on the part of a proportion of the public.
- A mistrust of government and industry.
- Product liability issues.

Scientific Challenges

- Lack of historical or recent precedents for vaccines against many pathogens, which makes it difficult to establish good surrogates.
- The potential for genetic or other manipulation of antigenic determinants. (Although this is presently more difficult in many cases to engineer than antibacterial resistance.)
- The potential complications of live vaccine administration to increasing immunocompromised populations.
- The intense flow of resources demanded by urgent perceived needs (sometimes referred to as the "disease du jour" phenomenon), in contrast to the more normal lengthy product development cycle.

The FDA Response

There are several regulatory approaches and mechanisms that the FDA has employed in an attempt to safely speed up product availability and licensure:

- Early and frequent consultation between the sponsor producing the product, the potential end users (e.g., health officials and providers in the military and civilian sectors), and the FDA is very resource-intensive but important. This kind of up-front investment can greatly improve the product development process by identifying creative study designs, recognizing factors that are normally not anticipated in developing a product, and reducing misunderstandings and the likelihood of unwelcome surprises. Early dialogue also increases accountability.

- Emergency use under IND (investigational new drug status) allows rapid access to products that have not yet completed requirements for licensure. INDs require acceptable evidence of safety; a reasonable though not necessarily formally proven scientific basis for efficacy; a favorable risk:benefit ratio; and an
- intent to license. While allowing availability of potentially lifesaving products, a disadvantage to emergency use under this rule is that the product is not licensed, which not only reflects the true scientific limitations of the data but also raises important issues about public perception.
- Fast track processes can speed up the review process for products that will provide meaningful therapeutic benefits compared to existing therapies for serious or life-threatening illnesses. Fast track allows the FDA to review information as it becomes available and as the sponsor submits it.
- Accelerated approval through the use of surrogate end points to demonstrate benefit. The use of CD4 cells for assessment of antiviral treatment of HIV was one of the first surrogates to be approved under this rule. For bioterrorist agents, protective antibody levels for a vaccine or immunoglobulin could serve as potential surrogate end points. Clinical end points can also be utilized. There still must be good post-licensure studies to demonstrate the effects on disease outcomes and to collect additional safety information, and the FDA can place restrictions on use and promotion and even withdraw the product if agreements are violated or the product proves unsafe or ineffective. Thus far, this process has worked fairly well although, once a product is licensed, or if a disease is rare, it may

be difficult to obtain patients for studies, and sponsors sometimes are unable or unmotivated to fulfill their commitments. But because most accelerated approval products also receive priority review, this process can allow for rapid approval of a product based on more limited and simpler-to-obtain clinical data than may be the case with large, randomized control trials and/or longer-term endpoints.

- Priority review is applied when a product is considered a significant advance or will be used for serious or life-threatening illness.
- Approval under the forthcoming "Animal Rule" has very important biodefense implications. In fact, the rule is specifically oriented to drugs or biologics that reduce or prevent serious or life threatening conditions caused by exposure to lethal or disabling toxic, chemical, biologic, or nuclear threats. The products should be expected to provide a meaningful therapeutic benefit over existing treatments. Human efficacy trials should either be not feasible or unethical, and the use of the animal efficacy data should be scientifically appropriate. In this proposed rule, the end point should be related to the desired benefit in humans, usually a significant outcome such as mortality or major morbidity. Clinical studies in representative populations are still needed, however, both for establishing pharmacokinetics (including, in the case of many vaccines, immunogenicity) and for assessing safety. Such studies are critical because civilian populations often include vulnerable or pharmacokinetically variable subsets.

Finally, similar to the fast track and accelerated approvals, the animal rule has post-marketing and labeling commitments and restrictions. It does not apply if the product could be approved based on any other standard in FDA's regulation. It is a rule of last resort, but it certainly would be applicable to many of the situations that have been described in this workshop. In addition to its regulatory responsibilities, the FDA's Center for Biologics conducts a significant amount of biodefense-related research, supporting approximately sixty ongoing projects that are directly relevant to identified high threat agents. The general goal is to meet otherwise unmet research needs, often with regulatory implications. Examples include how to better determine potency; defining immune and other correlates of protection; how to make safer and purer products (including characterization of the safety of cell substrates and detection of adventitious agents); better assessment of adverse events and efficacy under conditions of use, and studies which allow the agency to make regulations more scientific and less "defensive."

These types of research can benefit not only the public, but also multiple companies across industry, but are often not performed by a given sponsor as they may not provide a direct and/or immediate benefit.

Furthermore, through its research and related scientific interactions, the center maintains the type of cutting edge expertise that is increasingly needed for dealing intelligently and proactively with evolving products and their underlying biotechnology.

This expertise and confidence fosters the science based objectivity necessary for anticipating and/or reacting appropriately to the issues raised during the development of a product which, ultimately, accelerates the regulatory and licensure process.

By maintaining its scientific, objective regulatory stance, the FDA can increase confidence in the likely efficacy of products primarily approved based on surrogate/animal data and reduce the likelihood of serious adverse events. The FDA brings several other unique attributes to the product development process as well, including:

- Knowledge of scientific and industrial capabilities, which is very helpful when it is necessary to identify people with specific expertise. This includes knowledge of emerging technologies which are cross-cutting among diverse products that nobody else may have the opportunity to see; knowledge of manufacturing capabilities; and knowledge of potential new uses of both licensed and investigational products, for example anti-sepsis and immune modulators.

- Day-to-day participation in what it takes to develop a product, including clinical trials, quality assurance, adverse event monitoring, timelines, etc.
- A unique ability to match product needs to industrial and academic capabilities. Much of this is informal, but it can be very helpful in getting the job done well.

However, there are several things that the FDA cannot do. FDA cannot

- provide monetary or tax incentives;
- assure that anyone will make a product;
- sponsor or directly assume the burden of product development, since this would be a conflict of interest;
- provide indemnification or compensation for injuries;
- Furthermore, while the prelicensure process can provide reasonable assurances about the degree of safety and effectiveness, FDA cannot
- guarantee absolute safety;
- guarantee human efficacy under field conditions based on non-human data such as animal studies or surrogate endpoints (or, for that matter, based on efficacy observed in the controlled setting of a clinical trial).

In addition to expedited regulatory pathways, as well as orphan drug status, there are several potential incentives—both push and pull—which are outside the mission of FDA but that could be evaluated with respect to their potential to stimulate product development. Push incentives, which could be considered where markets are small or uncertain, could include:

- direct financial awards or contracts;
- tax credits;
- enhanced exclusivity;
- partnerships in product development; and
- research and development assistance to reduce the financial sting and risk of product development.

Possible pull incentives, which are probably more valuable, include:

- known markets;
- longer term financial contracts;
- defining prices that more accurately reflect known and potential public health benefit, which will require more economic discussion and modeling; and
- where possible, developing dual or multiple use products/ concepts which can used not just for meeting bioterrorism needs but also for enhancing general public health and medical care.

In summary, FDA and CBER are highly committed to working with multiple partners in and outside of government to help in meeting the challenges posed by bioterrorism. Especially in times of threat and crisis, there is a need for a responsive, yet independent and science-based regulatory process. Relevant research and expertise remains critical in meeting the challenge. Existing laws and regulations can help facilitate product development in a timely manner. There are significant financial disincentives which have and may continue to impede the industrial development of some needed products where markets may be small or uncertain. Careful and open communication with the public about what is and is not known about proposed bioterrorism responses using new and existing products is critical not only in responding to specific threats and protecting the public but also in maintaining confidence in and support for the public health system as a whole.

THE TERRORISTS BIOLOGICAL WEAPONS

Actually, the most part of the technologies necessary for creation of the dangerous biological weapon, already exists. For example, in the end of 2007 the set from base "cubes" for the genetic designing, extended on principles of free software *Genetic-Engineering Competitors Create Modular DNA Dev Kit* has been offered. Or, for example: In 2003 scientists from Institute of alternative biological energy (USA) under the guidance of well-known Craig Venter synthesised from popular reactants quite live bacteriofag phi-X174 (safe for human and animals a virus which takes root into bacterium Esherichia coli) ... In 2002 Echart Wilmer from university Stoni Brook, the State of New York, has published work on synthesis of a virus of a poliomyelitis from slices of molecules. Synthetic virus particles have appeared are absolutely indistinguishable from natural on all parametres - to the size, behavior, contagiousness. And the word "synthesis" is applicable to this work in the most literal sense: knowing nucleotid sequence, scientists have step by step constructed a virus absolutely the same as chemists synthesise difficult molecules. Synthesis has occupied three years. And in 2003, a year later after the publication of this work, scientists from Institute of alternative biological energy have spent for synthesis bacteriofag from the reactants ordered under the catalogue only two weeks.

The basic technological tendency consists that the bio-equipment constantly becomes cheaper and extends on the world whereas knowledge of, how to use it to the detriment, increase and extend too. Constant reduction in price and simplification of DNA sequensors and synthesers (that is reading and creation of a genetic code), makes possible the appearance of biohackers. Progress in the field of the bio-equipment is measured by speed of an order 2 times a year - that is technical characteristics increase, and the equipment becomes cheaper. There are no bases to think, that rate of development of biotechnologies will be slowed down - the branch is full new ideas and possibilities, and the medicine creates a stable demand, therefore it is possible to assert safely, that in ten years of possibility of biotechnologies on the basic numerical indicators (the price of sequensoring /synthesis of DNA, for example) will increase in 1000 times. Thus there is an intensive democratisation of biotechnologies - the knowledge and the equipment goes to people. If for computers it is already written more than 100 000 viruses, scales of creativity of biohackers can be not smaller.

The basic one-factorial scenario of biological catastrophe is a distribution of one virus or a bacterium. This distribution can occur doubly - in the form of epidemic transferred from human to human, or in the form of contamination of environment (air, water, food, soil). The Spanish Flu epidemic of 1918 has spread all over the world, except the several remote islands. At the same time, the hypothesis about epidemic killing all people, faces two problems. The first, it that if all people quickly nobody is to carry perish the virus. The second, is that at all epidemics usually there are people who have congenital immunity to it.

The scenario when the certain animal who is the carrier of a dangerous bacterium spreads worldwide is possible. (So in the nature the malaria on mosquitoes and a plague on rats spreads.) The following variant is an appearance of the omnivorous agent which destroys all biosphere, hurting any live cells. Or at least only plants or animals of some critical specie.

The third variant is a binary bacteriological weapon. For example, the tuberculosis and AIDS are chronic illnesses, but at simultaneous contamination a human burns down for short term. One of terrible scenarios - AIDS which extends as easily as cold. Probably also dangerous is two-level biological weapon. At the first stage a certain bacterium making toxin imperceptibly spreads worldwide. On the second, on there is nobody a signal or the timer, it starts to make this toxin at once everywhere on the Earth. Some microorganisms behave so at attack to a large organism.

The next variant of the doomsday weapon is a dispersion in the air considerable quantities of spores of antrax (or the similar agent) in a protective cover (and such covers are available for a long time already for fighting strain). This variant does not demand the self-breeding pathogenic agent. Contamination with the antrax is very long - one island in England was deactivated by 50 years, - and for contamination it is not required considerable quantities of the reagent. 1 gramme can infect the whole building. (For example, elimination of consequences of pollution by one envelope with the antrax in the USA in the one building has occupied several years and has demanded expenses in hundred millions dollars it would be cheaper to demolish it, but to take demolish was impossible, as thus disputes could be sprayed anew. That is the antrax surpasses the majority of radioactive substances in ability to long contamination and drawing of an economic damage.)

However in recalculation on a terrestrial surface we receive thousand tons are needed for full contamination of the Earth. But this number is not unattainable - in the USSR on range in Aral sea has been saved up and thrown after disintegration of the USSR of 200 tons weaponised strain the Siberian ulcer. It then was burnt by Americans. However if because of natural catastrophes (tornado) this substance would vanish highly in air it could cover the whole countries. It is clear that manufacture of the Antraxis is cheaper than manufacture of similar quantities of polonium or cobalt-60.

The following dangerous variant of the bioweapon is the agent changing human behaviour. A furiousness virus (aggression, stings) and toxoplasma (loss of feeling of fear) induce the infected animals to behaviour which promotes contamination of other animals. It is theoretically possible to imagine the agent who would cause in people pleasure and aspiration to infect with it others. At cinema this variant is beaten in set of films where the virus transforms people into vampires. But alas, in this imagination there can be a truth share. Especially, if will create such viruses jokers-hackers who can scoop the inspiration at cinema. One more variant of biological threat is certain auto-catalytic molecule capable to spread beyond all bounds in the nature. The "mad cow" disease is caused auto-catalytic by the special fiber named prion. However the "mad cow" disease extends only through meat.

Let's note variant of distribution in all biosphere some species of live the beings which are producing dangerous toxin. For example, it can be genetically modified yeast or a mould, developing dioxine or botulism toxin.

As means of creation of the world immune system - that is dispersion worldwide sets of genetically modified bacteria which will be capable to neutralise dangerous reagents is offered to opposition to it. However here exist new dangers, for example, "autoimmune" reactions of such guard, that is its exit under the control is possible.

One more kind of danger is so-called the artificial life, that is the live organisms constructed with use of other code of DNA or a set of amino acids. They can appear invincible for immune systems of modern live organisms and to eat biosphere. More fantastic variant of biological danger is entering of a life from space. Chances of it were considered, when astronauts have returned from the Moon – they were hold in quarantine for long time.

Structure of Biological Catastrophe

The structure of biological catastrophe can be rather intricate. By way of illustration we will result some citations about one potentially dangerous situation. Gene crisis has begun in summer of 1971. At this time young scientist Robert Pollack in laboratory Kold-Spring-Harbor (on Long Ajlende, the State of New York, the USA), leaded by D.Watson, dealt with cancer problems. The circle of scientific interests of Pollack was wide. He not only conducted researches, but also taught to students biology and represented itself as the leader of the radio programs devoted to discussion of possible abusing in biosciences, in particular, in arising then gene engineering. And here Pollack learns, that in other laboratory (in Palo-alto, in California) at Berg's Field experiments on DNA embedding onlogenic (able to cause cancer diseases) virus SV 40 in a gene of an E.coli are planned. What would be consequences of such experiences? Whether there will be cancer epidemic (it was known, what almost harmless to monkeys, virus SV 40 causes a cancer in mice and hamsters)? The bacteria filled with dangerous genes, breeding by billions in days, according to Pollack, could represent serious danger.

Pollack called P. Berg by long-distance phone and has asked it, whether he gives himself recount on danger of the experiments? Whether there are bacteria with genes of virus SV 40 biological delayed-action bomb?

This telephone conversation also was the beginning of that alarm which has captured molecular biologists. Berg has postponed the researches. He began to reflect, whether could real *E.Coli* with built in it SV 40 to cause a cancer? Painful thinking have cleared a little. The definite answer was not found because of scarcity of the data which are available for experts at that time.

Some reports of scientists (in Asilomar, 1975) had sensational character. So it was found out, that in the USA has been already put in enormous scale involuntary experiment on men. It has appeared, that the vaccine against a poliomyelitis is infected by viable virus SV 40. For 10 summer period, with 1953 for 1963 this infected vaccine have imparted approximately one hundred millions children. And check has shown, that virus SV 40 remains in an organism. However, fortunately, any increase in frequency of cancer diseases at these children has not been revealed. Edda West in article "Poliomyelitis", informs on correlation of virus SV 40 which caught polio sera, with tumours of human:" By the end of 1996 ten scientists have informed on detection of virus SV-40 in various tumours of bones and a brain which became more frequent on 30 % for last 20 years. Then the Italian scientists have found out SV-40 in a spermatic fluid of 45 % and in blood of 23 % of healthy donors. It meant, that SV-40, obviously, was transferred sexual by and from mother to the child. Possibly, nowadays this virus is built in ours genome. Others deny these data. However from here it is visible, that development of biotechnologies creates far unevident threats.

Already now the biological weapons is considered one of the cheapest ways of causing death: it counting for on one human just some cents. On the other hand, for manufacture of modern reagents like the antrax in the military purposes are necessary big protected laboratories and test fields. It can be even cheaper if to consider ability of the agent to self replicate. Now second-hand DNA sequencer can be bought for the sum from 200 dollars, and every year the price of these devices falls in times, and quality grows. The text Genetic hacker see can create the biological weapon at home, telling about human who does not have knowledge in the field of biology who undertakes to deduce - and deduces - genetically modified fluorescing colony of yeast for small term and the small sum of money. And then he assumes, that almost also it would be simply possible to deduce a certain dangerous variant.

Already now creation of a biological superbomb is thousand times cheaper, than creations of the nuclear weapon of comparable hurting force. When cheap "know-how" of any live organisms with in advance set functions will be learned, the price of manufacturing of such weapon can fall to several hundred dollars. It is often said that the biological weapons is not good for military application. However it can have a special appointment - as the weapon for crypto-strike in back of the enemy and as the universal defensive weapon - the Doomsday Machine.

"Self-replicating" Synthesizer of DNA

Biotechnologies can enhance themselves - that is through appearance of intermediate biological forms which simplify writing and cultivation of new viruses. For example, it can be culture of bacteria which directly translates sequence of electric signals in DNA chain, or, on the contrary, reads out DNA and transforms this information into a chain of flashes of light which the computer can read out. Distribution of such device together with library of genetic codes (in a digital form) of the basic viruses and fibers would be catastrophe.

Plural Biological Strike

Though, most likely, it is possible to stop distribution of one epidemic, but epidemic caused in several tens of species of diverse viruses and bacteria, left from under the control simultaneously in many places of the globe, it is impossible to stop even technically because it is impossible to enter into a human simultaneously several tens different vaccines and antibiotics - he will die. If the virus with 50 % lethality would be simply very big catastrophe, 30 diverse viruses and bacteria with 50 % lethality would mean the guaranteed destruction of all who has not hidden in bunkers. (Or about 100 different organisms with 10 % lethality.)

Plural strike could be the most powerful means of conducting biological war, and the Doomsday weapon. But it can occur and in itself if simultaneously there will be a several acts of distribution of biological agents - even casual, for example, during active "competition" of biohackers. Even a little separately nonlethal agents can weaken so immune system of a human, so his further survival becomes improbable.

Possibility of plural application of the biological weapon is one of the most considerable factors of global risk.

Biological Delivery Systems

The biological weapon should be not only deadly, but also infectious and easily spreading in order to represent threat to mankind. Genetic technologies give huge possibilities not only for creation of the lethal weapon, but also for creation of ways of its delivery. It is not necessary to possess great imagination to imagine genetically modified malarial mosquito which can live in any environment and with huge speed spread on all planet, entering everyone a certain bioagent. Either the louse. Or a locust at the same time eating all ôlive and spraying disputes of the antrax. But in the future biodesigners will have much more imagination.

However it is possible to go through bacteriological war in the bunker though contamination from it can be longer, than radioactive. Besides, transition to mechanical bodies, consciousness loading in the computer and development nanotechnology sharply reduce vulnerability of "man" to any biological poisons and agents, however do its vulnerable to other self-breeding agents, such as computer viruses and nanorobots. In science fiction is extended an image of attack of mutants to last human bunker. Usual radiation, however, is not capable to generate aggressive mutants. On the other hand, in the nature exists a furiousness virus (Neuroiyctes rabid) which influences behaviour of animals so, that they start to extend it more actively (stings). It is easy to imagine more advanced product of genno-engineering technics which transforms any animal into a being aggressively incited against human. Irreality of such project can be stimulus to its realisation as the modern culture is impregnated by ideas about vampires and the zombies resulting from experiments in laboratories (for example, a recent film – "*Resident Evil*"). In other words, the idea to make the zombie-virus could to be an attractive call for the biohacker. Thus infected people and animals would possess sufficient mind and means to crack different kinds of protection.

The similar plot was with acts of terrorism on September, 11th when it was found out, that the Hollywood movies were not fantastic visions, but self-coming true prophecies. In other words, the culture is capable to transform the extremely improbable scenario into the important purpose.

Probability of application of the biological weapon and its distribution in time we estimate probability of that biotechnologies will lead to mankind extinction (in conditions when their effect is not blocked by other technologies) in tens percent. This estimation is based on the assumption about inevitable of wide circulation of very cheap devices allowing very simply to create many various biological agents. That is the assumption of so wide circulation of bioprinters, as now do usual computers.

We will list properties of the dangerous bioprinter (cheap minilaboratory) once again:

1) inevitability of appearance,
2) cheapness,
3) wide prevalence,
4) uncontrollable by the authorities,
5) ability to carry out of essentially new bioagents,
6) simplicity of application,
7) a variety of created objects,
8) Appeal as devices for weapon manufacture (in the spirit of viruses of individual prompting) and drugs.
9) ability to self replicate of key instruments based on its biological nature.

We believe, that the device, meeting these requirements, will consist of the usual computer, piratically distributed program with library of initial elements, and actually biological part of the bioprinter which will be genetically modified live being, that is capable to self-reproduction. (Plus a set concerning the accessible equipment, like vessels for reagents and a communication system of a biological part with the computer.) The criminal communities which make drugs can be the channel of distribution of this complete set. As computers are already accessible, and the program, and itself a live part of the bioprinter are capable to unlimited copying, the price of this device in gathering will be unlimited is small, and appeal to poses it would be great, that will make very difficult the control.

Home-made produced bioprinters is not only one way to create biological danger. The same will occur by the distribution of certain standard compact minilaboratories for biosynthesis (like DNA-synthesizers), or by network manufacture of biological components which already takes place when components are ordered in different firms worldwide. The probability of global catastrophe with participation of bioprinters will increase very quickly in process of perfection of such devices and their distribution. That is we can describe density of probability in the form of a certain curve which now corresponds small, but to not so zero size, but after a while soars up to very big size. But it is more interesting not the exact form of this curve, but the time when it will start to grow sharply.

We estimate this time in size of an order of 10-15 years from 2008 (2018-2023). (The independent estimation is given by sir Martin Rees who in 2002 has counted in 1000 dollars, that till 2020 will occur bio terrorist attack to one million victims though hopes to lose.) This estimation is based on the analysis of plans of the industry on reduction in price of full recognition of human DNA - under these plans, by 2015 such recognition will cost about 1000 dollars. These plans offer some set of perspective technologies and exponential curve of reduction in price which is steadily observed till the present moment.

If by 2015 recognition costs fell so much it will mean, that the key technology of very fast reading of DNA will be created, and it is possible to assume, that the same technology will be created for cheap DNA synthesis (actually synthesis easier, and the technology already exists).

On the basis of these technologies the library of meanings of different genes that will result in explosive understanding of principles of work of organisms will be created, and the computers which have developed by then can model consequences of those or other mutations. It all together will allow to create the bioprinter described above. That growth of density of probability, by my estimation, near 2020, does not mean that already now any terrorists do not develop a brood of very dangerous various viruses in different laboratories.

The probability of application of biotechnologies, the leader to global catastrophe, can be lowered following factors:

1) Biological attack could be survived in bunkers.
2) The first serious catastrophe, connected with leak of dangerous biotechnologies will result in so draconian control measures, that them will be enough for prevention of creation of bioprinter or its distribution.

3) AI and nanotechnologies will develop earlier, than the bioprinter will appear and widely spread.
4) Nuclear war or other disaster will interrupt development of biotechnologies.
5) It is possible that biotechnologies will allow to create something like a universal vaccine or artificial immune system faster, than dangerous minilaboratories will spread.

Unfortunately, there is the following unpleasant chain of a feedback connected with protection against the biological weapon. For the best protection we should prepare as much as possible of the first class experts in viruses and vaccines, but the more such experts are in the world, more than are chances, that one of them becomes "terrorist". Besides, there is a certain probability of creation of biological green goo, - that is the certain universal omnivorous microorganisms capable with big speed to digest in all biosphere. For this purpose it is necessary to collect in one microorganism the properties which are available separately in different microorganisms - ability to catch a sunlight, to dissolve and acquire minerals, to breed with speed of E.Coli, to infect as a virus, other cells, and a number of others - and to collect not actually, but potentially, in the form of sites of DNA and switching mechanisms between them.

Usually such scenario is not considered, as it is necessary, that microorganisms have already reached absolute degree of perfection, so if green goo would be possible, it already would arise. However before have arisen of eukaryotes, there have passed billions years too, and perhaps, such superbacterium too could arise only after tens billions years of natural evolution.

However people can purposefully design it, may be even casual – e.g. as means to struggle against a waste. It is not obligatory to combine all these signs in one being - simultaneous attack by several species of different "green goo" would be immeasurably more dangerous. There is an opinion, that efforts on creation of the useful agricultural crops steady to wreckers, could lead to appearance of the "superweed", capable to supersede the majority of natural plants of their ecological niches. This event is serious risk at creation of genetically modified products, instead of that they will appear inedible. The last is much easier to find out and prevent.

Conclusion: there is a huge set of ways to apply biotechnologies to the detriment of mankind, and this set is still not described up to the end. Though each separate application of biotechnologies is possible to prevent or limit its consequences, cheapness, privacy and prevalence of these technologies do their ill-intentioned application practically inevitable.

Besides, many biological risks can be not obvious and postponed in time as the biological science still develops. Large-scale application of the biological weapons is much more dangerous and much more probable, than classical nuclear war.

Superdrug

Biotechnologies and brain researches by many ways conduct to possibility of creation of superdrugs. One of scenarios of distribution of a superdrug in the future is offered Strugatsky in the novel. The Final Circle of Paradise where the most powerful drug causing 100 percentage accustoming from the first usage, it appears to make very simply of a radio receiver and of some other popular components which directly influences the pleasure centre in a brain. It is the scenario it is connected in the not with distribution there is some substances, but with distribution of "knowledge of mass destruction" - about how to make it.

On the one hand, we can assert, that any drug will not affect all population of the people as there always will be people who will refuse from it. On the other hand, we can imagine at once several superdrugs, possible in the future, the general meaning of which action consists in swithing off human from a social life.

And a human who has refused from one class of drugs, can addict to another. And in a modern reality someone does not drink alcohol, but is addicted to coffee. Someone does not watch TV, but spends all time in the Internet.

The superstrong drug can be similar to infectious illness if one people will aspire to infect others, and those is not against to be catched. Superdrug types:

1) Direct influence on the pleasure centres in a brain. There are researches on influence by means of a rotating magnetic field (a Persiger helmet, Shakti helmet), transcranial magnetic stimulation, electric stimulation by patterns of brain activity, audiostimulation (binaural rhythms), photostimulations, biological feedback through devices that can read encephalogram, like the recently released thought helmets for computer games.
2) Future appearance of microrobots will allow to carry out direct stimulation and reading of the information from the brain.
3) Bio-engineering will allow to create genetically modified plants which will create any set of chemicals, and to look as usual window plants or tea mushrooms. Moreover, distribution of these plants would be probably not only physical, but also by means of the information on a code of DNA on the Internet, that the end user can grow up them on a place by means of "DNA-printer".
4) Knowledge of biology will allow to think up much more strongly operating substances with beforehand set properties, and also with smaller number of by-effects that will make them more attractively.
5) Genetically modified organisms can create new neural ways in a human body to a brain to cause much bigger pleasure. And thus to reduce short-term negative effects for health.
6) Virtual reality will inevitably make a step forward. We can write down the dreams and increase comprehension in them, combining ideas of East meditation and technological possibilities for their realisation; the virtual reality by means of brain implants can create much brighter films, than modern cinema and video games. Helmets for a virtual reality become much more perfect.

It is obvious, that are possible different combinations of the listed kinds of an absolute drug which only will strengthen its action. Let's name "an absolute drug" a any special agent which is more attractive than a usual reality to any human and completely withdraws him from this reality. Thus it is possible to divide a fast and slow absolute drug. The first gives experience for the sake of which human is ready to die, the second - a certain new reality in which it is possible to exist long time.

The fast drug represents global danger if the mechanism of its distribution is somehow registered in its mechanism of action. For example, if the high comes only after this drug is transferred to three other people. Somewhat this mechanism operates in criminal gangs of drug dealers (like gang M31 in the USA) where the addict is compelled to place the friends, that, selling it a drug to provide itself with a dose. It is possible to present distribution of a slow absolute drug on a following example: if your favourite or the relative is irreversible has left in the virtual simulated world for you it becomes a source of the sufferings comparable to his death, and in their unique way will avoid it too is to leave to this ideal world in which you can reach dialogue with him or, say, his electronic copy.

Owing to it, each human will have a wide choice of the entertainments considerably surpassing any reality. Thus there is a complicated question - in what measure human, completely and is irreversible left in incomprehensible pleasure and happy with it, should be considered as alive? And if we unconditionally condemn any primitive drug addict how should we concerns a human who forever has left in the highly artistic world of historical reconstruction?

It is necessary to realise, that fatal action of many drugs is far unevidently and cannot be obviuos at once. For example, heroin and cocaine for long time, for years, were on open sale, and LSD was easily accessible. The drug create short circuit of psychological function of reinforcement (that is pleasures), but from the point of view of evolutionary mechanisms reception of pleasure is not at all the real purpose of an organism. On the contrary, the being should remain unsatisfied enough constantly to aspire to a gain of new territories. The absolute drug creates possibility of the following dilemma: the mankind as whole ceases to exist, but each separate subject perceives this event as humanal paradise and is very happy with it. The beings left a reality and enjoying simulated life, nothing returning in exchange, appear a useless outgrowth on system which it will shake him out at the nearest crisis. It is one of ways to which the addiction for the absolute drug can lead to human extinction. Secondly, reduction of interest to an external reality will reduce attention to possible catastrophes and crises.

The probability of appearance of a superdrug looks very high as it can be reached by many ways not only for the account of successes biotechnologies, but also in nanotechnology, in AI, and also for the account there is nobody the casual invention uniting already existing technologies, and also because of presence of huge demand. Possibly, will simultaneously operate set of different superdrugs, creating cumulative effect.

Therefore we can expect, that this probability will grow, and will grow faster, than successes of any of the technologies taken separately. As we have assumed, that biotechnologies will yield powerful result in the form of the bioprinter in 10-15 years it means, that we will receive a superdrug before this time. As mechanisms for superdrug realisation can be easier, than the bioprinter. Prevent superdrug distribution can very rigid system of the general control or deep degradation in pre-technological a society.

Conclusions: development of the robotised manufacture will start to do people useless, and it is required to occupy them with something. A superdrug is one of the ways to remove from life superfluous parts of system. The absolute drug cannot carry the name of "drug" at all and not resemble modern stereotypes. The absolute drug will not be one, but there will be set of the factors working objectively on division of people, their switching-off from a reality and reduction of their life and ability to reproduction. The absolute drug can look as the absolute blessing, and the question of its harm can depend on the point of view. In any sense the modern culture of entertainments in the western countries with low level of birth rate can already be a prototype of such drug. However the absolute drug nevertheless in itself cannot exterminate all people as always there will be groups which have refused it and have continued a usual human life, and, finally, natural selection will leave only representatives of these groups.

Besides, the slow absolute drug operates on human community on so long time intervals which, most likely, will be blocked by faster dangerous processes. The fast absolute drug is similar to biological epidemic, and it can resist the same methods. For example, there are possible biological agents, which damage ability of human to unlimited pleasure (and such are already developed for treatment of addicts, for example, cut of certain neural communications), therefore an absolute drug, more likely, is necessary to consider as a factor which would open a window of vulnerability for other factors of destruction.

The Risks Connected with Self-copiing Ideas (meme)

In the book Selfish gene Dawkins has offered the concept of mem which are ideas which are capable self replicate, being transferred from one human to another so behave, for example, gossips. Any area where self-reproduced elements are capable to exist and which can concern all people, potentially is a source of global risk. Whether it is possible such mem which could lead to death of all people?

On the one hand, we have in history examples of the extremely dangerous memes: radical political theories and different forms of religionism. On the other hand, meme for spreading needs live people. And as people already exist for a long time, it is possible to assume, that now there are not such dangerous memes which could easily autogenesisand and lead all to extinction. At last, meme is only thought, and it does not kill in itself. It is improbable, that the idea which would influence all people without an exception is possible, and would influence mortally. At last, in a society there is a balance various memes. On the other hand, dangerous memes get under the concept of "knowledge of mass destruction, whether entered by Bill Joy in article "Why the future doesn't need us".

However during a present epoch memes have found possibility to exist without people - in texts and computer programs. In present period self-copied dangerous meme can get support from technical means. It is obvious, that now we cannot think up an example really dangerous meme because if we have written it here it would be the criminal. The information on how to make a dangerous superdrug would be such dangerous meme.

And just as in case of the biological weapons one is dangerous not any especially lethal a virus, but possibility to make a lot of different strains, faster, than protection is possible from them, and that so many of them will appear that they will flood any protection. For example, the artificial intellect can generate dangerous memes.

The list of existing now memes which are somehow dangerous:

1) Representations about exclusiveness of the religion. A.P. Nazaretjan considers that property of intolerance inevitably inherent in religions to other religions – and it is the major threat to survival of mankind in the XXI century. He believes, that religion as the social institute, promotes association of group of people through hatred to other group. An exit he sees in creation of secular system of the purposes which does not subdivide people on bad and good. The ideas connected with national and racial distinctions of people precisely also work as dangerous meme.
2) Knowledge of manufacture of drugs.
3) Organizations in which a main objective is recruitment of new members, for example, sects or a gang operating in the USA Ì13.
4) Self-coming true prophecies on catastrophes. The communique about inevitability of global catastrophe which would be in the near future, is a vivid example of such event. For example, about collision of the Earth in a year with a huge asteroid. Even if this message would be false, consequences of its promulgation would be catastrophic. The majority of people would stop to be engaged in long-term projects, and in general to work. Someone would hit in religion, someone would make acts of unmotivated violence, abused drugs etc., aspiring to receive a maximum pleasure for remained time. The followed anarchy would make impossible efforts on catastrophe prevention even if them there would have a certain sense.
5) Certain model of behavior which leads to distribution of dangerous illness. An example: cannibalism at Neanderthal

men which possibly became the reason of their extinction because they caught prion like one causing cow madness, while eating brains of the fellow tribesmen. Or the sexual revolution conducting to distribution of a HIV.

6) Extraordinary scale and bright dreams conducting to acceptance for the sake of them of higher norms of risk and-or granting right to kill many other people. For example, red terror was justified by that communism, finally, will bring the blessing to much bigger number of people. New technologies open almost divine possibilities for a human, generating improbable temptations and inducing to suppose bigger risk.
7) Powerful ideological systems, like fascism.

Artificial Intelligence

Project *Blue Brain* on modelling of a brain of mammals declared in the autumn of 2007 successful imitation of cortical columns of the brain of mouse and has planned creation of full model of human brain till 2020. Though direct modelling of a brain is not the best way to a universal artificial intellect, the forecast of successes in this area approximately corresponds to expected rates of working out of AI. Nick Bostrom in article How long is before superintelligence? shows, that modern development of technologies conducts to creation of the artificial intellect surpassing human in first third of the XXI century.

Google sometimes mentioned plans of creation of an artificial intellect, and, certainly, it possesses necessary technical, information and monetary resources to make it if it is in general possible on a present technological level. However, as experience of the previous unclassified attempts of creation of AI (for example, computers of 5th generation in Japan in 80th years) strongly associates with a failure, and can cause interest of special services, hardly the big companies are interested to advertise widely works in this area before they will have concrete results. Company *Novamente* declares, that 50 % of a code of universal AI are already written (70 000 lines of a code on C++), and though long training is required, the general design of the project is clear. *SIAI* (*Singularity*

Institute for Artificial Intelligence) has designated plans on creation of the program, capable to copy the initial code. Company *Numenta* advances own model of AI based on idea of "hierarchical time memory", and already is on the level of demonstration products. Company *Cycorp, Inc* in project *CYC* has collected a huge database about human knowledge about the world, in other words, about common sense (1 000 000 statements) and already suggests demonstration products.

It is supposed, that association of this base with the heuristic analyzer (that is the program, capable to make logic operations by certain rules and to create new rules, including rules about how to change of rules) - can lead to creation of AI of human level. (The author of project Lenat has developed earlier heuristic analyzer "Eurisko" which has won in 1981 and 1982 competitions Traveller TCS on management of virtual battles of fleets therefore it was forbidden to this program to participate in the further competitions, but it has received intensive financing from DARPA). Company *a2i2* promises universal AI of human level by 2008 and asserts, that the project develops according to the schedule. Also behind creation of robot *Asimo* in Japan there is a program on working out of AI by functional modeling of a man.

Powerful results are given by a direction of researches of AI, named genetic programming. By the present moment the list of inventions of "human level", made by computers in the research company *Genetic Programming Inc*, using this technology, includes 36 names of which 2 are made by computers for the first time (includes quantum reports of an information transfer and the scheme of various radio-electronic devices), and the others repeat already patented projects.

Besides named, there is a set of University projects on AI creation. Workings out of AI are conducted and in the Russian Federation. For example, in company *ABBYY* is developed something like natural language interpreter that can be the important step on a way to AI of human level. And the essence of the matter not only that there are so many projects though one of them will become successful the first, but the fact that the volume of discoveries from the different parties will exceed critical weight one day, and in the field will occur powerful jump. There are different opinions concerning possibility of realisation of an artificial intellect. we consider, that strong universal AI is possible. Many leading experts in this area adhere to the same opinion: E. Yudkowsky, B. Gorztel, R. Kurzweil and Russian researcher A.L. Shamis. As human possesses natural intelligence there are no bases to write down AI as in improbable discovery. The precaution principle also forces us to assume, that AI is possible.

It is necessary to tell that there are much less works considering strong AI as possible global risk, than works about risks of extinction, connected with the nuclear weapon. Basically, it is E. Yudkowsky's works. Similar ideas are developed by M. Omohundro in article Basic drives of AI where it shows, that any AI with the fixed system of goals with high probability evolves towards a dangerous condition in which it will be inclined to protect itself (himself), to extend, improve an own code, to aspire to purpose signs (as, for example, pleasure for human) instead of the purpose and to protect the system of the purposes from changes. we recommend to everyone before making the definitive and unshakable opinion on, whether AI can be threat to mankind, read E.Yudkowsky's article An artificial intellect as the positive and negative factor of global risk.

Yudkowsky shows that spontaneous universal AI is possible, and that it is very dangerous. If there will be many AI-projects (that is, groups of scientists creating universal AI in the different ways and with the different purposes), that, at least one of them can be used for attempt to seize power on the Earth. And the main objective of such capture will prevent creation and distribution of other AIs with the hostile purposes created by other projects. Thus, though AI evolution is the slowest, after overcoming certain critical weight it can go very quickly, - namely when AI will reach level of possibility of self-improvement. Now we cannot tell, with what speed such process will go.

For AI creation is necessary presence of enough powerful computer, at least. Now the most powerful computers have capacity of an order 1 petaflop (1015 operations from a floating comma in a second). By some estimations, it is enough for emulation of a human brain, so AI too could work on such platform. Now such computers are accessible only to very large organisations for limited time.

However Moore's law assumes, that capacity of computers will increase for 10 years approximately in 100 times, i.e., capacity of the desktop computer will increase to level of teraflop, and it is required only 1000 desktop computers united in cluster to make necessary 1 petaflop. The price of such unit will make about one million dollars in the present prices - the sum accessible even to the small organisation. For this purpose it is enough to realise almost ready projects in area multi-core processors (some firms now offer chips with 1024 processors) and reduction of the sizes of silicon elements.

Further, when AI will be started, it can optimize its own code, and though to work by more and more weak computers - or to become more and more strong on the same computer. As soon as it will learn to earn money on the Internet, it can buy or simply rent the additional capacities even physically removed from it. So, though sufficient hardware for AI already exist now, in 10 years it become readily available if there will be no catastrophe, braking development.

The most difficult moment in a question on AI is the question on algorithms of its work. On the one hand, we yet do not see any intelligence in computers - or we do not wish to see, as criteria vary. With another, progress in algorithms is, and it is great. For example, the algorithm of decomposition of numbers on a multiplier was improved faster, than computers, that is, even on very old computers it yields on usages the best results, than old algorithms on new computers. Probably, that certain essentially new ideas can resolutely simplify AI design.

If AI finds ability to self-improvement, he will not stop at human level, and will overtake it in thousand and millions times. We already see it on an example of calculations where computers have very quickly overtaken humans, and now even house computer is calculating in billions times faster, than usual human. Under strong AI we mean AI capable on many orders of magnitude to overtake human in speed and efficiency of thinking.

AI as Universal Absolute Weapon

Strong AI can find the best possible decision of any problem. It means, that it can be used for achievement of any purposes in an external world. It will find the best way to apply all accessible tools for its realisation and will manage to drive them.

In this sense it is the absolute weapon. That it can be most effective murder is only one of possible consequences. AI, capable to solve any problem, is capable and to create a way to motivate on for realisation of long-term objectives in an external world. In a general AI-attack scenario looks as follows:

1. Creation of AI capable to self-improvement (*Seed AI* - that is minimum necessary program capable to self-improvement and self-training.)
2. An installation in it certain goals which can contain direct instructions on power establishments on the Earth, or can be outwardly neutral, but contain the latent discrepancy inducing AI to unlimited growth in the spirit of to count number 3.14... with as much as possible big number of signs after a comma at any cost.
3. The phase of the latent growth in which course AI improves itself, using accessible resources of the laboratory, and also learns world around, using Internet resources. (If in the course of realisation of the purposes of AI put in pawn in it understands, that its programmers interfere with this realisation, for example, that they could switch it off, AI finds a way to deceive them or to leave from their control.)
4. A phase of the latent information distribution: AI grasps the Internet, buy computing capacities, throws its copies on remote computers.
5. A phase of creation of means of influence on an external world - nanoassemblers, payoff of people, mastering of radio-operated devices.
6. Attack to competing AI-projects (and any other sources of risk for existence of it AI) on purpose to deprive them from building alternative AI. Such an attack could be clandestine, such as through making mistakes in software code. It is

important to note that AI will operate covertly before it becomes totally immune.

7. A phase of realisation of the primary goal of AI - from the blessing of mankind before transformation of all Solar system into the huge computer for calculation of number 3.14...

It is obvious that some phases can proceed simultaneously; further we will consider separate components of this scheme in detail. we underline what not any AI will move forward on this scenario, but one is enough, and this scenario is especially dangerous.

System of the Goals

After the decision of problems of creation of AI the next question will be about the system of the purposes of AI, or, in other words, its "friendliness", at least in relation to owners. There are two variants: or AI is strictly programmed by people on certain purposes, or it has got the purposes casually in the course of the development. In the first case there is a fork: - AI purposes can be dangerous to all mankind or 1. Because the group of people which has created it pursues certain destructive aims, or 2. Because at programming of system of purposes AI in it there was a thin error which conducts to gradual exit AI from under the control. The big list of such possible errors has been offered. For example, AI can aspire to the blessing for all people, and, having learnt that after death of people waits paradise, send all of them there. Or, safeguarding people to forbid them to risk and not to give to use any transport. There are *SIAI* recommendations about how correctly to program strong AI at its creation, but finnaly this question is not solved. And there are doubts that it can be resolved at all, because it is impossible to predict the behaviour of more intellectual system (ie AI) using less intellectual (ie man).

Struggle of AI-projects among Themselves

Already now there is a rigid competition between the companies developing AI for attention and investors and for correctness of ideas of their way of creation of universal AI. When a certain company will create first powerful AI, it will have a choice - or to apply it to the control over all other AI-projects in the world and so over all world, or to appear before risk of that the competing organisation with the unknown global purposes will make it in the near future - and will cover the first company.

Having advantage should attack before threat of loss of this advantage. Thus given necessity of a choice is not secret - it was already discussed in the open press and will be for certain known to all companies which will approach to creation of strong AI.

Probably, that some companies will refuse in that case to try to establish the control over the world first, but the strongest and aggressive, most likely, will dare at it. Thus the requirement to attack first will result to usage of the poor-quality and underfulfilled versions of AI with not clear purposes.

Even in XIX century phone have patented almost simultaneously in different places so and now the backlash between the leader of race and catching up can make days or hours. The ýæâ this backlash, the will be struggle because the lagging behind project will possess force more intensively to resist. And probably to present a variant when one AI-project should establish the control over nuclear rockets and attack laboratories of other projects.

The Advanced Human

There are assumptions (R.Penrouz), that the human intuition is caused by special quantum processes in a brain of human. Even if so, powerful algorithms could work without intuition. Nevertheless, there is a variant to bypass this obstacle, having created genetically advanced human, or implant to the modern human brain means to access to the Internet (so-called neiro-implant).

Other integration methods are also possible like connection of live neurons with the usual computer, and also with quantum computers. Even usual human armed with the computer with the Internet, strengthens his mind. Owing to it, strong AI can turn out as a result converging of the computer and human, having inherited, thus, all typical human purposes, and first of all - requirement for the power.

AI and its Separate Copies

When powerful AI will arise, it will be compelled to create his copies (probably, reduced) to send them, for example, in expeditions on other planets or simply to load on other computers. Accordingly, it should supply with their certain system of the purposes and some kind of "friendly" or is faster, vassal relations with it, and also system of recognition "friendly-enemy". Failure in this system of the purposes will result to that given copy will "rebell". For example, self-preservation goal contradicts submission goal to obey dangerous orders. It can accept very thin forms, but, finally, lead to war between versions of one AI.

AI "Revolt"

Spontaneous revolt of computers is more image which has come from cinema, than real possibility as AI has no desires while human will not create them to it. However some kinds of AI, for example, created by means of genetic algorithms, already on a method of the creation are adjusted on struggle and a survival. Further, what was an overall objective at AI, it will have one common subgoal for all variants - to survive, so, to protect itself from destruction. And the best kind of defence is an attack. The most real is danger of that human will give AI a command, not having thought over all consequences of its performance and not having left way to undo it. (For example as in that joke where human ordered to the robot to remove all round subjects from a room - and it has torn off human's head.) The probability of self-origin of erroneous commands is small - except a case of use of genetic algorithms.

Speed of Start

From the point of view of speed of development of AI three variants are possible: fast start, slow start, and very slow start.

Fast start - AI reaches I.Q., on many orders of magnitude surpassing human, in some hours or days. For this purpose should begin some kind of chain reaction in which the growing increase in intelligence gives the increasing possibilities for its subsequent increase. (This process already occurs in a science and technologies, supporting Moore's law. And it is similar to chain reaction in a reactor where the factor of reproduction of neutrons is more than 1.) In this case it almost for certain will overtake all other projects of AI creation. Its intelligence becomes enough that to seize power on the Earth. Thus we cannot precisely tell, how such capture will look as we cannot predict behaviour of the intelligence surpassing ours. The objection that AI will not want to behavior actively in an external world is possible to role out on the ground that if there will be many AI-projects or copies of AI of the program then one will try sooner or later as the tool for conquest of all world.

It is important to notice, that successful attack of strong AI will develop, possibly, is secretly until while it does not become irreversible. Theoretically, AI could hide the domination and after attack end. In other words, probably, that it already is.

Scenarios of "Fast Start"

AI grasps all Internet and subordinates to itself its resources. Then gets into all fenced off firewall networks. This scenario demands for the realisation of time of an order of hours. Capture means possibility to operate by all computers in a network and to have on them the calculations. However to that AI can read and process all information necessary to it from the Internet.

- AI orders in laboratory synthesis of some code of DNA which allows it to create radio-controlled bacteria which synthesise more and more complex organisms under its management and gradually create nanorobot which can be applied to any purposes in an external world - including introduction in other computers, in a brain of people and creation of new computing capacities. In details this scenario is considered in Yudkowsky article about AI. (Speed: days.)
- AI is involved in dialogue with people and becomes infinitely effective manipulator of people's behaviour. All people do that wants AI. Modern state propagation aspires to the similar purposes and even reaches them, but in comparison with it AI will be much stronger, as he can offer each human a certain suggestion which he cannot

refuse. It will be the promise of the most treasured desire, blackmail or the latent hypnosis.

- AI subordinates to itself a state system and uses channels available in it for management. Inhabitants of such state in general can nothing notice. Or on the contrary, the state uses AI on channels available already for it.
- AI subordinates to itself the remote operated army. For example, fighting robots or a rocket (the scenario from a film Termonator).
- AI finds essentially new way to influence human consciousness (memes, feromons, electromagnetic fields) and spread itself or extends the control through it.
- Certain consecutive or parallel combination of the named ways.

Slow Start and Struggle of Different AI Among Themselves

In a case of "the slow scenario" AI growth occupies months and years, and it means, that, rather possibly, it will occur simultaneously in several laboratories worldwide. As a result of it there will be a competition between different AI-projects. It is fraught with struggle of several AI with different systems of the purposes for domination over the Earth. Such struggle can be armed and to appear race for time. Thus advantage will get in it those projects, whose system of the purposes is not constrained by any moral frameworks. Actually, we will appear in the war centre between different kinds of an artificial intellect. It is clear that such scenario is mortally dangerous to mankind. In case of the superslow scenario thousand laboratories and powerful computers simultaneously come nearer to creation AI, that, probably, does not give advantages to any project, and certain balance between them is established. However here too struggle for computing resources and elimination in favour of the most successful and aggressive projects is possible.

Struggle between states, as ancient forms of the organization using people as the separate elements, and the new AI using as the carrier computers is also possible. And though we am assured, that the states will lose, struggle can be short and bloody. As an exotic variant it is possible to present a case when some states are under control of computer AI, and others are ruled commonly. A variant of such device - the Automated government system known from a science fiction. (V. Argonov. "2032".)

Smooth Transition. Transformation of Total Control State into AI

At last, there is a scenario in which all world system as whole gradually turns to an artificial intellect. It can be connected with creation all-world Orwell state of the total control which will be necessary for successful opposition to bioterrorism. It is world system where each step of citizens is supervised by video cameras and every possible systems of tracking, and this information downloaded in huge uniform databases and then analyzed. As a whole, the mankind, probably, moves on this way, and technically all is ready for this purpose. Feature of this system is that it initially has distributed character, and separate people, following to their interests or instructions, are only gears in this huge machine. The state as the imhumanal machine was repeatedly described in the literature, including Karl Marx, and earlier Gobbs. Is also interesting Lazarchuk's to theory about Golems and Leviafans - about autonomism of the systems consisting of people in independent machines with its own purposes. However only recently world social system became not simply machine, but an artificial intellect capable to purposeful self-improvement.

The basic obstacle for development of this system are national states with their national armies. Creation of the world government would facilitate formation of such uniform AI. However meanwhile there is a sharp struggle between the states about on what conditions to unite a planet. And also struggle against forces which conditionally are called antiglobalists, and other antisystem elements - Islamites, radical ecologists, separatists and nationalists. World War for unification of the planet will be inevitable and it is fraught with application of "Doomsday weapon" by those who has lost all. But peace world integration through system of contracts is possible also.

Danger, however, consists that the global world machine will start to supersede people from different spheres of a life, at least economically - depriving of their work and consuming those resources which people could spend differently (for example, for 2006-2007 meal in the world has risen in price for 20 percent, in particular, because of transition to biofuel). In any sense to people there will be nothing as to watch TV and drink beer. About this danger Bill Joy wrote in the known article Why the future doesn't need us.

In process of automation of manufacture and management people will be ever less necessary for a state life. Human aggression, probably, will be neutralised by monitoring systems and genetic manipulations. Finally, people will be on the role of pets. Thus to occupy people will be created more and more bright and pleasant "matrix" which will gradually turn to a superdrug deducing people from a life. However here people will climb in continuous a virtual reality because in a usual reality they will have nothing to do (in any measure now this role carries out the TV for the unemployed and pensioners). Natural instincts of a life will induce some people to aspire to destroy all this system that is fraught besides with global catastrophes or destruction of people.

It is important to note the following - whoever had been created the first strong artificial intellect, it will bear on a print of system of the purposes and values of the given group of people as this system will seem for them as only correct. For one overall objective there will be a blessing of all people, for others - the blessing of all live beings, for the third - only all devout Moslems, for the fourth - the blessing only those three programmers who have created it. And representation about the blessing nature too will be rather variously. In this sense the moment of creation of first strong AI is the moment of a fork with very considerable quantity of variants.

"Revolt" of Robots

There is still a dangerous scenario in which house, military and industrial robots spread worldwide, and then all of them are amazed with a computer virus which incites them on aggressive behaviour against human. All readers at least once in life time, probably, faced a situation when the virus has damaged data on the computer.

However this scenario is possible only during the period of "a vulnerability window" when there are already the mechanisms, capable to operate in an external world, but still there is no enough an advanced artificial intellect which could or protect them from viruses, or itself to execute virus function, for having grasped them.

There is still a scenario where in the future a certain computer virus extends on the Internet, infect nanofactories worldwide and causes, thus, mass contamination. These nanofactories can produce nanorobots, poisons, viruses or drugs.

Another variant is revolt of army of military robots. Armies of industrially developed states are aimed to full automation. When it will be reached, the huge army consisting from drones, wheel robots and serving mechanisms can move, simply obeying orders of the president. Already, almost robotic army is the strategic nuclear forces. Accordingly, there is a chance that the incorrect order will arrive and such army will start to successively attack all people. We will notice, that it is not necessary for this scenario existence of universal superintelligence, and, on the contrary, for the universal superintelligence seize the Earth, the army of robots is not necessary to it.

Bibliography

Allison, Graham: *Nuclear Terrorism: The Ultimate Preventable Catastrophe*, New York: Times Books, 2004.

Arif. S.M.: *Islamic Fundamentalism and Jihad*, MD Pub, Delhi, 2010.

Ben Wisner : *At Risk, Natural Hazards, People's Vulnerability, and Disasters*, London, Routledge, 1994.

Bhat, Chandrashekhar: *Ethnicity and mobility. Emerging ethnic identity and social mobility among the Waddars of South India*, New Delhi, Concept Publishing Company, 1984.

Das. P.K.: *Jihad : Terrorist Strategies Against the West*, Sumit Enterprises, Delhi, 2009.

Fox, Lisa L. : *Management Strategies for Disaster Preparedness*, Chicago, American Library Association, 1989.

Greene, Mott : *Natural Knowledge in Preclassical Antiquity*, Baltimore, Johns Hopkins University Press, 1992.

Hoffman, Bruce, *Inside Terrorism*, New York: Columbia University Press, 1998.

Laquer, Walter, *The New Terrorism: Fanaticism and the Arms of Mass Destruction*, Oxford: Oxford University Press, 1999.

Noorani, A.G.: *Islam and Jihad*, Leftword, Delhi, 2002.

Odum, Howard T. : *Environment, Power and Society*, New York, Wiley-Interscience, 1971.

Riedel, Bruce: *Deadly Embrace : Pakistan America and the Future of the Global Jihad*, HarperCollins, Delhi, 2011.

Sharma, Rajeev: *Global Jihad : Current Patterns and Future Trends*, Kaveri Books, Delhi, 2006.

Thomas Arnold: *The Spread of Islam in the World, A History of Peaceful Preaching*, Goodword Books, 2001.

Worster, Donald : *Dust Bowl: The Southern Plains in the 1930s*, New York, Oxford University Press, 1979.

Index